Fraud & Abuse Investigations Handbook for the Healthcare Industry

Robert A. Griffith, Esquire and
Paul W. Shaw, Esquire

© April 2000
American Health Lawyers Association
1025 Connecticut Avenue, NW
Suite 600
Washington, DC 20036-5405
Phone: (202) 833-1100
Fax: (202) 833-1105
E-mail: info@healthlawyers.org
Web site: www.healthlawyers.org

ISBN: 0-918945-43-7

All rights reserved. No part of this publication may be reproduced, stored in a retrieval system, or transmitted, in any form or by any means, electronic, mechanical, photocopying, recording, or otherwise, without the express, written permission of the publisher.

DISCLAIMER
"This publication is designed to provide accurate and authoritative information in regard to the subject matter covered. It is provided with the understanding that the publisher is not engaged in rendering legal or other professional services. If legal advice or other expert assistance is required, the service of a competent professional person should be sought" — from a declaration of the American Bar Association.

RELATED TITLES OF INTEREST

Log onto Health Lawyers Web site at www.healthlawyers.org and click Publications
to order the following or obtain more information.

Physician Recruitment and Retention: Reconciling Legal Tensions Between Tax Law and Fraud and Abuse Issues, 2nd Edition
© 2000, 1995, 386+ pages, softbound, Practice Guide

Physician Fraud and Business Issues
© 2000, 185 pages, softbound, Issues Collection

Managed Care Compliance Guide
© 1999, 247 pages and disk, 3-ring binder, Practice Guide

Best Practices Handbook in Advising Clients on Fraud and Abuse Issues
© 1999, 94 pages, softbound, Practice Guide

Administrative Sanctions for Healthcare Fraud and Abuse
© 1999, 140 pages, spiral bound, Expert Series

Long Term Care Antifraud and Abuse Compliance Manual
© 1999, 149 pages, spiral bound, Expert Series

False Claims Act & the Healthcare Industry: Counseling & Litigation
© 1999, 438 pages, hardbound, Cornerstone Series

Healthcare Fraud: Investigations and Enforcement Issues
© 1999, 298 pages, softbound, Issues Collection

Healthcare Provider Compliance Issues
© 1999, 154 pages, softbound, Issues Collection

Stark II Regulations: A Comprehensive Analysis
© 1998, 40 pages, spiral bound, Expert Series

Legal Issues in Healthcare Fraud and Abuse: Navigating the Uncertainties, 2nd Edition
© 1997, 1994, 403 pages, softbound, Cornerstone Series

Healthcare Model Compliance Manual
© 1999, 1998, 1997, 318+ pages with disk, 3-ring binder, Practice Guide

Medicare and Medicaid False Claims: Legal Complexities and Developing Issues
© 1996, 54 pages, spiral bound, Expert Series

State Illegal-Remuneration and Self-Referral Laws
© 1996, 160 pages, spiral bound, Expert Series

Healthcare Fraud and Abuse: Compliance and Enforcement, 1999 Program
© 1999, 3-ring binder, Health Lawyers' Education Program

Healthcare Fraud and Abuse: Compliance and Enforcement, 1998 Program
© 1998, 3-ring binder, Health Lawyers' Education Program

ABOUT THE AUTHORS

Robert A. Griffith is a partner at Schwartz and Griffith in Boston, Massachusetts, and specializes in the representation of healthcare providers in all matters concerning fraud and abuse investigations including prosecutions, overpayment demands, billing, compliance, and discipline. He began his career as a Massachusetts Assistant Attorney in one of the first Medicaid Fraud Control Units in the nation. With over twenty years experience as a trial attorney in this specialized area of law, Mr. Griffith has participated in over 250 healthcare fraud and abuse investigations and prosecutions in no fewer than seventeen different state and federal jurisdictions.

In private practice in Boston, Massachusetts since 1982, Mr. Griffith is the author of numerous articles and book chapters on health law topics in the area of fraud and abuse and a frequent speaker at health law continuing education programs for the legal and medical professions. Robert A. Griffith presently serves on the Board of Directors of the American Health Lawyers Association. Mr. Griffith is also a former Chairperson of the Massachusetts Bar Association's Health Law Section and the Medicine and Law Committee of the Tort and Insurance Practice Section of the American Bar Association. Mr. Griffith is a graduate of St. Bonaventure University 1974 and Boston College Law School 1978.

Paul W. Shaw is a member of the litigation and health law departments of Brown, Rudnick, Freed & Gesmer in Boston, Massachusetts, where he concentrates in representing businesses and professionals in healthcare fraud and abuse investigations. Mr. Shaw has represented numerous healthcare clients involved in criminal fraud and abuse investigations by the federal government and state Medicaid Fraud Control Units in Massachusetts and elsewhere in the United States. These clients include clinical laboratories, hospitals, durable medical equipment suppliers, physicians, medical practice groups, home health agencies, and other healthcare providers.

Mr. Shaw has authored numerous healthcare articles for trade and professional journals and is a frequent presenter at AHLA conferences. He has written and lectured extensively on issues of healthcare fraud and abuse, with particular emphasis on statistical sampling and extrapolation procedures. Mr. Shaw is a member of the American Health Lawyers Association Task Force that is developing a Model Physician Compliance Plan for use by physician practices, and has developed and implemented compliance plans for hospitals and other industries.

Mr. Shaw graduated from Georgetown University Law School in 1975, after graduating *magna cum laude* from the University of Massachusetts at Amherst, where he was elected to Phi Beta Kappa. He served as an Assistant Attorney General in the Criminal Bureau of the Massachusetts Attorney General's Office from 1975 through 1982, where he was Chief of the Regulatory Crimes Unit. He is an Adjunct Professor at Suffolk Law School, where he teaches a course on healthcare fraud and abuse. Prior to joining Brown Rudnick, Mr. Shaw was a founding partner in the Boston law firm of Schwartz, Shaw and Griffith.

ACKNOWLEDGMENTS

We would like to thank a number of people who contributed to the development and publication of this book. First, we would like to thank Will Harvey, Acquisitions Editor and Manager of Non-Dues Publications of the American Health Lawyers Association, for approaching us with the concept for this publication. Without Will's foresight, experience, guidance, and considerable patience, this project would never have been completed. For the countless hours spent editing and organizing the contents of this publication we extend our heartfelt appreciation to Rob Truhn, AHLA Production Editor and Editor of *Health Lawyers News*. Last, but certainly not least, we thank Jerome B. Tichner, a former associate with Schwartz, Shaw and Griffith, presently with Brown Rudnick Freed & Gesmer, for his many hours of research, editing, and proofreading.

We also thank our many colleagues in the American Health Lawyers Association for their friendship and encouragement on this project. In particular, we would like to thank Phil Pomerance of Hinshaw & Culbertson in Chicago, who graciously allowed us to adapt materials he has presented over the years at AHLA seminars. Of course, as with many projects of this size, it could not have been accomplished without the motivation and reassuring support of our family of friends in the organization, including Leslie Allison, Nyda Brook, David Greenberg, Alan Gilchrist, Alice Gosfield, Anne Hoover, Patricia Jacobsen, James Kelly, Marilou King, Michel LaFond, Peter Leibold, Laurie Levin, Lawrence Litwak, Nicholas Messuri, Claire Obade, Mark Rust, James Sheehan, Howard Sollins, Sanford Teplitsky, Elizabeth Turqman, and James Wieland. Thank you for all you have done.

TABLE OF CONTENTS

About the Authors

Acknowledgments

1. **Introduction** 1

2. **The Statutory Framework for Fraud and Abuse Investigations** 3
   2.1 **Federal Criminal Statutes** 3
       2.1.1 Health Insurance Portability and Accountability Act of 1996 3
             2.1.1.1   Health Care Fraud Statute 3
             2.1.1.2   False Statements Relating to Healthcare Matters 3
             2.1.1.3   Obstruction of Criminal Healthcare Investigations 4
             2.1.1.4   Theft and Embezzlement Relating to Healthcare Benefit 4
       2.1.2 Medicare and Medicaid Patient Protection Act of 1987 4
             2.1.2.1   Anti-Kickback Provisions 5
       2.1.3 False Claims Act 5
       2.1.4 False Statements 6
       2.1.5 Mail and Wire Fraud 6
       2.1.6 Obstruction of Justice 7
   2.2 **State Law** 7
   2.3 **Civil Enforcement Actions** 7
       2.3.1 Civil False Claims Act 7
             2.3.1.1   Qui Tam Actions 8
       2.3.2 Administrative Sanctions 9
             2.3.2.1   Civil Monetary Penalties 9
             2.3.2.2   Exclusions 10

3. **Overview of Enforcement Agencies** 11
   3.1 **Department of Health and Human Services** 11
       3.1.1 Health Care Financing Administration 11
       3.1.2 Office of the Inspector General 11
   3.2 **Department of Justice** 12
       3.2.1 U.S. Attorney General's Office 12
       3.2.2 Federal Bureau of Investigation 12
   3.3 **State Programs** 13
       3.3.1 Medicaid Fraud Control Units 13
       3.3.2 Divisions of Medical Assistance (State Medicaid Administrators) 13
   3.4 **Other Entities Involved in Detecting Fraud and Abuse** 14
       3.4.1 Carriers and Intermediaries 14
       3.4.2 Peer Review Organizations 14
   3.5 **Private Enforcement** 14
       3.5.1 Qui Tam Suits 15
   3.6 **Cooperative Government Activities** 15

4.	**Requests for Documents and Investigatory Subpoenas** 17
4.1	**Request for Information or Assistance by the OIG** 17
4.2	**Demand for Immediate Access by the OIG or State Medicaid Enforcement Agency** 17
4.3	**Subpoena from the OIG** 18
4.4	**HIPAA Subpoenas** 19
4.5	**Civil Investigative Demands** 20
4.6	**Grand Jury Subpoenas** 21

5.	**Responding to the Requests for Documents** 22
5.1	**Contacting the Government** 22
5.2	**Review and Analysis of the Document Request** 23
5.3	**Ensuring the Integrity of the Requested Documents** 24
5.4	**Responding to the Document Demand** 24
	5.4.1 Document the Scope of the Subpoena 24
	5.4.2 Determine the Location of Potential Documents 25
	5.4.3 Appoint an Independent Custodian 25
	5.4.4 Provide Written Instructions to the Custodian and Document Searchers 25
	5.4.5 Advise Company Personnel About the Issuance of the Document Request 26
	5.4.6 Provide Written Instructions That No Relevant Documents Are to be Destroyed 26
	5.4.7 Consultations Between the Custodian and Counsel Regarding Questions Relating to the Scope of the Subpoena 26
	5.4.8 Counsel Should Personally Review the Gathered Documents 27
	5.4.9 Keep a Record of the Documents and Materials Produced to the Government . . 27

6.	**Investigations** 28
6.1	**Informing Employees of an Investigation** 28
6.2	**Sudden Appearances by Agents** 29
6.3	**Providing Access to Records** 30
6.4	**Search Warrants** 30
	6.4.1 Practical Tips 31
	6.4.2 Advice in the Event of a Search 31
6.5	**Electronic and Video Surveillance** 33
	6.5.1 Tape Recording Conversations 33
	6.5.2 Video Surveillance and Telephone Wiretaps 34

7.	**Issues and Advice for Discussion During an Investigation** 35
7.1	**Multiple Representation and Fee Issues** 35
7.2	**Retaining Auditors, Experts, and Other Consultants** 38
7.3	**Hiring an Attorney for the Employees** 38
7.4	**Notifying the Government that the Employees Are Represented by Counsel** 39
7.5	**Joint Defense Agreements** 40
	7.5.1 Elements of a Joint Defense Agreement 41

8.	**Pre-Judgment Asset Seizures and Payment Suspensions**	**43**
8.1	Background	43
8.2	Fraud Injunction Statute; Freezing and Protecting Assets	43
	8.2.1 Anatomy of a §1345 Action	47
8.3	Suspension of Payments to Providers	49
8.4	Use of Criminal Forfeiture for Healthcare Offenses	50
	8.4.1 Practice Note	50
9.	**Civil Audits and the Use of Statistical Sampling**	**53**
9.1	How a Statistical Sampling Audit is Initiated	53
9.2	How a Statistical Sampling Study is Conducted	54
9.3	Challenging Statistical Sampling	56
9.4	Practical Suggestions for Confronting a Statistical Sampling Study	58
	9.4.1 Re-Examination of the Audited Cases	58
	9.4.2 Having a Medical Consultant Review the Medical Findings	58
	9.4.3 Retaining an Expert Statistician	59
9.5	HCFA Consent Settlement Procedures	59
9.6	Conclusion	60
10.	**Affirmative Defense Techniques**	**61**
10.1	Assessing the Information Available	61
	10.1.1 Testimonial Evidence	61
	10.1.1.1 Conduct followup interviews and obtain *affidavits*	62
	10.1.1.2 Track all witness interviews conducted by the government	63
	10.1.2 Documentary Evidence	68
	10.1.2.1 Track issues raised by the government's document requests/subpoenas	68
	10.1.2.2 Quantify the information developed	68
	10.1.2.3 Address all issues raised by the government	69
10.2	Implementing an Offense	69
	10.2.1 Providing the Government with Exculpatory Evidence	69
	10.2.2 Position Statements with Memorandum of Law	70
	10.2.2.1 Legally	70
	10.2.2.2 Factually	70
	10.2.3 Declaratory Judgment Action	70
11.	**Voluntary Disclosures and Settlement Options**	**72**
11.1	Voluntary Disclosure	72
	11.1.1 Making the Decision to Disclosre	72
	11.1.1.1 Legal Duty to Disclose Discovered Overpayments	72
	11.1.1.2 The Strategic Benefits of Disclosure	73
	11.1.1.3 Potential Negative Consequences of Disclosure	75
	11.1.1.4 The Risks of Not Disclosing	75
	11.1.2 How and To Whom to Disclose	76
	11.1.2.1 Carrier/Intermediary Disclosures	76

| | | 11.1.2.2 | Voluntary Disclosure Protocol | 76 |

11.2 Settlement Agreements 77
    11.2.1 Plea Agreement (Criminal Settlement) 77
    11.2.2 Civil Settlement 78
        11.2.2.1   Corporate Integrity Agreements 79

EXHIBITS

(Chapter 3)
I.	Example of OIG Special Fraud Alert
II.	Example of OIG Annual Work Plan

(Chapter 4)
III.	Example of OIG Written Request for Records
IV.	Example of OIG Subpoena Duces Tecum
V.	Example of DOJ Subpoena Duces Tecum
VI.	Example of Search Warrant
VII.	Example of HIPAA Subpoena Served at Conclusion of Search
VIII.	Example of Grand Jury Subpoena

(Chapter 5)
IX.	Example of Letter Confirming Document Production Agreements
X.	Example of Letter Identifying Independent Custodian of Records
XI.	Example of Memorandum to Custodian of Records
XII.	Example of Instructions to Document Searchers
XIII.	Example of Cover Letter Specifying Produced Documents
XIV.	Example of Memorandum Specifying Produced Documents

(Chapter 6)
XV.	Example of Letter re: Notice of Potential Interview
XVI.	Example of Memorandum to Staff re: Potential Investigation
XVII.	Example of Memorandum to Key Personnel re: Search Warrants
XVIII.	Examples of Application for Search Warrant and Supporting Affidavit
XIX.	Example of Search Warrant
XX.	Example of Receipt for Property Seized

(Chapter 7)
XXI.	Example of Memorandum Outlining Potential Conflict of Interest
XXII.	Example of Waiver of Potential Conflict of Interest
XXIII.	Example of Engagement Letter for Auditor
XXIV.	Example of Marking Material System Preserving Privilege
XXV.	Examples of Joint Defense Agreements

(Chapter 8)
XXVI.	Example of Verified Complaint for Injunctive Relief and Supporting Affidavit
XXVII.	Example of Temporary Restraining Order
XXVIII.	Example of Preliminary Injunction

(Chapter 9)
XXIX.	Example of HCFA Notice of Overpayment Based on Random Sampling
XXX.	Example of Appeal to a Carrier for Hearing

XXXI.	Example of Notice Describing Options for Consent Settlement Procedure

(Chapter 10)

XXXII.	Example of Chart of Investigation of Physician Practices
XXXIII.	Example of Position Statement Letter to U.S. Attorney's Office with Memorandum of Law
XXXIV.	Example of Declaratory Judgment Action

(Chapter 11)

XXXV.	Examples of Voluntary Disclosure Involving Employee Dishonesty
XXXVI.	Example of Plea Agreement
XXXVII.	Example of Civil Settlement Agreement
XXXVIII.	Example of Corporate Integrity Agreement

1. INTRODUCTION

The numbers are nothing short of staggering. While total healthcare expenditures approach approximately one trillion dollars each year, the General Accounting Office has estimated that healthcare fraud may account for as much as 10% of all expenditures, or as much as $100 billion every year.[1] As more money escapes an already strained system, efforts to detect and punish fraud that undermines both the cost and quality of healthcare have increased significantly.

Passage of the Health Insurance Portability and Accountability Act of 1996 ("HIPAA") significantly expanded the powers of the federal government to investigate healthcare fraud and abuse. HIPAA represents an unprecedented Congressional mandate to pursue an endemic fraud crisis in the healthcare industry and a significant increase in the weapons of war available to the government.

The cornerstone of the HIPAA fraud and abuse provisions is found in the legislative directive for a Medicare Fraud and Abuse Program to be administered by the Attorney General and the Secretary of the Department of Health and Human Services ("DHHS"). In January 1997, Attorney General Reno and Secretary Shalala released the "Health Care Fraud and Abuse Control Program and Guidelines," effective January 1, 1997. A central premise of the guidelines relevant to enforcement actions was the recognition of coordinated federal, state, and local enforcement programs and investigations to address healthcare fraud investigations in multiple jurisdictions. The HIPAA fraud and abuse program guidelines further direct the coordinated pursuit of criminal, civil, and administrative remedies. Three years have passed since the inception of these coordinated actions.

In January 2000, DHHS and the Department of Justice ("DOJ") released the annual report for FY 1999 for the Health Care Fraud and Abuse Control Program. There was a 16% increase in the number of healthcare fraud criminal indictments filed in 1999 (371) over the previous year.[2] A total of 396 defendants were convicted. Ninety-one new civil cases were filed in 1999 and 2,278 civil matters were pending. The federal government also won or negotiated more than $524 million in judgments, settlements, and administrative impositions in various healthcare fraud cases and proceedings. Approximately $369 million of the $490 million collected in 1999 were returned to the Medicare Trust Fund, and an additional $4.7 million was returned to Medicaid. Changes in the law resulting from HIPAA resulted in the exclusion of 2,976 individuals and entities from Medicare, Medicaid, and other federally sponsored healthcare programs. Those excluded either have faced or will face additional participation and contractual problems with a host of state, federal, and private programs.

---

[1] U.S. Department of Justice Health Care Fraud Report, Fiscal Years 1995 & 1996, p. 4.

[2] Department of Health and Human Services and the Department of Justice Health Care Fraud and Abuse Control Program Annual Report for FY 1999, Pg. 2.(hereinafter "DHHS/DOJ Report"), found on the Web at www.hhs.gov/oig/press/hipaa2.htm.

In almost every instance, the case was developed in part through a government-directed investigation. Despite the government's remarkable track record in this area, many in the healthcare industry question whether fraud and abuse is as rampant as claimed, and whether a substantial portion is, in some part, attributable to a Byzantine set of poorly drafted rules, regulations, and guidelines. It is no great revelation that, given today's statutory arsenal, many innocent and unintended acts can easily be and often are "characterized and alleged" as falling within the broad penumbra of healthcare fraud and abuse. Understanding the process of a fraud and abuse investigation, and acquiring a basic understanding of the issues and practical steps to employ when you or your company becomes involved, is the first step towards a successful outcome.

This Practice Guide is designed to provide administrators, executives, medical directors, office managers, physicians, and medical practice managers with a broad overview of healthcare fraud investigations, supplementing the authors' discussion with a comprehensive set of sample government documents, affidavits, and subpoenas, as well as typical and helpful letters and memoranda generated by experienced healthcare fraud and abuse defense attorneys. Understanding the powers, procedures, and remedies available to law enforcement entities is critical for healthcare industry executives, personnel, and attorneys who find themselves participating in these focused investigations as a "target," "subject," "witness," or counsel.

2. THE STATUTORY FRAMEWORK FOR FRAUD AND ABUSE INVESTIGATIONS

Myriad statutes empower the federal government to pursue healthcare fraud and abuse on criminal, civil, and administrative bases. The following is a brief overview of the statutes most commonly used to prosecute and sanction healthcare fraud.

2.1 FEDERAL CRIMINAL STATUTES

2.1.1 Health Insurance Portability and Accountability Act of 1996

Congress's passage of HIPAA established a number of new offenses relating to healthcare fraud. Specifically, HIPAA contains the following criminal provisions.

2.1.1.1 *Health Care Fraud Statute*

18 U.S.C. § 1347 sets forth criminal penalties applicable to all-payer healthcare benefit programs, including private insurance plans. Under this provision, penalties may be imposed for knowingly and willfully executing or attempting to execute any scheme or artifice to 1) defraud any healthcare benefit program or 2) obtain by means of false or fraudulent pretenses any money or property owned by or in the custody or control of any healthcare benefit program.[1] **For purposes of this statute, "Health care benefit program" is defined as**

> Any public or private plan or contract, affecting commerce, under which any medical benefit, item or service is provided to any individual, and includes any individual or entity who is providing a medical benefit, item or service for which payment may be made under the plan or contract.[2]

Penalties under this section include the imposition of fines and significant terms of imprisonment. Violations resulting in serious bodily injury may give rise to 20-year sentences.

2.1.1.2 *False Statements Relating to Healthcare Matters*

18 U.S.C.§ 1035 is a false statement statute applicable to all payer health benefit programs or plans. Under this statute, criminal penalties may be imposed for making knowing and wilful false statements "in connection with the delivery or payment of health care benefits, items or services."[3] Penalties include fines and imprisonment up to five years.

---

[1] *See* 18 U.S.C. §1347.

[2] 18 U.S.C. § 24.

[3] 18 U.S.C. § 1035.

2.1.1.3 *Obstruction of Criminal Healthcare Investigations*

18 U.S.C. § 1518 prohibits the obstruction of federal healthcare offense investigations. Criminal penalties may be imposed under this section upon individuals engaging in, or attempting to willfully prevent, obstruct, mislead, or delay the communication of information or records relating to a federal healthcare offense to a criminal investigator.[4] Penalties under this section include fines and imprisonment up to five years.

2.1.1.4 *Theft and Embezzlement Relating to Healthcare Benefit*

18 U.S.C. § 669 establishes criminal penalties for the knowing and willful theft or embezzlement from, or in relation to, a healthcare benefit program. Penalties under this section include fines and imprisonment up to 10 years; where the property involved does not exceed $100 in value, the term of imprisonment would not exceed one year.[5]

2.1.2 Medicare and Medicaid Patient Protection Act of 1987
42 U.S.C. § 1320a-7b(a)

This statute proscribes six specific types of conduct including the making of false statements, the concealment of information with the intent to induce improper federal payments, improperly converting federal payments, and submitting claims for services provided by unlicensed individuals. Violation of any provision of this statute is a felony punishable by a $25,000 fine and/or imprisonment up to 5 years.[6]

This section's most commonly enforced provision prohibits individuals from "knowingly and wilfully mak[ing] or caus[ing] to be made any false statement or representation of a material fact in any application for any benefit or payment under [the Medicare or Medicaid programs]." As claims containing *any* false statements regarding material facts are actionable under this provision, many activities beyond the blatant billing for unrendered services may lead to violations. Examples of other prohibited conduct under this provision include misrepresenting services actually rendered (e.g., "upcoding"), and falsely certifying that certain services were medically reasonable and necessary.

---

[4] 18 U.S.C. § 1518.

[5] 18 U.S.C. § 669.

[6] 42 U.S.C. § 1320a-7b(a).

2.1.2.1 *Anti-Kickback Provisions*
42 U.S.C. § 1320a-7b(b)

Included within the Medicare and Medicaid Patient Protection Act of 1987 is the federal Anti-Kickback Statute. This act prohibits the knowing and wilful solicitation, receipt, offer, or payment of remuneration (i.e, kickbacks, bribes or rebates) to induce either the referral of individuals to a party who shall furnish or arrange the furnishment of items or services reimbursable under Medicare or Medicaid or to induce the purchase of items or services payable by Medicare or Medicaid.[7] A violation of any provision of this Act represents a felony punishable by a $25,000 fine and/or imprisonment up to 5 years. The term remuneration refers to *any form* of economic benefit, including: reduced rent, compensation guarantees, equipment loans, the provision of administrative and billing services, and participation in ventures offering the opportunity to generate fees.

Because the literal wording of this statute prohibits a number of transactions generally necessary or beneficial to the healthcare industry, Congress authorized DHHS to create "safe harbor" exceptions permitting certain practices that might otherwise be prohibited. For an in-depth analysis of the application of the anti-kickback law and its various safe harbors, the authors recommend *Legal issues in Healthcare Fraud and Abuse: Navigating the Uncertainties*.[8] Healthcare providers are cautioned to scrutinize any business arrangement where any direct or indirect payment or other economic benefit is related to patient referrals.

2.1.3 False Claims Act
18 U.S.C. § 287

The False Claims Act ("FCA") represents the primary tool used by the federal government to prosecute fraudulent billing practices under Medicare and Medicaid. The statute prohibits presenting a claim to the United States that is known to be "false, fictitious or fraudulent."[9] Violations of the FCA are felonies punishable by significant fines and imprisonment terms up to 5 years.

To prove a violation of the FCA, the government must establish the following elements:

- the defendant presented a claim against the United States or any agency or department of the United States;
- the claim was false, fictitious, or fraudulent; and

---

[7] 42 U.S.C. 1320a-7b(b).

[8] (2nd ed. 1997), by Carrie Valiant and David Matyas (published by the American Health Lawyers Association).

[9] 18 U.S.C. § 287.

- the defendant knew or should have known the claim was false, fictitious, or fraudulent.[10]

While some courts have held that the Government must prove the defendant knew of the falsity of the claims to prove violations of this section, others rule that knowledge can be inferred from reckless disregard or conscious avoidance of the truth.

2.1.4 False Statements
18 U.S.C. § 1001

The government frequently utilizes this statute prohibiting false statements as a vehicle to prosecute healthcare fraud. Specifically, the statute prohibits the making of any false, fictitious or fraudulent statements to the United States or any agency thereof.[11] This prohibition extends to *any* false statement, either oral or written, thereby allowing for a very broad range of prosecution. The expansive reach of this statute allows it to be applied not only against individuals submitting claims containing false representations, but also against witnesses or others who lie to the Federal Bureau of Investigation ("FBI") agents during the course of investigations regarding those claims.

2.1.5 Mail and Wire Fraud
18 U.S.C. § 1341
18 U.S.C. § 1343

As correspondence with Medicare and Medicaid almost always involves the use of mail and electronic wiring systems, parties submitting false claims to the government will frequently be the subject of prosecution under the mail and wire fraud statutes. Government programs and private providers invariably utilize the mail or electronic wire systems to send or receive payments, explanation of benefit forms, and other related documents. Consequently, these two statutes, which prohibit the use of the mail or the wires to further "schemes" to defraud, are often applied against parties submitting false claims.

Notably, false claims submitted to and/or schemes to defraud or submit claims to private health insurance companies and government entities will implicate these statutes. The mail and wire fraud statutes cover the entire range of fraudulent conduct punishable under the False Claims Act, including:

- billing for services that were not rendered;
- filing claims for services billed at inflated rates; and

---

[10] *See Id.*

[11] 18 U.S.C. § 1001.

- billing for services that were not medically reasonable and necessary.[12]

Violations of either the mail or wire fraud statutes are subject to a fine of up to $250,000 and/or imprisonment of up to five years. In addition, mail and wire fraud violations are considered predicate offenses under the Racketeer Influenced and Corrupt Organizations Act ("RICO").[13]

2.1.6 Obstruction of Justice
18 U.S.C. § 1518
18 U.S.C. § 1505

Obstruction, in any material way, of a criminal investigation involving potential federal healthcare offenses or of Medicare audits or investigations represents a felonious act. Obstruction generally occurs when a healthcare provider fails to produce subpoenaed records; alters, enhances, or destroys records during the course of an investigation; or induces a witness not to cooperate with criminal investigators. Conviction under these obstruction statutes may result in fines and/or imprisonment of up to 5 years.

2.2 STATE LAW

In addition to the various federal criminal provisions used against providers filing false Medicare and Medicaid claims, a number of state enforcement provisions exist. Applicable state laws range from provisions addressing general larceny to statutes specifically designed to fight healthcare fraud. For example, a number of states have enacted state Medicaid False Claims Acts and state Medicaid anti-kickback laws patterned after federal statutes.[14] In addition, more than 40 states have created special units dedicated to the prosecution of Medicaid fraud.

2.3 CIVIL ENFORCEMENT ACTIONS

2.3.1 Civil False Claims Act

Similar to the criminal FCA, the government may, in addition to seeking criminal sanctions, pursue a provider under the civil False Claims Act ("civil FCA").[15] As a result of its penalty provisions, this represents one of the most powerful enforcement tools the federal government has at its disposal in connection with healthcare fraud. Under the civil FCA, any person or entity knowingly making a false claim to the government (i.e., to Medicare), is liable for mandatory civil

---

[12] Carrie Valiant, Esq. and David E. Matayas, Esq, *Legal issues in Healthcare Fraud and Abuse: Navigating the Uncertainties*, p. 159 (1997).

[13] 18 U.S.C. § 1961.

[14] *See, e.g.,* Mass. G.L. c. 118E, §§ 40, 41.

[15] 31 U.S.C. § 3729

penalties and fines. The mere filing of a false claim will trigger liability under the civil FCA, even if payment is never made or received.

The penalty provision of the civil FCA mandates that *each individual false claim submitted* gives rise to penalties between $5,000 and $10,000; this can also be coupled with penalties equaling treble the damages incurred by the government. Consequently, each false "line item" claimed can result in thousands of dollars of liability. In cases where providers submit significant numbers of claims (e.g., hospitals or laboratories), total exposure to liability can amount to millions of dollars.

To establish liability under the civil FCA, the government must prove the following:

1) the provider presented or caused to be presented to an agent of the United States a claim for payment;
2) the claim was false or fraudulent; and
3) the defendant knew that the claim was false or fraudulent.

Importantly, the knowledge requirement for civil liability under the civil FCA is often lower than under the criminal statute.[16] The civil FCA defines "knowing" and "knowingly" as either actual knowledge or the "reckless disregard of the truth or falsity of the information."[17] Under these definitions, honest mistakes are not subject to the civil FCA. However, the careless submission of a series of improper claims may constitute reckless disregard, and so lead to liability.[18] The DOJ has stated that where billing errors, honest mistakes, or negligence result in improper claims, the provider may be asked to return the funds but without penalties.

2.3.1.1 *Qui Tam Actions*

The qui tam or "whistleblower" provisions contained within the civil FCA contribute significantly toward making the civil FCA the most commonly used statute in civil enforcement of healthcare fraud.[19] Qui tam provisions allow private persons (called "relators") to bring civil actions for violations of the FCA on behalf of the United States, and to receive a percentage of the funds obtained from FCA defendants. These significant awards provide substantial incentive to report (or "blow the whistle" on) fraudulent billing practices. Private persons satisfying the requirements of this section who report directly and independently obtained information of fraudulent billing to the government are generally entitled to receive either between 15% - 30% of the recovery from a government proceeded action, or between 25% -30% of the recovery from an action conducted by

---

[16] 31 U.S.C. § 3729(b).

[17] *Id.*

[18] *See, e.g.,* United States ex rel. Hochman v. Nackman, 145 F.3d 1069 (9th Cir. 1998).

[19] *See* 31 U.S.C. § 3730(b).

the whistleblower.[20] As a result, qui tam cases are frequently the basis for initiating a government investigation of healthcare fraud.

Under the statute, a "qui tam plaintiff" is required to file the complaint in federal court under seal. The complaint and a written disclosure of substantially all material evidence in the plaintiff's possession must be served on the government. The complaint is not served upon the named defendant. The complaint remains under seal while the United States Attorney's Office investigates the allegations in the complaint. The government's initial review period is sixty days, but can be extended by the court on motion of the government with the plaintiff's assent. During the period the case is under seal, the government determines whether the allegations have merit and intervention is warranted. It is not uncommon for a qui tam complaint to remain under seal for several years while the government investigates and/or develops the case.

2.3.2 Administrative Sanctions

2.3.2.1 *Civil Monetary Penalties*

Pursuant to the Civil Monetary Penalty Law ("CMP Law"),[21] DHHS is authorized to administratively impose civil monetary penalties ("CMPs") and assessments against providers making false or improper claims. These penalties apply to a broad range of conduct, including the making of claims to Medicare or Medicaid for items or services that the party submitting the claim either *knows* or *should know* were not provided as claimed. Under HIPAA, penalties under this section were increased in 1996 from $2,000 to $10,000 per claim, and an additional penalty was raised from two three times the amount claimed.[22] For certain actions, civil penalties may be as high as $50,000 per act.

In practice, CMP actions are often brought against providers convicted of criminal violations. This approach is frequently utilized because criminal convictions represent prima facie evidence of false claims.

Medicare is required to notify appropriate state licensing agencies, the state Medicaid program, and peer review and professional organizations of the imposition of CMPs against providers and request action be taken against the provider. These notices have a strong potential to inspire collateral action. Resignation in advance from certain organizations may minimize the number of organizations who receive notice.

---

[20] *See* 31 U.S.C. § 3730(d).

[21] 42 U.S.C. § 1320a-7a.

[22] Pub. L. No. 104-191.

2.3.2.2 *Exclusions*

DHHS is also empowered to exclude providers from participation in the Medicare and Medicaid programs under certain circumstances.[23] Exclusion from the Medicare program is an effective deterrent. The mere threat of this daunting sanction often leads to settlement, illustrating why very few healthcare cases actually proceed to trial.

Conviction of a criminal offense related to the delivery of an item or service under the Medicare or Medicaid program will result in a **mandatory** exclusion for a minimum period of five years.[24] There is no maximum period of exclusion. By law, a "conviction" for the purposes of exclusion includes findings of guilt, pleas of guilt, pleas of nolo contendere, and/or entry into "first offender programs."[25]

DHHS is also empowered to issue non-mandatory or "permissive" exclusions from the Medicare and Medicaid programs. For example, a conviction for financial misconduct relating to the general delivery of healthcare or a conviction for obstruction of a healthcare investigation may result in permissive exclusion.[26] HIPAA established minimum periods of exclusion for various categories of convictions ranging from one to three years.

---

[23] Social Security Act § 1128; 42 U.S.C. §1320a-7.

[24] 42 U.S.C. § 1320a-7.

[25] Social Security Act § 1128(i); 42 U.S.C. §1320a-7(i)..

[26] 42 U.S.C. § 1320a-7(b).

3. OVERVIEW OF ENFORCEMENT AGENCIES

A substantial number of administrative and criminal investigative agencies are involved in a cooperative effort to identify, investigate, and act upon instances of fraud and abuse. These include the DOJ, the FBI, the DHHS Office of Inspector General ("OIG"), all local Medicare Carriers or Intermediaries, all 48 state Medicaid Fraud Control Units ("MFCUs"), every "single state agency" administering the Medicaid Program, and private individuals recently energized by the potential windfall due a relator in a qui tam case.

3.1 DEPARTMENT OF HEALTH AND HUMAN SERVICES

3.1.1 Health Care Financing Administration

The Health Care Financing Administration ("HCFA") is a federal agency within DHHS. Established in 1977, HCFA maintains the consolidated responsibility of administering both the federal Medicare and Medicaid programs.

HCFA is responsible for issuing interpretations of the Social Security Act, as well as providing guidance to the various Medicare carriers and intermediaries administering the Medicare program at the local level. As part of its role, HCFA oversees Medicare overpayment appeals during which providers contest audit results, payment denials, and cost allowance denials issued by carriers or intermediaries. Counsel should be aware that in addition to pursuing administrative initiatives focused on preventing healthcare fraud, HCFA works hand-in-hand with the DOJ and the OIG to combat fraud and abuse at the federal level.

3.1.2 Office of the Inspector General

The OIG is an investigative agency responsible for investigations of suspected fraud and abuse in the Medicare program. Investigators of this agency probe areas of suspected fraud and abuse by interviewing potential witnesses, gathering documents, and analyzing claim/payment trends regarding providers under scrutiny. This agency wields considerable power—including the ability to impose administrative sanctions such as CMPs, as well as to exclude providers from federal healthcare programs. In 1999 alone, OIG excluded 2,976 individuals and businesses from the Medicare/Medicaid programs.[1]

The OIG does not have the power to bring criminal prosecutions or civil enforcement actions. The OIG may refer cases to the DOJ for criminal or civil action, but the decision to prosecute rests with the United States Attorney's Office for the federal district concerned.

---

[1] DHHS/DOJ Report, Pg. 10.

In addition to investigating fraud and abuse, the OIG attempts to deter such activities by issuing Special Fraud Alerts regarding particular areas of concern.[2] The office has also developed public sample compliance programs setting forth guidelines under which various types of providers are advised to operate.[3] These guidelines discuss "risk areas" noted by the OIG, as well as recommendations regarding specific billing requirements and procedures. The OIG also publishes an annual work plan identifying the goals and focus areas of the agency.[4]

3.2 DEPARTMENT OF JUSTICE

The primary investigative/enforcement agency in the United States is the DOJ. Healthcare fraud and abuse has become a primary target of the DOJ during the last ten years. In fact, on its list of priorities, the DOJ has placed healthcare fraud and abuse as second only to violent crime. Two investigative branches exist within this agency: the U.S. Attorney General's Office and the FBI.

3.2.1 U.S. Attorney General's Office

The Attorney General's Office maintains local offices throughout the United States and has established a number of healthcare fraud units specifically devoted to the pursuit of healthcare fraud and abuse. Local U.S. Attorneys investigate and prosecute civil and criminal violations and may utilize any number of various statutes to target healthcare providers and suppliers. Demonstrating its focus on healthcare fraud and abuse, in 1993 the U.S. Attorney General appointed a Special Counsel for Health Care Fraud to organize and oversee the DOJ's efforts in this area. In 1999, the Attorney General established a National Health Care Fraud Task Force to coordinate efforts by federal and state law enforcement agencies.[5]

3.2.2 Federal Bureau of Investigation

The FBI is the primary law enforcement agency for the federal government, and it is committed to the deterrence and prosecution of healthcare fraud and abuse. In 1999, the FBI handled over 1,500 healthcare related cases and over 500 agents were assigned full time to this area.[6] Under HIPAA, several hundred million dollars has been allocated to the FBI for its healthcare fraud efforts. The FBI has jurisdiction not only to investigate crimes involving the federal Medicare/Medicaid

---

[2] *See* Exhibit I.

[3] For example, in 1999 the OIG has issued guidances relating to home health agencies and durable medical equipment suppliers. These and other guidances can be found within the OIG's Web site: www.dhhs.gov/progorg/oig.

[4] *See* Exhibit II.

[5] *See* DHHS/DOJ Report, Pg. 8.

[6] *See Id.* at 22.

programs but also commercial insurance carriers such as Blue Cross/Blue Shield. Through the use of federal statutes prohibiting the use of the mails or wires to commit fraud, as well through provisions of HIPAA, the FBI is able to pursue companies and individuals suspected of defrauding private insurers.

Procedurally, the FBI does not have independent authority to prosecute violations. Consequently, the FBI coordinates with and conveys its investigative findings to the U.S. Attorney General's office. Together, these two arms of the DOJ act as the federal government's primary weapon against fraud or abuse. The effectiveness of this collaboration is clear. In 1999, 371 new criminal prosecutions were filed, while 396 defendants were convicted in healthcare fraud related crimes.[7]

3.3 STATE PROGRAMS

Medicaid is a partially federally funded health insurance program administered by each state through a "single state" agency. Consequently, although the DOJ has jurisdiction over Medicaid fraud, a majority of Medicaid fraud cases are handled by the offices of the individual state Attorneys General.

3.3.1 Medicaid Fraud Control Units

Currently, 48 states have established MFCUs to detect and prosecute fraud. These units, which primarily operate within the states' Attorneys General offices, are authorized to investigate fraud against the Medicaid and Medicare programs.[8] MFCUs receive referrals from a variety of sources, including the "single state" agencies administering the Medicaid program in each state, private contractors administering aspects various aspects of the Medicaid program, and other various regulatory agencies such as those overseeing health, mental health, retardation, and social services.

3.3.2 Divisions of Medical Assistance
(State Medicaid Administrators)

In the Medicaid program, fraud and abuse is generally detected by the state agency administering the program (e.g., Massachusetts' Division of Medical Assistance). These agencies routinely audit providers to determine if they are operating within the program's rules and regulations. The various types of providers routinely audited include:

---

[7] *See Id.* at 2.

[8] At the time of publication, three states had not formed Medicaid Fraud Control Units. These states were Idaho, Nebraska, and North Dakota.

- physicians;
- durable medical equipment providers;
- home health agencies; and
- nursing homes.

If cases of fraud are uncovered during the course of audits, these state agencies are required by federal law to refer the case for criminal investigation to the state MFCU.

3.4 OTHER ENTITIES INVOLVED IN DETECTING FRAUD AND ABUSE

3.4.1 Carriers and Intermediaries

Although HCFA administers Medicare, it does not directly handle the processing and payment of the millions of claims submitted each month. Instead, HCFA contracts with private insurance companies to administer the claims processing and payment functions for the Medicare program. Specifically, HCFA contracts with insurers to act as fiscal intermediaries to Medicare Part A providers and as Medicare carriers to Medicare Part B providers.[9]

Medicare carriers and intermediaries play a significant role in the identification of fraud and abuse. These agencies review the claims and cost reports submitted by participating providers as well as the supporting documentation. As such, they are in an ideal position to identify the errors, inconsistencies, and irregular billing patterns frequently associated with fraud and abuse. Each carrier and intermediary has a fraud and abuse unit charged with investigating and identifying potentially fraudulent practices. Upon the discovery of potential abuse, these agencies will either perform an independent investigation and audit, or convey their findings to the appropriate government agencies.

3.4.2 Peer Review Organizations

Private peer review organizations contract with HCFA and states to engage in the review of physician services. These organizations attempt to identify physicians operating below the standard of care or outside professional standards and have the ability to recommend that such providers be sanctioned.

3.5 PRIVATE ENFORCEMENT

HCFA encourages private citizens to participate in the mounting deluge against healthcare fraud. The government provides a bounty of up to $1,000 for any fraud and abuse uncovered as a

---

[9] Part A providers include, but are not limited to, hospitals, skilled nursing facilities, home health agencies, and hospices, whereas Part B providers include, but are not limited to, physicians, physicians assistants, durable medical equipment suppliers, and clinical laboratories.

result of a Medicare recipient's complaint.[10] Additionally, HCFA has established various fraud reporting mechanisms such as fraud telephone hotlines to provide easy access for beneficiaries suspecting fraud or abuse.

Private commercial carriers have also begun to initiate actions under the federal RICO statute that was originally enacted to fight organized crime.[11]

3.5.1 Qui Tam Suits

Private enforcement of healthcare fraud and abuse has reached an all-time high due in large part to amendments made in 1986 to the FCA. In 1986, Congress created significant incentives for private individuals to assist the government in bringing fraud and abuse claims. These amendments empower private individuals (known as relators) to file qui tam suits on behalf of the government and have led to enormous recoveries for the government and the relators. In 1999, the federal government paid more than $44 million to relators under the qui tam provisions of the FCA.[12]

3.6 COOPERATIVE GOVERNMENT ACTIVITIES

Historically, with regard to the investigation of healthcare fraud, little cooperation took place between the various federal agencies, or between federal and state prosecutors. This has changed significantly as we enter the new millennium. In 1996, HIPPA mandated that a Fraud and Abuse Control Program be initiated.[13] This program is designed to:

- coordinate federal, state, and local law enforcement to control healthcare fraud and abuse;
- conduct investigations, audits, evaluations, and inspections relating to the delivery of and the payment for healthcare;
- facilitate the enforcement of the Medicare and Medicaid exclusion, CMPs, and the Anti-Kickback Statute;
- provide industry guidance, including the issuance of new safe harbors, fraud alerts, and advisory opinions relating to fraudulent healthcare practices; and
- establish a national data bank for reporting and disclosure of final adverse actions against healthcare providers.[14]

---

[10] This incentive is detailed on every Medicare Explanation of Medical Benefits form.

[11] 18 U.S.C. §§ 1961-1968 (1999).

[12] DHHS/DOJ Report, Pg. 5.

[13] Pub. L. No. 104-191.

[14] DOJ Health Care Fraud and Abuse Control Program and Guidelines (effective date January 1, 1997), at p.1.

Additionally, in 1999, a National Health Care Fraud Task Force was established to coordinate efforts by federal and state agencies. As a result, the DOJ and OIG now participate in working groups that meet regularly to establish enforcement priorities.

The result of these efforts is that federal prosecutors filed 371 indictments in healthcare fraud cases in 1999, a 16% increase over 1998. The Health Care Fraud and Abuse Control Program Annual Report for FY 1999 disclosed that 396 defendants were convicted of healthcare fraud related crimes in 1999, while 2,278 civil matters were pending and 91 new civil cases were filed. The incentive for this activity is the $369 million in funds returned to the Medicare Trust Fund.

4. REQUESTS FOR DOCUMENTS AND INVESTIGATORY SUBPOENAS

In the vast majority of cases, healthcare fraud investigations involve a variety of requests for documents and investigatory subpoenas. It is not unusual that the receipt of a request for records, or subpoena duces tecum, will be the first notice a provider receives that he, she, or it, is the subject of an investigation(s). This section outlines the various tools used by law enforcement agencies to obtain documentary material during the course of an investigation.

4.1 REQUEST FOR INFORMATION OR ASSISTANCE BY THE OIG

The various regional offices of the OIG conduct investigations of Medicare fraud and abuse. By statute, the OIG has broad authority to request access to examine a healthcare provider's books and records.[1] As a result, the OIG is not required to issue a summons in order to gain access to records or information, but may simply submit a request in writing to the provider. In general, denial of the request can and often will result in eventual suspension or exclusion from the federal health programs.[2]

The OIG's authority with regard to access requests is limited to obtaining documentary materials related to the Medicare program. As a rule of thumb, recipients of such a request should ensure that **only** the materials the OIG is authorized to examine and has requested are provided. While there may be many other considerations bearing on the issue of whether or not additional documents should be provided, this decision is best made after careful consideration of a number of issues, including patient confidentiality, privacy, and privilege, agency jurisdiction, a thorough grasp of the direction of the investigation, and the related factual issues.

4.2 DEMAND FOR IMMEDIATE ACCESS BY THE OIG OR STATE MEDICAID ENFORCEMENT AGENCY

In accordance with 42 U.S.C. § 1320-7 and 42 C.F.R. § 1001.1301, a healthcare provider may be penalized for failing to grant "immediate access" (i.e., within 24 hours) upon reasonable request to the OIG or a MCFU for the inspection and copying of records, documents, or other data within these agencies' authority. Among other requirements, "reasonable requests" must be written, submitted during normal business hours, presented by and signed by an OIG or state MCFU representative, and must detail the scope, authority and effective date of the request.[3] However, if the agency reasonably believes the documents sought are in imminent risk of being

---

[1] 5 U.S.C. Appendix 3.

[2] An example of a typical OIG written request for records is appended as Exhibit III.

[3] 42 U.S.C. § 1320-7(b)(12) and 42 C.F.R. § 1001.1301.

altered or destroyed, providers are not entitled to the 24-hour time frame in which to grant access to the records.[4] The penalty for failure to comply with a request for access entails a ninety-day minimum exclusion from the Medicare and Medicaid programs.

4.3   SUBPOENA FROM THE OIG

The OIG also has broad administrative subpoena power. Under the authority of the Inspector General Act, each Inspector General has the power to subpoena the production of "all information, documents, reports, answers, records, accounts, papers and other data and documentary evidence" pertinent to an Inspector General's investigation.[5] While the power to compel the production of documentary material is very broad, the Inspector General Act does not empower the OIG to depose witnesses. As a result, most witnesses are contacted at a time and place and under circumstances considered most favorable to the government's task at hand and simply interviewed.

Many may consider an OIG and/or FBI interview far less daunting than a deposition or an appearance before the grand jury; however, in the authors' experience, the simple interview with an unsuspecting and unprepared witness often results in the most damaging testimony. An unsuspecting and unprepared witness is more likely to be nervous, anxious to appear cooperative, less able to provide accurate testimony when relevant documents are not available for reference, and more likely to assume, project, and otherwise offer less than sanguine testimony. In addition, the statements are rarely recorded and, therefore, at the very least subject to only the interviewer's interpretation.[6]

OIG subpoenas can be served by any investigator or auditor from the OIG. In addition, a subpoena can be issued to any person or entity that may have relevant information, even if that entity is not directly involved in Medicare or Medicaid programs.[7]

In the context of healthcare fraud investigations, it is significant that information obtained pursuant to an Inspector General subpoena can be shared with other government agencies, such as the DOJ. As a result, OIG subpoenas are more widely used than grand jury subpoenas, as information obtained by the United States Attorney pursuant to a grand jury subpoena can be disseminated to other agencies only upon a showing of "particularized need."[8] Understanding

---

[4] *Id.*

[5] 5 U.S.C. app. 3, 6(a).

[6] A sample OIG Subpoena Duces Tecum is appended as Exhibit IV.

[7] *See* US v. Art-Metal-USA, 484 F.Supp. 884 at 886-887 (D.N.J. 1980). "The failure to comply with an OIG subpoena is grounds for exclusion from the Medicare program. 42 U.S.C. § 1320a-7."

[8] *See* United States v. Sells Engineering, Inc, 463 U.S. 418 (1983).

that information obtained pursuant to an OIG subpoena can be disseminated to other agencies provides substance to the warning we provided earlier in this chapter about providing access to information above and beyond the request. This information can, and if relevant will, be provided to other agencies with the jurisdiction to take action.

An OIG subpoena for documents can be used during the course of any OIG investigation and the information obtained shared with the DOJ. As a matter of policy, once an OIG investigation becomes the subject of a federal criminal investigation, the United States Attorney's office generally will obtain documentary information either by means of a grand jury subpoena or a HIPAA subpoena.

4.4 HIPAA SUBPOENAS

One of the most important enforcement tools provided to the DOJ is the "health care fraud subpoena."[9] As a result of HIPAA, since 1996 the DOJ has been authorized to issue healthcare fraud subpoenas to obtain records during the course of a federal healthcare fraud investigation. The authority to issue these subpoenas duces tecum is delegated to one or more specifically designated Assistant United States Attorneys within each district. HIPAA subpoenas have become the principal investigatory tool of local United States Attorneys' offices during joint civil and criminal healthcare fraud investigations.[10] HIPAA subpoenas are easily identified by the following language, which typically appears above the signature of the U.S. Department of Justice official signing the subpoena.

> Issued under authority of Sec. 248 of the Health Insurance Portability and Accountability Act of 1996, Public Law No. 104-91
> (18 U.S.C. § 3486)

The government can require not only the production of documents but also other "tangible things" (*i.e.* date stamps, signature stamps, computers, floppy disks). "Tangible things" is a broad term and certainly subject to even broader interpretation in the future as the case law surrounding HIPAA continues to grow. The government also has the authority to require custodians of records to testify concerning the production and authentication of such records. The authority granted by this statute is very broad, and has been upheld against arguments that it constitutes an unreasonable search and seizure under the Fourth Amendment, which requires a showing of probable cause.[11]

---

[9] *See* 18 U.S.C. § 3486.

[10] An example of such a subpoena is appended as Exhibit V.

[11] *In re Subpoena Duces Tecum*, W.D. Va. Nos. 1:99MC00005; 1:99MC00006, (6/23/99).

HIPAA, which was in part designed to overcome the secrecy requirements imposed on grand jury investigations, authorizes the United States Attorney to share any information obtained with civil and administrative enforcement agencies. As a result, these summonses are frequently used during the course of joint criminal and civil investigations by the FBI and the OIG, including cases where there is an ongoing grand jury investigation or other criminal investigation. Indeed, when confronted with a HIPAA subpoena, the only safe assumption is that the investigation is "multi-agency."

Frequently, federal agents executing federal search warrants on a healthcare provider will issue a HIPAA subpoena at the conclusion of the search as a "clean up" measure to insure that all the records sought by the search warrant are eventually turned over to the government.[12]

Finally, the practitioner should be aware that HIPAA affords protection to providers who comply with a "health care fraud subpoena."[13] The statute explicitly provides immunity from civil liability to an entity that complies in good faith with a subpoena and produces the materials requested. This is an absolute grant of immunity that overrides any federal or state laws governing the confidentiality of medical records.

4.5 CIVIL INVESTIGATIVE DEMANDS (CIDs)

Since 1986, the DOJ's Civil Division is authorized to issue Civil Investigative Demands ("CIDs") during the course of investigations conducted under the FCA.[14] These administrative subpoenas can be issued by the Attorney General on any individual who may possess information relevant to a false claims act investigation. CIDs are, however, somewhat limited. Specifically, a CID is limited to use in the investigation of violations of the federal civil FCA and cannot be used in conjunction with a criminal grand jury investigation. However, information obtained pursuant to a CID can be disclosed to other attorneys, including prosecutors, within the DOJ.

By statute, CIDs are used as investigatory tools only before a suit has been filed under the FCA.[15] Once the government files suit under the FCA or intervenes in a qui tam action, discovery proceedings are subsequently governed by the ordinary rules of civil procedure.

---

[12] Exhibits VI and VII are examples of a search warrant and a HIPAA subpoena served at the conclusion of the search.

[13] 18 U.S.C. § 3486.

[14] 31 U.S.C. § 3733.

[15] See 31 U.S.C. § 3733(a)(1).

The powers granted to the DOJ are broad. A CID can require a party subject to it to:

- produce documents for inspection and copying,
- provide written answers to written interrogatories relating to the documentary material, and
- give oral testimony concerning the documentary materials.[16]

While the scope of a CID is broad, a party subject to a CID can still assert any applicable privilege as well as seek to quash the CID for failure to comply with the statutory requirements for its issuance. Because authorization to issue a CID must be obtained from the Attorney General, CIDs are administratively burdensome and not particularly favored for use in criminal health fraud investigations. HIPAA subpoenas are utilized more frequently.

4.6 GRAND JURY SUBPOENAS

Grand jury subpoenas are issued during the course of ongoing criminal investigations. Generally, the issuance of a grand jury subpoena indicates that the government has conducted at least a preliminary investigation and is determined to proceed with a criminal investigation. The issuance of a grand jury subpoena or a HIPAA subpoena rather than a search warrant indicates the prosecutor does not believe the subject will destroy or conceal the documents referenced in the subpoena. Unlike other types of summonses, a grand jury subpoena can be issued for the testimony of witnesses as well for the production of documentary material.[17]

Documents produced and testimony given to a grand jury are subject to the requirements of grand jury secrecy embodied in the Federal Rules of Criminal Procedure.[18] Given the powers of the United States Attorney and Office of Inspector General to issue administrative subpoenas during the course of a healthcare fraud investigation, grand jury subpoenas are less frequently used during a healthcare fraud investigation involving parallel criminal and civil investigations (where the potential exists for a civil enforcement action as well as criminal prosecution). Generally, a grand jury subpoena will be issued after criminal prosecutors have clearly identified the targets of the healthcare fraud investigation, and the government wants to secure the testimony of witnesses under oath prior to actually returning criminal indictments.

---

[16] *See Id.*

[17] An example of a grand jury subpoena to testify and bring documents is appended as Exhibit VIII.

[18] (Fed.R.Crim.P. 6(e)(3)(C)). [Documents and testimony] . . . can only be shared with civil or administrative agencies upon a showing of "particularized need." *See* United States v. Sells Engineering, Inc., 463 U.S. 418, 444-445 (1983).

5. RESPONDING TO THE REQUESTS FOR DOCUMENTS

Recipients of either a request for production of documents or an investigatory subpoena should **immediately** notify experienced counsel **in every instance**. The authors state this emphatically. **Do not** attempt to handle the matter initially, or simply try to determine if there is an actual need to notify or retain counsel. The receipt of a request or subpoena for records is a critical development; the handling and outcome of this situation could determine the path, pace, and result of future events (i.e. disposition of the case, continued investigation, filing of civil suit, or criminal indictment). It is not unusual that some of the most serious errors a provider can make often occur at this stage. If there is only one overriding concept the reader gains from this chapter, it should be to **immediately** notify counsel upon receipt of a request for documents or an investigatory subpoena.

5.1 CONTACTING THE GOVERNMENT

An initial review of the request for production of documents or the investigatory subpoena issued to the provider will often apprise counsel of the scope of the investigation. For example, a subpoena directed at billing records regarding patients who have received evaluation and management services is a strong indication the investigation is focused on the appropriateness of the code levels submitted for those services. On the other hand, a subpoena for business records related to the leasing of rental space to healthcare providers and/or suppliers is a strong indication the investigation is centered on whether or not the rental charge was in fact an inducement for the referral of services prohibited by the Anti-Kickback Statute.

Accurately interpreting the government's past and future course of actions, based upon its present course of action and the information sought, can be likened to a game of chess. The level of sophistication is determined by the players' experience and foresight. An attorney's anticipation of governments' investigative strategy is essential at this stage, and it is an extremely rare instance when the uninitiated novice triumphs over the master.

Identifying which governmental agencies are involved in the investigation is an important step in determining and anticipating future events. Identification of the agency involved can provide clues as to the investigation's nature. For example, a document request or subpoena issued by the OIG will, in many circumstances, be a clear indication that the investigation is still in the early stage. Alternatively, the receipt of a HIPAA subpoena is definite confirmation that the United States Attorney is conducting the investigation, indicating a more serious scenario. Irrespective of one's initial assessment of the subpoena, counsel should contact the government agent named in the request or subpoena as soon as possible. If there is an attorney involved (such as an Assistant U.S. Attorney or a DOJ or MFCU attorney), counsel should arrange a conference as soon as possible.

Contacting the government will usually enable counsel to more quickly determine the nature and scope of the investigation, although this is not a hard and fast rule. It is not unusual to hear experienced defense counsel lament about the fact that it is easier to gain critical information from a more experienced than less experienced prosecutor. Understand, however, that the amount of information disclosed by prosecutors to defense attorneys in an investigation is determined by facts too numerous to list here but certainly include:

- the nature, stage, and relative importance of the investigation;
- the particular person or entity that is the target or subject of the investigation;
- the progress made to date;
- the need for additional information or evidence;
- the prosecutor's prior relationship with defense counsel;
- defense counsel's reputation; and, of course,
- the individual style and personality of the individuals involved.

One of the first tasks at hand during the initial meeting or conversation with the government representatives is to determine whether the investigation is criminal and/or civil in nature, the specific issues under investigation and, if possible, the government's theory of the case. Healthcare fraud and abuse counsel often spend countless hours developing intricate scenarios and plans designed to elicit as much information as possible during the initial conference with the government. The inquiries are generally directed at the length and progress of the investigation as well as the client's status and that of the employees (i.e., target, subject, or witness). Keep in mind, however, that if a qui tam False Claims Action has been filed under seal, it is highly unlikely that counsel will be advised of this fact. Where the initial contact from the government is a HIPAA investigatory subpoena, a good indication exists that such an action was filed against the provider. Therefore, some thought should be given to which particular individual(s) may have filed the action, when the action was filed, what position they occupied, and what information may have been accessed.

5.2 REVIEW AND ANALYSIS OF THE DOCUMENT REQUEST

One of the first tasks at hand is a review of the scope of the request/subpoena. Requests/subpoenas will generally seek production of a series of generic categories of documents. For example, they may seek lists of employees, various specified patient records, billing records, remittance advices for a particular procedure of code, provider manuals, and bulletins issued by the Medicare carrier. The OIG or United States Attorney will often use a "stock" list of documents it seeks during the course of a healthcare fraud investigation. For some providers, certain of those categories may not exist and the government should immediately be informed of this fact.

If a subpoena is facially overbroad both in terms of the categories of documents requested and the time period involved, a reasonable attempt should be made to narrow the scope of the subpoena, including consideration of a motion to quash for overbreadth. Where compliance with the subpoena is either unreasonable or impossible, counsel should notify the government as soon as possible, carefully documenting the unreasonableness or impossibility of compliance.

Generally, subpoenas call for the production of the documents within a short period of time, such as 14 to 30 days from issuance. Typically, the government will be flexible on extending the date of production, particularly with voluminous documents involving a significant time period. Another solution would be to ask that the production of records be staggered over a reasonable period of time. Where voluminous records are requested for an extended time period the government, in the authors' experience, has been receptive to initially selecting and reviewing a sample of the requested records, deferring inspection of the remainder for some agreed upon time. This allows the healthcare provider or supplier to postpone delivery of the remaining requested records until after the initial grouping has been evaluated, with the hope that no further records will be sought.

5.3 ENSURING THE INTEGRITY OF THE REQUESTED DOCUMENTS

Nothing is more critical to the successful outcome of an investigation than to ensure that the documents, items, and other materials summonsed are not altered or destroyed. Too often, a healthcare client will panic upon receipt of a subpoena and either make "additions" to a clinical record, or otherwise withhold or destroy potentially incriminating material. In other cases, providers may falsely represent that the documents requested could not be found. Altering or otherwise enhancing the records will necessarily give rise to charges of obstruction of justice, thereby eliminating any defense based upon the quality of the records themselves. The gathering, reviewing, and production of requested materials in response to a subpoena or other discovery demand must be handled carefully to avoid obstruction of justice allegations.

It is almost standard fare that during the course of a healthcare fraud investigation the government will attempt to determine whether the provider has engaged in obstruction of justice by such conduct. While complicated billing patterns based upon technical requirements of the Medicare laws may not rise to the level of a criminal charge, nothing will result in a criminal prosecution faster than the destruction, alteration, or enhancement of documents. Indeed, in more than a few cases, the United States Attorney has concluded that, even though the underlying facts do not support either criminal or civil prosecution for healthcare fraud, obstruction of justice charges for interference with the investigation were warranted. Consequently, it is imperative that health care providers circulate a written memorandum to the provider's employees that emphasizes the importance of fully complying with the subpoena. One additional benefit of a written memorandum is documentary proof of the employer's good faith intentions should an employee alter, enhance, or destroy records on his or her own.

5.4 RESPONDING TO THE DOCUMENT DEMAND

Our checklist for responding to document demands includes the following:

5.4.1 Document the Scope of the Subpoena

Many subpoenas are drafted by persons with limited knowledge about the provider's business and the specific types of records maintained by the business. In most instances, therefore, it is beneficial for counsel to meet with the government agent or attorney who issued the subpoena in an attempt to clarify any ambiguities and, if appropriate, discuss narrowing the subpoena's scope. In situations where a CID or HIPAA subpoena requests myriad documents, counsel will negotiate directly with the designated Assistant United States Attorney who issued the subpoena. In the authors' experience, the government will limit the scope of a subpoena if the provider can demonstrate valid reasons why compliance with the literal terms of the subpoena is overburdensome. In other cases, the government will generally allow the provider to stagger production over time.

In all cases, counsel must confirm, by means of a letter, any agreements reached with the government regarding the scope and manner of production. CIDs and subpoenas are not self-enforcing. Documenting the efforts to negotiate a reasonable scope for the discovery demand will only enhance one's position if the government seeks court enforcement.[1]

5.4.2 Determine the Location of Potential Documents

Many large providers have documents and records stored at numerous locations or sites. Immediately determine whether records or other responsive documents are located at the office(s), in storage, or in the possession of a third party (such as a billing agent or accountant), and how long retrieval will take.

5.4.3 Appoint an Independent Custodian

In any case where the government has requested a large number of documents, a key employee should be appointed as custodian for the purpose of gathering the documents requested. This person should be uninvolved in the underlying allegations and should have authority to obtain documents from the highest levels of the company. The custodian should be informed that he or she may be questioned under oath by the government about the search for records and the response made to the subpoena. It is advised that the appointment and duties be in writing so as to eliminate any question about the custodian's responsibilities.[2]

It is vital that the organization carefully select not only the custodian but all other employees involved in the document gathering and review process. Any employee with access to crucial documents has the potential to file a qui tam lawsuit. In the world of the federal FCA, knowledge is power. As a general rule, most organizations should rely on the smallest control group possible.

5.4.4 Provide Written Instructions to the Custodian and Document Searchers

As every unrecorded conversation is subject to each participant's interpretation, providers should avoid supplying the custodian with undocumented oral instructions regarding the particular records to be gathered. The custodian and any other individual responsible for locating the relevant

---

[1] A sample letter is appended to this chapter as Exhibit IX.

[2] *See* Exhibit X.

documents should receive written instructions that are clear, easy to follow, and incorporate any arrangements the provider (through counsel) has reached with the government.[3] All such requests should contain the following:

- a detailed description of the various types of documents;
- the time period covered by the subpoena; and
- the potential location of the documents.

Requests to company employees regarding file searches should also be in writing, and the custodian should receive written confirmation from each department queried that responsive documents have been produced or exhaustively searched for. Negative results should be documented. All instructional memoranda should be drafted with the clear expectation that they will ultimately be provided to the grand jury or investigating agency.

5.4.5 Advise Company Personnel About the Issuance of the Document Request

In most small businesses, document requests and/or the receipt of a subpoena will rapidly become a matter of common knowledge. While every company has varying concerns, some thought should be given to informing some or all of the employees about the request and the company's commitment to full compliance. Counsel should be available to answer any employee concerns or questions.

5.4.6 Provide Written Instructions That No Relevant Documents are to be Destroyed

Apart from any intentional destruction of documents, it is usually advisable that the healthcare provider under subpoena suspend any general document destruction policies routinely practiced by the provider or the provider's staff until it is determined if those documents scheduled for destruction are responsive to the subpoena. This applies to e-mail messages as well, if covered by the subpoena. Instruction memoranda should also address the often overlooked "Post-It" notes that, depending upon the language of the subpoena, may have to be produced.

5.4.7 Consultations Between the Custodian and Counsel Regarding Questions Relating to the Scope of the Subpoena

In virtually every case, questions will arise about whether or not particular documents fall within the scope of the subpoena and must be produced. In all instances, instructions to employees or the provider should be documented by counsel.

---

[3] Sample instructions to the company custodian and document searchers are appended as Exhibits XI and XII.

5.4.8 Counsel Should Personally Review the Gathered Documents

After the custodian has assembled all potentially responsive documents, they should be reexamined by counsel to determine if they are in fact responsive to the request. This crucial step ensures that no document protected by the attorney-client privilege or attorney-work product doctrine is inadvertently produced and no unnecessary documents disclosed. At this stage, a privilege log will be created, listing any documents withheld under a claim of privilege. A privilege log will identify:

- the person who wrote the document;
- the named recipient;
- the date;
- a brief description of the subject matter of the document; and
- the privilege or doctrine relied upon.

5.4.9 Keep a Record of the Documents and Materials Produced to the Government

All documents produced (even originals) should be Bates stamped and copied, potentially eliminating any dispute as to what was or what was not produced to the government. A cover letter and detailed memorandum specifying the documents being produced should be addressed to the government by counsel and, where applicable, Bates stamped numbers referenced.[4] A signed receipt for the delivery of the records should be obtained in every case.

---

[4] A sample cover letter and applicable memorandum are attached as Exhibits XIII and XIV.

6. INVESTIGATIONS

Investigations represent one of the least controlled areas of government activity. Consequently, investigations can be very intrusive, disruptive and time consuming. Techniques employed include interviewing employees, searching for documents pursuant to search warrants and electronic surveillance. Investigations may take place at any time including after a grand jury has convened and also after an indictment has been issued. While undergoing an investigation, however, providers can benefit by paying close attention to the questions asked and the information sought by the government. Keeping close track of what the government is looking for can provide a rough roadmap of the scope of the investigation which can be quite valuable during future negotiations and communications with the government.

6.1 INFORMING EMPLOYEES OF AN INVESTIGATION

The most commonly used interview technique in healthcare fraud and abuse investigations is the "after work hours" interview. Investigators employ this tactic of approaching employees at home in the mornings, evenings, or on weekends in the hopes of catching them off guard and at a location where he or she will be more likely to talk than at work. Employees confronted at home will usually cooperate with investigators and provide extensive interviews due to nervousness, uncertainty, and the general assumption that they should cooperate with the government. The deliberate or accidental failure to inform employees of an investigation leaves them ill-informed of their rights, responsibilities, and the proper information with which to protect themselves.

In all but the most extenuating circumstances, employees should be informed of the investigation and advised of their rights as soon as possible. Advance disclosure tends to reduce the shock and surprise when employees are contacted at home, and ensures that they have a thorough understanding of their rights and obligations.

Employers should be cautioned to keep a more than comfortable distance from any activity that the government might misconstrue as obstructing justice. In the authors' experience, the government is much more likely to take a dim view of an employer advising the employee of his or her rights than that of independent counsel advising the employee of these rights. Consequently, advice to employees during fraud and abuse investigations should almost always be provided by counsel, usually via letter or memorandum to eliminate any potential confusion over what was or was not stated.[1] In general, we recommend employees be advised of the following:

- Absent a grand jury subpoena, the employee has the choice whether to be interviewed. The employee cannot be compelled to make a statement. However, neither the employer nor counsel should instruct or advise employees not to speak with investigators.

---

[1] Examples of such letters and memoranda are appended as Exhibits XV-XVII.

- It is the employee's decision whether or not to speak with government agents.

- If the employee is contacted by an agent and elects to be interviewed, the employee has a right to consult an attorney *before* each and every conversation and is also entitled to have an attorney present during any interview.

- In the event the employee elects to be interviewed by a government agent, the employee must provide full and truthful information in response to any questions asked. Failure to do so can and most likely will result in criminal charges.

- Employees should be *asked* to immediately contact counsel for the provider if the employee is approached by anyone requesting information.

6.2   SUDDEN APPEARANCES BY AGENTS

While many audits involve just a review of documents and records submitted by a provider in response to written requests of an auditor, there are numerous occasions when an auditor or agent will appear at a provider's office or, as stated above, at an employee's home demanding records and/or an interview. As previously outlined in the chapter on requests for documents, both the OIG and the state MFCU have the authority to gain "immediate access"[2] to a provider's office upon reasonable request in writing for the purposes of examining records, documents, and other data pertaining to the Medicare and Medicaid programs.[3]

In the event an agent appears at the door, we advise the following be accomplished:

- Insist the agent confer with provider's counsel to advise him of the agent's identity, purpose, and authority.
- Have counsel present during any interview or questioning.
- Record all documents produced, examined, and/or copied.

In any event, once counsel is contacted, he or she will usually possess enough experience to request the auditor/agent not ask any questions until counsel has arrived and advise the client of that fact. If counsel cannot attend the meeting, an interview can always be scheduled at a later convenient date.

---

[2] "Immediate access" does not mean that government agents can simply appear at the premises and demand access. "Immediate access" is defined as being within 24 hours of the request unless the investigator believes the records will be altered or destroyed. 42 C.F.R. §1001.1301.

[3] Failure to comply with an OIG request for access to records can result in permissive exclusion from the Medicare and Medicaid programs. Similarly, failure to grant immediate access to the state MFCU can result in exclusion from the Medicare and Medicaid programs for a minimum of ninety days.

6.3 PROVIDING ACCESS TO RECORDS

While many healthcare fraud investigation units routinely share details of the investigation, these disclosures are usually made by the attorney in charge. The agent or auditor will often refuse to disclose any details about the underlying case. This is often accomplished through the perfunctory statement that the records are being requested pursuant to an "ongoing investigation." The refusal notwithstanding, counsel should nonetheless make every effort (within reason) to find out the nature of the investigation at the time access is requested.

Where at all possible, do not allow the agent free run of the office, as the agents often use this opportunity to gather the additional evidence required to obtain a federal search warrant. Tactfully seat the agent in a conference room or office if possible, and provide only the requested records. Where possible, try to adhere to the following guidelines:

- Neither the provider nor its employees should discuss the case with the agent. This is a task best suited for counsel.

- The provider should request that all substantive questions be presented in writing for review by counsel or presented directly to counsel.

- Always obtain a card—or name, unit or department, address, and telephone number— for each agent and auditor present.

- Be wary of providing the agent with access to patient medical records beyond the particular program with which the agent is affiliated. If the agent is employed by the state MFCU, he or she may not be entitled to the medical records of patients whose services were paid for by a private insurance program without a signed consent form from the patient. Seek the assistance of counsel in these matters.

6.4 SEARCH WARRANTS

A search warrant authorizes designated law enforcement personnel, such as agents from the FBI, to enter onto private property and search for the evidence specified in the warrant. The issuance of a search warrant is a very serious matter, as it indicates that the government has an ongoing criminal investigation, and has convinced a judge or magistrate that "probable cause" exists to believe a crime was committed and that evidence will be found during the search of the specified location. In the context of healthcare fraud investigations, many federal prosecutors maintain they seek search warrants only when there is a likelihood the target of the search will destroy, alter, or conceal evidence if served with an investigatory subpoena or a subpoena to produce the material to a grand jury.[4]

---

[4] Subpoenas of this sort rely upon the party served to provide the requested information within a particular period of time rather than in an immediate fashion.

To obtain a search warrant, the government must submit an application and an affidavit setting forth the facts of the investigation and the reasons why it is believed that evidence or the proceeds of a crime are located at the place sought to be searched.[5]

At the time a search warrant is executed, the agents must provide the owner or controller of the place to be searched with a copy of the warrant.[6] At the conclusion of the search, the agent in charge must provide a receipt for any property taken.[7] Government agents are also required to file a fully detailed inventory of the property seized with the court "promptly" after the search, as well as providing a copy of this inventory to the person from whom or from whose premises the property was taken upon request.

While they are powerful government tools, search warrants themselves provide little information about the nature of government investigations. Even though the application for the warrant and the appended affidavits submitted to secure the warrant set forth the evidence accumulated by the government, courts generally seal these documents. Alternatively, one can examine the types of documents seized and the questions asked by the agents to gain insight into the nature and scope of the investigation.

6.4.1 Practical Tips

If at all possible, counsel should be present during the execution of a search warrant to witness and monitor the process. Government agents frequently attempt to interview employees during the course of a search, but the search warrant itself provides no authority to detain an employee during a search for the purpose of questioning. Investigative techniques of this sort are employed to extract as much information as possible. In most instances, they work quite well. The risks to a provider posed by these tactics make it advisable for provider's counsel to brief key employees about the potential for a search and their respective rights in the event a search is conducted or they are contacted by the government.[8]

6.4.2 Advice in the Event of a Search

To prepare staff for the possibility of a search warrant being executed at the employee's home or provider's place of business, the following is a list of practical instructions:

---

[5] Under the Fourth Amendment and Fed.R.Crim.P. 41(c), both the application and the warrant itself must describe "with particularity" the place to be searched and the items seized. Examples of an application for a search warrant and supporting affidavit in a case that was unsealed at the time of indictment are appended as Exhibit XVIII.

[6] An example of a warrant is appended as Exhibit XIX.

[7] Exhibit XX. *See* Fed.R.Crim.P. 41(d).

[8] Exhibits XV-XVII contain examples of the information one might want to convey by memoranda.

- Be polite, courteous, and cooperative without surrendering the rights and responsibilities we have discussed in this handbook.

- Do not refuse entrance to the investigators. Instead, create and keep a record of what they do, view, ask, and seek.

- Request a copy of the actual search warrant, as well as any attachments that specify the areas to be searched and the items to be seized.

- Obtain the name and business card of the agent in charge of the search. If possible, obtain the names and business cards of all others who assist in the search.

- Do not attempt to conceal, destroy, or remove from the premises any documents or property during the course of the search.

- A warrant authorizes agents to search and seize property only. ***IT DOES NOT PROVIDE AGENTS WITH THE AUTHORITY TO COMPEL AN INTERVIEW WITH THE OWNER OF THE SEARCHED PREMISES OR THE EMPLOYEES.***

- Refer all substantive questions posed by an agent to counsel.

- Do not volunteer information.

- The warrant will authorize the agents to search specific premises or portion thereof and seize specific property. Keep track of the areas being searched and the items seized.

- If the agents appear to go beyond the warrant's scope either in the areas searched or the items seized, bring this to the attention of the head agent. However, under no circumstances should you interfere with the search even if it apparently has exceeded the scope of the warrant. There are circumstances that may justify searches in areas beyond those described in the warrant, but they are beyond the scope of this handbook.

- Agents are required to provide a receipt for all property seized. The owner of the property is entitled to an inventory of the property seized.

- Employees may agree to be interviewed during a search. In most circumstances, an employee should not be instructed to decline an interview. However, the employee can decline on his or her own. Keep track of who was interviewed and, where possible, all questions and responses.

6.5 ELECTRONIC AND VIDEO SURVEILLANCE

Those subject to criminal investigation must be aware of the significant possibility of government-initiated electronic surveillance. The federal electronic surveillance statutes, commonly referred to as Title III statutes, are codified at 18 U.S.C. §§2510-2522 (1999).[9] Given the significant Fourth Amendment implications in the Government's use of wiretaps and "bugs," these statutes impose significant procedural requirements upon prosecutorial personnel who seek to use such devices.[10]

These statutes establish minimum federal procedural safeguards regarding the use of electronic surveillance devices. States, although unable to diminish the stringency of these federal procedural laws, are entitled to enact stricter regulations.[11] Where investigators violate procedural rules pertaining to electronic surveillance, the provider may be in a position to suppress the evidence as "ill-gotten fruits" of an illegal surveillance. Keep in mind, however, that Title III rules do not apply to every form of electronic surveillance.

6.5.1 Tape Recording Conversations

18 U.S.C. § 2516 enables the Attorney General and certain designated staff members to authorize applications to federal courts for orders approving the interception of wire or oral communications. Additionally, 18 U.S.C. § 2511(2)(c) provides that "it shall not be unlawful under this chapter for a person acting under color of law to intercept a wire, oral, or electronic communication, where such person is a party to the communication or one of the parties to the communication has given prior consent to such interception...." Simply stated, the Federal Government may intercept and record a conversation so long as it has been ordered by a federal judge or where one party consents to such monitoring.[12]

---

[9] These federal statutes were enacted in reaction to Berger v. New York, 388 U.S. 41 (1967) and Katz v. United States, 389 U.S. 347 (1967), which discussed the constitutionality of police investigative techniques in view of the Fourth Amendment of the Constitution of the United States.

[10] For specific procedures, *see* 18 U.S.C. §§ 2511, 2515, 2516 2518(10) and 2520.

[11] *See* U.S. v. Mora, 821 F.2d 863, n.3 (1st Cir. 1987) citing United States v. Smith, 726 F.2d 852, 856 (1st Cir.).

[12] *See* United States v. White, 401 U.S. 745 (1971); United States v. Caceres, 440 U.S. 741, 750-751 (1979), *See also* United States Attorney's Manual, Department of Justice, October 1997, § 9-7.301.

State practices, however, differ from jurisdiction to jurisdiction. Certain states prohibit so-called "one party consensual interception,"[13] whereas others allow it.[14] Again, is a matter for discussion with counsel.

6.5.2 Video Surveillance and Telephone Wiretaps

Video surveillance has increased in the last few years as technology has improved. Unlike wiretapping and "bugging," video surveillance — particularly silent video surveillance — is not clearly within the scope of Title III. Federal courts have differed in their determinations of whether Title III applies to video surveillance.[15] As such, under some circumstances investigators may not be bound by the same stringent procedural safeguards that govern other methods of surveillance. Although some question exists as to the freedom of investigators to utilize video surveillance, the government has generally attempted to temper the unrestricted use of this tool by implementing internal guidelines.

The U.S. Attorney's Office states:

> When court authorization for video surveillance is deemed necessary [by the appropriate Department of Justice personnel], it should be obtained by way of an application and order predicated on Fed. R. Crim. P. 41(b) and the All Writs Act (28 U.S.C. §1651). The application and order should be based on an affidavit that establishes probable cause to believe that evidence of a Federal crime will be obtained by the surveillance. In addition the affidavit should comply with the provisions of the Federal electronic surveillance statutes.[16]

In general, one should assume that if an investigation is ongoing, investigators are or may be listening and watching. Anyone involved should be advised to consider the nature of their conversations and to confer with counsel if questions arise. It is significantly easier to avoid providing the government with unnecessary and unrequested information rather than attempting to suppress the admittance of such evidence during a hearing or trial.

---

[13] *See, e.g.,* Commonwealth v. Blood, 400 Mass. 61, 507 N.E.2d 1029 (1987)

[14] *See* Louisiana v. Vince No. 98-1892 (La.App. 1 Cir. 6/25/99), 1999 WL 486950 (La.App. 1 Cir.)).

[15] *See* U.S. v. Mesa-Rincon, 911 F.2d 1433 (10th Cir 1990) (applying the requirements of Title III to video surveillance); U.S. v. Taketa, 923 F.2d 665 (9th Cir. 1991) (discussing the fact that silent video surveillance is not aural in nature and as such does not fall under Title III).

[16] United States Attorney's Manual, Department of Justice, October 1997, §9-7.200.

7. ISSUES AND ADVICE FOR DISCUSSION DURING AN INVESTIGATION

Prior to the development of strategies for defending a health care investigation, a number of basic issues must be addressed. Who is being represented by counsel? What are the terms of that representation? Should each owner of the entity under investigation be represented by the same counsel? What are the risks involved in joint representation? These specific issues, and a number of other important concerns must be addressed at the onset of any investigation.

7.1 MULTIPLE REPRESENTATION AND FEE ISSUES

The targets of many healthcare fraud investigations are either small, closely-held businesses or medical practices consisting of a partnership of several physicians or other healthcare professionals. The close relationships of the players involved often foster the desire to engage in collaborative defense efforts. Such efforts, however, raise potential conflict of interest issues that must be considered by counsel prior to entering into a representation agreement.

Initially, counsel will assess whether he or she can represent both the entity and the principals involved, or whether separate counsel must be retained by each potential client. This decision involves consideration of strategic implications and governing ethical rules, and is made difficult by the fact that during the preliminary stages of the case, insufficient information may exist to determine the full potential exposure of each principal. Compounding the problem is counsel making decisions regarding joint representation when faced with potential clients who may not understand the possible need for separate counsel. The issue of adding legal fees only serves to complicate the considerations.

Representation of multiple clients by a single firm provides some advantages for clients. Joint representation ensures equal access to information, the ability to implement a consistent defense strategy, and often provides for efficient allocation of defense costs by eliminating extra fees stemming from multiple lawyers having to familiarize themselves with the facts and laws involved in the case. Engaging in multiple client representation carries significant risks, however, that can result in the lawyer's disqualification from representing any of the participating clients, including the corporate entity.

At the core of any decision to represent multiple clients is the fact that a potential conflict of interest may exist in a situation where a law firm represents more than one party to an issue in the dispute. This is particularly true when the multiple parties are all targets of the same investigation. Lawyers' decisions to represent multiple clients are generally governed by the American Bar Association's *Model Rules of Professional Conduct* ("MRPC"), which have been widely adopted in jurisdictions around the United States. Counsel must also consult the disciplinary rules for his or her particular jurisdiction. MRPC Rule 1.7, which discusses conflicts of interest and addresses scenarios involving multiple client representation, reads as follows:

> Model Rule 1.7:
> (a) A lawyer shall not represent a client if the representation of that client will be directly adverse to another client, unless:
> 　　(1) the lawyer reasonably believes the representation will not adversely affect the relationship with the other client; and
> 　　(2) each client consents after consultation.
> (b) A lawyer shall not represent a client if the representation of that client may be materially limited by the lawyer's responsibilities to another client or to a third person, or by the lawyer's own interests, unless:
> 　　(1) the lawyer reasonably believes that the representation will not be adversely affected; and
> 　　(2) the client consents after consultation. When representation of multiple clients in a single matter is undertaken, the consultation shall include explanation of the implications of the common representation and the advantages and risks involved.

Under this section, an attorney must (1) consider whether joint representation will in any way affect the ability to represent *any* of the clients, (2) consult with *each* client about the potential risks and advantages of engaging in such representation, and (3) obtain consent to the joint representation from *each* client. Ultimately, if an attorney feels that he or she cannot conscientiously represent each of the clients, then the attorney must not engage in such multiple representation.

Complicating matters further, counsel must consider the potential for a conflict of interest to arise after joint representation has been initiated. In these scenarios, counsel must terminate representation of at least one of the clients in conflict, and often must terminate representation of all of these clients. Specifically, under MRPC Rule 1.9, the attorney must generally acquire consent of the former client in order for the representation to continue. This is a very difficult hurdle if such consent had not been obtained prior to the termination.[1] In many cases, even if such consent had been obtained, courts may prohibit the representation from continuing.

Prior to entering into a joint representation arrangement, counsel must be aware of the risks involved, and advise the potential clients accordingly. Accompanying the potential conflicts and risks of termination discussed above are a number of other risks. For example, government prosecutors generally do not like joint representation of targets because of the difficulty such representation poses to employing a "divide and conquer" strategy of getting one target to cooperate

---

[1] In some cases, lawyers attempt to have clients participating in a joint representation sign written agreements under which the client consents to the lawyers right to continue representation of the organization even if a conflict is discovered and representation of the client is terminated. The validity of such agreements have had mixed success, however, and are likely to be frowned upon by the courts if motions for disqalification are filed. *See* Jeffery D. Wohl, *Ethical Obligation of Employment Lawyers*, PLI Litigation and Administrative Practice Course Handbook Series, Pg. 1056-1057, October-November, 1999.

in the investigation. It is not unusual, therefore, for a prosecutor to offer leniency to one of several jointly represented targets primarily for the purpose of inducing the retention of separate counsel. Additionally, prosecutors may seek to have the presiding judge order the targets to obtain separate representation. Courts facing such motions assess whether the clients have been informed fully of the risks involved in multiple representation and of their rights to retain separate counsel. The court needs to be assured that the clients' actions constituted a knowing waiver of their right to be represented by counsel unhindered by any potential conflicts of interest. In some cases, courts have held that it is impossible for jointly represented clients to receive effective representation, and have ordered the clients to obtain individual counsel. In other cases, courts permit the clients to make their own decision regarding what is in their best interests.

An additional risk of entering into multiple representation is that one of the represented clients may choose to cooperate with the government and testify against the others. If such a scenario arises, the attorney would be placed in the position of having to cross-examine a former client. During such cross-examinations, however, attorneys may generally not utilize information received in confidence. This restriction could prevent the remaining client from receiving complete representation from that attorney.

Because clients must be informed of these risks, counsel will provide the clients with a written memorandum setting forth the pros and cons of joint representation.[2] Only after the clients and the attorney have independently decided that joint representation is permissible and mutually beneficial may they enter into a representation agreement. Counsel will usually obtain written waivers of the potential conflict of interest from each client.[3] Irrespective of the execution of these waivers, the joint representation must cease if at any point either the client or the law firm determines that adequate representation of each individual client is no longer possible.

A second scenario resulting in potential conflicts of interest arises when a corporation and its employees are targets of an investigation and the corporation agrees to pay the legal fees of the employees. In such a situation, it is possible to allege the attorney's loyalties will be divided between his client (the employee) and the party paying the attorney (the corporation). Such scenarios are governed by MPRC Rule 1.8, which states:

> A lawyer shall not accept compensation for representing a client from one other than the client unless: (1) the client consents after consultation; (2) there is no interference with the lawyer's independence of professional judgment or with the client-lawyer relationship; and (3) information relating to the representation of the client is protected as required by Rule 1.6.

---

[2] *See* Exhibit XXI.

[3] *See* Exhibit XXII.

Therefore, when a corporation pays the employee's legal fees, the attorney may accept such payment only with the permission of the employee, and the attorney may not allow the corporation's payment of the employee's fees to influence the representation.

Both counsel and each potential client must weigh the benefits to be gained from joint representation and the resulting economies of scale against the potential conflicts of interest. In most cases, counsel must determine whether the potential conflict prevents him or her from adequately representing the interests of each client. If so, counsel must avoid entering into the representation.

7.2   RETAINING AUDITORS, EXPERTS, AND OTHER CONSULTANTS

In more than a few healthcare fraud investigations, it will be advisable to retain the services of an auditor, expert, and/or consultant to assist in formulating a defense to the government's investigation. In order to protect information or documents prepared by the consultant from involuntary disclosure to the government, the attorney will retain the consultant pursuant to an engagement letter setting forth the scope of the project and the obligations of the expert/consultant. Such a letter establishes the nature of the work to be performed and can protect the confidentiality of any communications occurring between the client and the agent. Courts have held that communications made between a client and an agent in furtherance of legal services are to be considered privileged communications.[4]

Irrespective of the terms of the engagement letter, it is very important that counsel control all information provided to the consultant. To avoid any inadvertent waiver of the work-product privilege, all information sent to the consultant should be clearly marked as attorney-client privileged and confidential. It is recommended that counsel utilize a marking system for this purpose, and inventory all documents and other materials provided to the consultant.[5] In many instances, counsel will want to be present during any interviews conducted by the consultant with the client or the employees in order to preserve the attorney-client privilege with regard to the communications.

7.3   HIRING AN ATTORNEY FOR THE EMPLOYEES

Often the aforementioned risks regarding multiple client representation necessitate separate representation of the organization, its principals, and the organization's non-targeted employees. At the onset of an investigation, counsel may initially notify prosecutors that its representation extends to the healthcare provider "and all its employees" in order to limit the ability of government investigators from directly contacting employees. However, where multiple representation is impractical, it is recommended that the healthcare provider under investigation promptly retain an attorney to represent all the "non-target" employees who are potential and/or likely witnesses.

---

[4] *See* In re Grand Jury Proceedings Under Seal v. U.S., 947 F.2d 1188 (4th Cir. 1991); U.S. v. Schwimmer, 892 F.2d 237 (2nd Cir. 1989); U.S. v. Kovel, 296 F.2d 918 (2nd Cir. 1961). *See also* In re Grand Jury Proceedings Under Seal v. U.S., 947 F.2d 1188 (4th Cir. 1991); U.S. v. Schwimmer, 892 F.2d 237 (2nd Cir. 1989); U.S. v. Kovel, 296 F.2d 918 (2nd Cir. 1961). A sample engagement letter for an auditor is appended as Exhibit XXIII.

[5] *See* Exhibit XXIV.

Retaining one attorney to represent all non-target witnesses provides a number of strategic benefits to the provider. Initially, retaining one attorney to represent all non-target employees reduces the provider's costs and enables the retained attorney to develop a solid understanding of the facts and subtleties involved in the case. Additionally, it is likely that the attorney for the witnesses will develop a relationship with the attorney for the providers, enabling them to reach an understanding concerning government investigative activities. If representation of the employees is arranged by the provider, employees should be informed of the following:

- That an attorney has been retained for their benefit and that the attorney is available to give advice to any employee desiring representation with regard to the investigation.

- That they may seek the advice of the retained attorney either in advance of, at the time of, or following any contact by government investigators.

- That at any time they are contacted by an investigator they have the right to decline to be interviewed without counsel being present. **Note: A Provider should never instruct or in any way suggest that an employee not answer questions, as this may be construed as obstruction of justice.**

- Employees should also be advised that each has a right to individual counsel of his or her own choosing. (Note that under some circumstances it may be appropriate for the provider/client to pay for an employee's individual attorney.)

This advice can be included within the same memorandum used to advise employees of the investigation (see Exhibit XVI). Any memorandum should include the name of the attorney for the employees to contact.

As a final measure, counsel must determine if any particular employee requires separate counsel (e.g., target employees or employees facing potential individual exposure due to their role or position). This analysis likely will require reevaluation as the investigation develops and counsel learns more about the facts.

7.4 NOTIFYING THE GOVERNMENT THAT THE EMPLOYEES ARE REPRESENTED BY COUNSEL

Every jurisdiction has ethical rules that prohibit an attorney from directly contacting a person who is represented by counsel. In order to develop some control and oversight of the government's access to information, either the healthcare provider under investigation or counsel must notify the prosecutor and government investigators as soon as possible that the entity is represented by counsel. Furthermore, it is strongly recommended that the independent counsel retained to represent the provider's employees is asked to immediately notify the investigating agency of the employees' representation, as well as to notify the investigating agency to avoid any direct contact with those employees.[6] Generally, this will prevent the investigating agency from being able to interview employees without counsel present.

7.5 JOINT DEFENSE AGREEMENTS

Particularly in fraud and abuse investigations (which often involve multiple targets and potential defendants, complex legal issues, and voluminous documentary evidence), it is beneficial that uninhibited communication exists among counsel for the various targets and subjects of an investigation. Counsel for these various parties will often find it beneficial to exchange information and documents, as well as to share in the costs and tasks involved in presenting a defense. Experience has demonstrated that the targets of an investigation can better present a coherent and plausible defense when each party acts in unison towards common goals or strategies. Joint defense tactics allow parties to coordinate their approaches.

However, it is essential when engaging in joint defense activities to ensure that communications within the group remain confidential under the attorney-client privilege and work-product doctrine. One means of achieving these goals is by the use of a "Joint Defense Agreement." Under such an agreement, counsel and their clients agree to the confidential exchange of information, thus extending the attorney-client privilege and work-product privilege among all the clients. A joint defense agreement allows for more efficient representation by giving parties the tactical advantage of confidential exchange of information in the possession of others. It also allows parties facing the same opponent, or who have legal interests in common, to pool resources necessary for experts, research, or any other information relevant to their cases. For example, counsel may choose to divide analysis of witness statements or other voluminous information so as to avoid redundant efforts. Frequently, these agreements result in saving time, money, and effort.

Specifically, joint defense agreements allow counsel to communicate confidential statements made by the client to participating attorneys under the protection of the attorney-client privilege. Such arrangements generally fall under an exception to the rule that divulging confidential information to third parties waives the attorney-client privilege. Joint defense privileges have been recognized in every jurisdiction in which the issue has been raised.[7]

---

[6] In the past, the U.S. Department of Justice has on occasion ignored ethical rules regarding contact with represented parties, and initiated direct contact with the employees or former employees of a target even though the witness being contacted is represented by counsel. The Justice Department has claimed that its attorneys are not subject to the ethical prohibitions of local or state bars and courts. Every federal court that has addressed this issue has rejected the government's position, holding that federal prosecutors may not initiate or maintain contact with represented persons. *See* U.S. ex. rel O'Keefe v. McDonnell Douglas Corp., 132 F.3d 1252 (8th Cir. 1998); *In the Matter of Howes*, 940 P.2d 159 (N.M. 1997); *DOJ Attempts Back Door Approach to Contact With Represented Persons*, 22 Champion 9 (March, 1998).

[7] *See generally* United States v. Bay State Ambulance and Hospital Rental Service, 874 F.2d 20, 28-29 (1st Cir. 1989); *In re Grand Jury Subpoenas*, 902 F.2d 244, 248-49 (4th Cir. 1990); United States v. McPartlin, 595 F.2d 1321, 1336-1337 (7th Cir. 1979).

Counsel should be aware that certain risks do exist with regard to entering into a joint defense agreements. For example, if a member of a joint defense agreement becomes a witness for the government, a likelihood exists that the remaining joint defense attorneys will be disqualified.[8] Additionally, there is a possibility that a party to the agreement will breach the joint defense agreement and reveal to the government privileged information learned during joint defense strategy sessions.[9] In such scenarios, if the remaining members of the agreement are unable to show that information was secured through a breach of privilege and not some other non-privileged source — a difficult showing — there will be no way to exclude the information from use, and the remaining defendants may be severely prejudiced against.

Another pitfall that counsel should be aware of with regard to these agreements involves the potential for adverse relationships to develop among joint targets. Under the joint defense or common interest "privilege," communications between parties and their attorneys are not protected if a falling-out occurs at a later date.[10] Additionally, a joint defense attorney's relationship with former members of the agreement may hinder the attorney from conducting certain rigorous cross-examinations. This may ultimately result in a court's determination that the attorney's client was denied the effective assistance of counsel.[11]

7.5.1 Elements of a Joint Defense Agreement

Joint defense agreements will vary according to the particular needs of the joint defense members. Although courts will occasionally retroactively infer joint defense arrangements to protect communications, a written agreement is clearly in the best interests of all parties to a joint defense agreement.[12] To be effective, the agreement should be signed by the parties and their attorneys setting forth the scope, limits, and obligations under the agreement.[13]

---

[8] *See* Matthew D. Forsgren, *The Outer Edge of the Envelope: Disqualification of White Collar Criminal Defense Attorneys Under the Joint Defense Doctrine*, 78 Minn.L.Rev. 1219, at 1222 (1994).

[9] *See, e.g.*, United States v. Melvin, 650 F.2d 641 (5th Cir. 1981).

[10] *See In the Matter of a Grand Jury Subpoena Duces Tecum Dated November 16, 1974*, 406 F.Supp 381 (S.D.N.Y. 1975)

[11] United States v. Agosto, 675 F.2d 965, 969-71 (8th Cir. 1982).

[12] United States v. McPartlin, 595 F.2d 1321, 1336-37 (7th Cir. 1979); Continental Oil Co. v. United States, 330 F.2d 347, 350 (9th Cir. 1964).

[13] Two sample agreements are appended as Exhibit XXV.

At a minimum, a joint defense agreement should declare the following:

- the common interest of the parties;

- that the parties are making disclosures with the understanding that they are covered by the joint defense doctrine;

- that materials previously confidential will remain confidential when communicated to members of the agreement or their counsel;

- that members may not disclose information obtained under the joint defense agreement;

- that members may withdraw from the agreement, but that information obtained under the agreement will remain privileged;

- that counsel intends to pursue the separate but common interests of their clients; and

- waivers by all defendants of the right to representation by counsel free of undivided interests to avoid disqualification of defense counsel. Such waivers will usually defeat a subsequent claim for disqualification.[14]

---

[14] United States v. Bicoastal Corp., 1992 U.S. Dist. LEXIS 21445 (N.D.N.Y. Sept. 28. 1992); United States v. McDade, 1992 U.S. Dist. LEXIS 11447 (E.D.Pa. July 30, 1992); United States v. Anderson, 790 F. Supp. 231 (W.D. Wash. 1992).

8. PRE-JUDGMENT ASSET SEIZURES AND PAYMENT SUSPENSIONS

The enactment of HIPAA and subsequent changes and alliances by federal and state prosecutorial units have altered the traditional path of a fraud and abuse investigation.[1] Providers are now far more likely to be targeted for a particular type of action early in the investigative stage. Cases that might have languished at the Carrier's Fraud and Abuse Unit are now earmarked for direct referral to the OIG or US Attorney's Office. Coordinated efforts between federal (DOJ, US Attorney's Office, OIG, Drug Enforcement Agency, Food and Drug Administration, etc.) and state (State Attorney General Offices, MFCUs, Medicaid, state board of registration in medicine, etc) are far more prevalent. If it is believed that the provider has engaged in a pattern of fraudulent conduct, a criminal investigation may be conducted with the assistance of the FBI and local United States Attorney's Office without the provider ever being contacted by the investigators. Too, often the provider will ignore "early warnings" of the criminal investigation such as notices from patients that they have been contacted by OIG agents.

8.1 BACKGROUND

Prior to the enactment of HIPAA, while the Government had an array of civil remedies available to seize assets in connection with any mail fraud investigation (including healthcare fraud) before instituting a criminal prosecution, these remedies were not pursued in a consistent manner by the various United States Attorneys. Instead, the government primarily relied on criminal prosecutions, and focused on obtaining restitution only at the conclusion of the case.

However, with the enactment of HIPAA, federal prosecutors were given a mandate to employ non-traditional remedies and parallel criminal and civil proceedings. The enforcement tools provided by HIPAA are designed to promote non-traditional remedies to protect and recover assets, as well as to deter fraudulent schemes. This remedy is being employed more frequently with drastic results.[2]

8.2 FRAUD INJUNCTION STATUTE; FREEZING AND PROTECTING ASSETS

18 U.S.C. § 1345, the fraud injunction statute, is an important weapon in the government's arsenal because it authorizes the government to seek and the courts to enjoin fraudulent conduct and the seizure assets during the pendency of the government's investigation *before* indictment. The particular provision allowing for pre-indictment injunctions and seizures was originally enacted in

---

[1] Pub. L. No. 104-191.

[2] *See* United States v. DBB, Inc. 180 F.3d 1277 (11th Cir. 1999); *See also* United States v. Anastasio, No. 399CV1163 (D. Conn July 30, 1999).

1984 as part of the Comprehensive Crime Control Act of 1984.[3] Originally intended as a tool to combat mail fraud, the provision empowered federal courts to act with a broad remedial mandate to protect the public and the United States from present and future fraud schemes, including the freezing of assets, during a criminal investigation. These remedies can be sought and implemented before an indictment, whenever there is a substantial potential for injury during the pendency of *an investigation*. While a "§ 1345" proceeding is civil in nature, it can only be initiated in instances where specified *criminal* violations exist; a civil cause of action for fraud provides no original or independent basis for a § 1345 action.

HIPAA amended 18 U.S.C. § 1345 to expressly make the statute applicable to federal healthcare offenses. The statute provides injunctive relief when a person is "committing or about to commit a Federal health care offense."[4] The statute also permits the government to bring a civil action in any federal court:

> if a person is alienating or disposing of property, or intends to alienate or dispose of property, obtained as a result of a Federal health care offense or property which is traceable to such violation, the Attorney General may commence a civil action in any Federal court –
> (A) to enjoin such alienation or disposition of property; or
> (B) for a restraining order to —
>   (i) prohibit any person from withdrawing, transferring, removing, dissipating, or disposing of any such property or property of equivalent value, and
>   (ii) appoint a temporary receiver to administer such restraining order.[5]

The HIPAA amendments explicitly expand the availability of § 1345 injunctions in federal healthcare offense investigations to prevent the dissipation or alienation of assets obtained as a result of a "federal health care offense".[6] Accordingly, the new amendments provide two independent avenues for seeking injunctive relief in criminal investigations involving federal healthcare offenses: (1) When a person is committing or about to commit a federal healthcare offense; or (2) when a person is alienating or disposing of assets, or intends to do so, obtained as a result of a federal health care offense violation, or traceable to such a violation.[7] Under § 1345(a)(2), the government can seek to protect the fraudulently obtained property or property of "equivalent value."

---

[3] Comprehensive Crime Control Act of 1984, P.L. 98-473(Oct. 12, 1984).

[4] 18 U.S.C. § 1345 (a)(1)(C).

[5] 18 U.S.C. § 1345(a)(2).

[6] The term "Federal Health Care Offense" is defined under 18 U.S.C. § 24 to include violations of multiple criminal statutes including: 18 U.S.C. § 287 (false claims), 18 U.S.C. § 1518 (obstruction of a federal healthcare fraud investigation), and 18 U.S.C. § 1035 (false statements in connection with the delivery of or payment for healthcare benefits, items or services).

[7] 18 U.S.C. § 1345(a)(1)

A recent court interpretation of the term "equivalent value" opened the door to the seizure of virtually any asset(s) equal to that obtained by the fraud. In July of 1999, the Eleventh Circuit Court of Appeals provided the broadest interpretation yet on the meaning of the term "equivalent value."[8] In that case, *United States v. DBB, Inc.* ("DBB"), a citizen brought a qui tam action against the defendants, directors and officers of various durable medical equipment providers, pursuant to the federal FCA and Florida law.[9] The complaint alleged that the individual defendants used the provider defendants to defraud the United States and the State of Florida through false Medicare and Medicaid claims.[10] The government claimed that the defendants obtained more than $7.2 million through their fraud.[11] The district court entered a temporary restraining order freezing all of the defendants' assets.[12]

The United States then filed an amended complaint and motion for a preliminary injunction which was allowed on the condition that the United States file a memorandum indicating which assets of the defendants were traceable to the alleged fraud.[13] The United States filed a motion to amend the injunction to freeze assets equivalent in value to the amount obtained by the defendants through fraud, regardless of whether the assets were traceable to the fraud.[14] The district court denied the motion, concluding that the plain language of § 1345(a)(2)(B) required the United States to freeze only those assets through a preliminary injunction that were traceable to the alleged healthcare offense. Both the United States and the defendants appealed the rulings of the district court.[15]

The issue on appeal was whether § 1345(a)(2)(B) authorized a federal court to grant injunctions freezing property of equivalent value whether or not it is traceable to the alleged federal healthcare fraud.[16] The Eleventh Circuit, interpreting the legislative intent of the statute, held:

In order to obtain relief, the United States must show that a defendant is alienating or disposing of property obtained through, or traceable to, health care fraud.

---

[8] United States v. DBB. Inc., 180 F.3d 1277 (11th Cir. 1999).

[9] *Id.* at 1279.

[10] *Id.* at 1279.

[11] *Id.* at 1279.

[12] *Id.* at 1279.

[13] *Id.* at 1279-80.

[14] *Id.* at 1280.

[15] *Id.*

[16] *Id.* at 1280.

Furthermore, under our interpretation, the two subsections provide broad avenues of relief that complement each other and further congressional intent. Subsection (a)(2)(A) offers the government the ability to prevent the sale or other disposition of a particular piece of property that it has traced to fraud. Subsection (a)(2)(B), on the other hand, explicitly provides broader relief for situations where the property obtained through fraud is not as easily identified. It allows the government to prevent the withdrawing, transferring, removing, and dissipating of an amount of the defendant's assets equal to that obtained through fraud and to have a temporary receiver appointed to administer the assets until a final judgment is reached.[17]

The Eleventh Circuit reversed and remanded the district court's decision.[18]

Shortly following the *DBB* decision, the District Court for the District of Connecticut adopted the reasoning of the Eleventh Circuit. In *United States v. Anastasio* ("Anastasio"), the federal court granted a temporary restraining order against a podiatrist for alleged fraudulent Medicare billing practices.[19] The temporary restraining order froze every asset for which the government had knowledge, including the podiatrist's residence, pension funds, and investment accounts, in addition to his business and personal bank accounts. The government immediately sought and obtained a preliminary injunction to continue the relief provided in the temporary restraining order, namely to keep the podiatrist's assets frozen pending further investigation of the alleged Medicare fraud.[20]

Federal courts have yet to agree on whether assets neither obtained from nor traceable to an alleged fraud, other than a federal healthcare offense, are subject to a preliminary injunction under § 1345(a)(2)(B). Prior to *DBB* and *Anastasio*, various district courts had taken the position that "any assets to be frozen must in some way be traceable to the allegedly illicit activity."[21]

In *United States v. Brown* ("Brown"),[22] the defendants, a physician, his sister, and his medical practice were charged with defrauding Medicare by, among other things, billing for services neither

---

[17] *Id.* at 1285-86.

[18] *Id.* at 1286.

[19] United States v. Anastasio, No. 399CV1163 (D. Conn. July 30, 1999).

[20] *Id.*

[21] United States v. Fang, 937 F. Supp. 1189, 1191 (D. Md. 1996) (analyzing § 1345(a)(1)); *see also* United States v. Savran, 755 F. Supp. 1165, 1183 (E.D.N.Y. 1991) (Interpreting the pre-1996 version of § 1345, the court held "the government must first demonstrate that a precise amount of proceeds from the fraudulent scheme were deposited in a specific bank account which also contained untainted funds,"); United States v. Quadro Corp., 916 F. Supp. 613, 619 (E.D. Tex. 1996) (citing United States v. Brown in holding that "a district court may freeze only those assets which the government has proven by a preponderance of the evidence to be related to the alleged fraud.").

[22] United States v. Brown, 988 F.2d 658, 659 (6th Cir. 1993).

performed nor medically necessary, double-billing, and "upcoding." The district court issued a temporary restraining order freezing the defendants' funds held at any financial institution with an exemption of $10,000 per month for business expenses.[23] Although the issue before the *Brown* court was whether 18 U.S.C. § 1345, as amended to cover banking law violations,[24] granted the district court authority to freeze a defendant's assets in a civil fraud suit that does not involve banking law violations, the court's holding with respect to the scope of injunctive relief available under the statute is telling.

The Sixth Circuit Court of Appeals held that the district court exceeded the proper scope of its injunction by freezing all of the defendant's funds, despite the fact that only 75% of the defendant's business was related to the tainted Medicare claims.[25] The Sixth Circuit held that "[t]he court may freeze only those assets related to the alleged fraud" and remanded the case to reevaluate the nature of the assets frozen.[26]

Despite the line of cases mandating some connection between the alleged fraud and the assets sought to be enjoined, the *DBB* decision is the first circuit court decision to address the scope of injunctive relief available under § 1345(a)(2)(B) in the context of a federal healthcare offense.[27] It is likely that federal prosecutors will rely heavily on *DBB* and the Eleventh Circuit's analysis to persuade other Circuits and District Courts to allow similarly broad seizures and injunctions in the future.

8.2.1 Anatomy of a § 1345 Action

The following is an outline of what to expect should a healthcare provider be subject to an action for preliminary injunctive relief under 18 U.S.C. § 1345.

1. The government will file a civil action in U.S. District Court under § 1345(a)(1) and/or (a)(2) and the venue will be governed by 28 U.S.C. § 1391(b), which incorporates the "substantial contacts" test. This test may be satisfied by a single act of mail or wire fraud if it is part

---

[23] *Id.* at 660.

[24] *Brown* was decided after the 1990 amendment of 18 U.S.C. § 1345 to included "banking law violation[s]", but before the 1996 amendment - the sole change of which was the addition of "Federal health care offense" as another violation that would trigger the availability of injunctive remedies to the Government.

[25] *Id.* at 664.

[26] *Id.*

[27] United States v. DBB. Inc., 180 F.3d 1277 (11th Cir. 1999).

of a scheme to defraud.[28] The complaint would be verified and may likely be supported by affidavit(s).[29]

Along with the complaint, the government will file an Ex Parte Motion for a Temporary Restraining Order ("TRO") and possibly a Motion to Seal the Pleadings. If the Ex Parte Motion for a TRO is allowed, the government will serve the healthcare provider, and possibly all affected banks and financial institutions, with copies of the pleadings. The Court may issue a ten-day restraining order, subject to a preliminary injunction hearing.[30]

2. The alleged violations must be predicated on a federal healthcare offense or one of the enumerated offenses in § 1345(a)(1), such as mail or wire fraud. The equitable remedies available under § 1345 are not available for past violations that have terminated.[31] Whether a conspiracy or fraudulent scheme has terminated is often a complicated area issue compounded by a body of legal theory and rulings that allows expanded theories by the government (not necessarily incorrect) as to the initiation, duration, and termination of these crimes. In any event, the fraudulent scheme must also be ongoing and there must exist a threat of continued perpetration.[32] The mere declaration by a defendant that the disputed activity has ceased or will cease does not preclude the issuance of an injunction.[33]

3. To obtain preliminary injunctive relief under § 1345, the government need not show a likelihood that it will prevail on the merits of its injunction action or that it has suffered irreparable harm. The government is only required to show that there is "probable cause" or a "reasonable probability" to believe that the defendants are violating or about to violate any of the sections specified in § 1345.[34] The injunction may enjoin future unlawful conduct and prevent the alienation or dissipation of assets.

4. The court is empowered to fashion broad remedial relief, including the prevention of the sale or disposition of assets and the appointment of a receiver. An injunction applies not only

---

[28] United States v. Hartbratt, 773 F. Supp. 1240 (S.D. Iowa 1991).

[29] *See* Exhibit XXVII.

[30] *See* Exhibit XXVII.

[31] United States v. William Savran & Associates, Inc., 755 F. Supp. (E.D.N.Y. 1991) at 1178.

[32] *Id.*

[33] United States v. Fang, 937 F. Supp. 1186 (D. Md. 1996) at 1200.

[34] *See* United States v. Fang, 937 F. Supp. 1186 (D. Md. 1996) (applying "reasonable probability" standard); United States v. William Savran & Associates, Inc., 755 F. Supp. 1165, 1177 (E.D.N.Y. 1991) (applying probable cause standard); United States v. Weingold, 844 F. Supp 1560, 1571 (D. N.J. 1994) (applying probable cause as the "controlling substantive standard" in a mail fraud case); United States v. Quadro Corp. 916 F. Supp. 613, 617 (E.D. Tex. 1996) (applying preponderance of evidence standard).

to the defendant, but prevents third parties from removing the defendant's assets.[35] The assets subject to seizure by the government under § 1345 are those obtained from or traceable to the fraudulent scheme and, arguably, assets equal to those obtained through the fraud, although not necessarily obtained from or traceable to the fraud themselves.[36]

5. The relief available will not necessarily be limited to simply a seizure of assets. The court could order the preservation of financial and accounting records, including bank records which detail the disposition of payments, and require the defendant to provide financial reports and other discovery detailing the sources and uses of funds and his or her financial condition.[37]

6. Prior to indictment, the injunction action will be governed by the Federal Rules of Civil Procedure. After indictment, control switches to the Federal Rules of Criminal Procedure.[38] The defendant may not remain silent at the preliminary injunction hearing without an adverse inference being drawn from his or her silence or the exercise of the Fifth Amendment privilege against self-incrimination.[39] An injunction may issue for a reasonable, but not indefinite, period of time. Because the sole basis for the injunction is a violation of specific criminal statutes, there must eventually be an indictment to sustain the injunctive relief.[40]

8.3 Suspension of Payments to Providers

An administrative remedy often used during healthcare criminal cases is the suspension of payment to the provider. It can be used at any stage of an investigation and usually has some impact on the ability of a provider to conduct business. The government has the authority to instruct the Medicare intermediary or carrier, as well as any state Medicaid program, to suspend payments to a provider "to protect the [Medicare or Medicaid] program against financial loss."[41] The suspension can be imposed upon "reliable evidence" that the circumstances giving rise to the need for suspension involve fraud or willful misrepresentation.[42] The provider is not entitled to prior notice of the proposed suspension nor any specification of the evidence upon which the determination was made to suspend payment. However, if the administrative suspension is imposed concurrently with

---

[35] United States v. DBB. Inc., 180 F.3d 1277, 1286 (11th Cir. 1999).

[36] *Id.* at 1285-86.

[37] Exhibit XXVIII. *See* United States v. Brown, 988 F.2d. 658, 660 (6th Cir. 1993); *see also* United States v. Anastasio, No. 399CV1163 (D. Conn. July 30, 1999).

[38] 18 U.S.C. § 1345(b).

[39] *Fang*, 937 F. Supp at 1199.

[40] *Fang*, 937 F. Supp at 1197 at n.11.

[41] 42 C.F.R. § 405.370(b).

[42] 42 C.F.R. § 405.371(b).

a civil action to freeze assets, it is likely the government would rely (at least in part) on the same affidavits and supporting materials as were utilized in the civil action.

8.4 Use of Criminal Forfeiture for Federal Healthcare Offenses

18 U.S.C. § 982 was also amended by HIPAA. This section authorizes the **forfeiture** of property that constitutes or is derived directly or indirectly from proceeds traceable to the commission of a federal healthcare offense. These criminal provisions authorize, in appropriate instances, the forfeiture of the "gross proceeds" of any federal healthcare offense.[43] The concept of "gross proceeds" includes property traceable to the property obtained directly from the offense. Significantly, the criminal forfeiture provisions authorize the pre-trial seizure of assets upon the filing of an indictment or information.

To invoke and sustain the *criminal* forfeiture provisions, the government must indict and obtain a conviction of a substantive offense; here, one of the enumerated federal healthcare offenses.[44] The forfeiture count must be contained in the indictment.[45] The defendant is entitled to a jury trial on the forfeiture issue, and a special verdict is required to be returned as to the extent of the interest or property subject to forfeiture.[46] The government's evidentiary burden is the "by a preponderance of the evidence" standard. If the jury finds against the defendant, the court, when imposing a sentence, is required to order forfeiture of the subject property.[47] Upon conviction, substitute assets may be forfeited if the forfeitable property has been dissipated.

8.4.1 Practice Note

When healthcare providers are subject to criminal investigations for fraudulent conduct, attorneys will usually address the potential for payment suspensions or preliminary injunctive relief during the course of the investigation. One foreseeable consequence of asset seizure and/or payment suspension is an impact on the provider's ability to pay for legal services. Attorneys will tend to be extremely cautious when advising a client about the government's ability to obtain preliminary injunctive relief, as any advice provided to a client resulting in a transfer of funds between and amongst the clients' accounts could present the appearance of impropriety on the part of the advising attorney. The attorney will seek to avoid providing any advice that may be utilized by the client to fraudulently transfer assets beyond the reach of the government. Improperly handled situations could result in the attorney being summonsed as a witness, or even a possible subject or target of the ongoing investigation, thereby jeopardizing the client's representation.

---

[43] 18 U.S.C. § 982(a)(6).

[44] United States v. Aramony, 88 F.3d 1369 (4th Cir. 1996).

[45] Fed. R. Crim. P. 7(c)(2).

[46] Fed. R. Crim. P. 31(e).

[47] 18 U.S.C. § 982(a)(6).

When confronting actual or potential asset seizures, it will be necessary to separate assets derived from activities not connected with the alleged fraudulent activity from those that may be. In the *Anastasio* case,[48] the defendant was able to prove that all of the funding for his pension funds had been derived from income earned prior to the date of the alleged fraudulent scheme. This type of evidence may prove useful in negotiations with the United States Attorney to modify any injunctive orders to allow for the use of these funds to pay salaries, necessary expenses, medical bills and/or insurance, and legal fees.

Once in place, an asset freeze may continue until such time as the parties can reach an agreement and the government concludes its investigation without pursuing an indictment or upon further order by the court. It is easily conceivable that an asset freeze could last several months and possibly years.

In *DBB*,[49] the District Court granted the government's motion for a TRO on September 8, 1998, freezing all of the defendants' assets. It also entered an order indefinitely extending the duration of the TRO until a ruling was entered on the motion for a preliminary injunction.[50] The defendants appealed the district court's indefinite extension of the TRO.[51] On July 14, 1999, and without elaboration, the Eleventh Circuit Court of Appeals found "no merit" in the defendant's argument and rejected it "without discussion."[52]

Only one court to date has addressed the issue of the need for a criminal proceeding to follow a preliminary injunction in a "timely fashion." In *United States v. Fang*,[53] the court stated that "Although [18 U.S.C. § 1345(a)(1)] contemplates the possibility of injunctive relief at any stage of the proceedings, as a practical matter, any preliminary injunction freezing assets will almost certainly be followed in timely fashion by a criminal proceeding. A permanent injunction freezing assets not followed by a criminal trial would be virtually impossible to justify and would undoubtedly invite serious constitutional challenge."[54] Attorneys should closely scrutinize the duration of an asset freeze to ensure that practical and constitutional considerations are afforded to their clients.

---

[48] United States v. Anastasio, No. 399CV1163 (D. Conn. July 30, 1999).

[49] 180 F.3d 1277 (11th Cir. 1999).

[50] *Id.* at 1279.

[51] *Id.* at 1280.

[52] *Id.*

[53] 937 F. Supp. 1189, 1191 (D. Md. 1996).

[54] *Id.* at 1197, n.11.

Despite the apparent breadth of the government's ability to reach assets of a healthcare provider, district courts arguably retain broad discretion to allow the healthcare provider, especially a sole practitioner such as a physician, access to sufficient funds to meet his or her needs which include the necessities of life and reasonable attorney's fees.[55] In *United States v. Fang*,[56] the court recognized that it was "in a position to minimize potential harm to a defendant by exercising its discretion to allow the defendant access to sufficient funds to meet his or her needs for living expenses, counsel fees, and by limiting the duration of the freeze."[57]

At the court's urging, the defendants and the United States in *United States v. Barnes* negotiated a "consent preliminary injunction" which exempted the payment of salaries to the defendant's employees and reasonable business expenses.[58] The United States District Court for the Northern District of Iowa held that the consent preliminary injunction was within the proper scope of 18 U.S.C. § 1345.[59] If not explicitly set forth in a temporary restraining order or motion for preliminary injunction under § 1345, the attorney representing a healthcare client should raise an exception of reasonable attorneys fees and business expenses. Any agreement with the United States Attorney to exempt certain assets from the breadth of a temporary restraining order or preliminary injunction should be entered into the record.

---

[55] United States v. Fang, 937 F. Supp. 1186, 1200 (D. Md. 1996).

[56] *Id.*

[57] *See also* United States v. Thier, 801 F.2d 1463 (5th Cir. 1986) (holding that although exemption of assets sufficient to pay a defendant's reasonable attorneys fees and necessary living expenses are not mandatory they are "factors that the district court judge must consider in deciding whether and to what extent to grant an asset-freezing injunction"); United States v. Brown, 988 F.2d 658, 660 (6th Cir. 1993) (permitting an allowance of $10,000 a month to the defendant for business expenses).

[58] 912 F. Supp. 1187, 1190 (N.D. Iowa 1996).

[59] *Id.* at 1198.

9. CIVIL AUDITS AND THE USE OF STATISTICAL SAMPLING

Many healthcare fraud and abuse investigations result not in the bringing of a criminal or civil enforcement action, but instead in a demand for overpayment[1] from Medicare, Medicaid, Blue Cross, other private insurers, OIG, and/or the U.S. Attorneys Office. The sums of money requested by such overpayment demands are often large, leaving providers angered, bewildered, and in many instances in search of the funds to pay. These occasionally staggering demands are often calculated through the use of an extrapolation of a sample audit of a provider's claims. Additionally, in criminal cases involving allegations of schemes to defraud Medicare or an insurance company, Medicare carriers and insurance companies routinely submit victim impact statements containing extrapolated sums during sentencing to establish the amount of loss. Therefore, it is vital for healthcare providers to have an understanding of extrapolation and the statistical sampling methods in order to develop effective challenges and defenses.

9.1 HOW A STATISTICAL SAMPLING AUDIT IS INITIATED

When an initial investigation reveals billing problems warranting an in-depth review of a provider's billing history, the government has two options: 1) performing a case-by-case review of the provider's patient files; or 2) conducting a statistical sampling of the provider's records. Statistical sampling is by far the more frequently utilized option. Difficulties, such as the time and expense required to perform case-by-case reviews, generally lead third-party payers to apply the more economical, although less reliable, statistical sampling techniques.

In an ongoing effort to reduce costs and manpower needs, Medicare has employed the use of statistical sampling techniques since 1972. HCFA formally adopted the use of the statistical sampling to project overpayments to Medicare providers in an administrative ruling issued in 1986.[2] Courts have further endorsed the use of these techniques, recognizing that "enormous logistical problems" exist when third-party payers are forced to initiate case-by-case record reviews of providers who have submitted literally thousands of claims during a calendar year.[3]

Although efforts to reduce governmental and other third-party payer costs have led to the general acceptance of statistical sampling in medical provider audits, providers should be cognizant

---

[1] Overpayments are generally defined as excess compensation paid because of improper billing practices. These include: a misused billing code, billing for non-covered services, billing for services that were medically unnecessary in relation to the diagnosis, and failure to have adequate documentation to verify the services provided. *See* Medicare Carriers Manual, Part B, Part 3, Section 7100.

[2] *See* HCFC Ruling No. HCFAR-86-1 (Feb. 20, 1986)

[3] Illinois Physicians Union v. Miller, 675 F.2d 151, at 157 (7th Cir. 1982). *See also* Rutherford v. Dept. of Social Services, 193 Mich. App. 326, 329, 483 N.W.2d 410 (1992); United States v. DeCosmo, Civil Action No. 82-631, slip op., at 10 (D.Colo. May 27, 1988); State of Georgia v. Califano, 446 F.Supp. 404 (N.D. Ga. 1977).

of the fact that such techniques do not always produce accurate or reliable results. In fact, the manner in which statistical sampling is performed may result in significantly exaggerated overpayment amounts that can and should be challenged.

9.2　HOW A STATISTICAL SAMPLING STUDY IS CONDUCTED

Medicare "Sampling Guidelines" contain a detailed technical explanation of the proper methods for establishing and conducting statistical sampling studies.[4] The following provides an elementary outline of how such studies are generally performed.

The parameters of a statistical study greatly impact the results generated by the study, and must initially be determined by the party conducting the audit. First, the insurer determines the items of service or types of billings to be reviewed during the sampling study. This entails the determination of whether the audit is to be purely random in nature, or whether the sampling shall be focused on particular code groupings. Next, the insurer establishes the "time reference" of the study. Time reference refers to the explicit beginning and ending dates of the period to be reviewed. Finally, the insurer determines the "universe" of claims so that the results of the study may be extrapolated and a total overpayment determination can be determined. The universe of claims merely refers to the total number of items of service that were actually paid during the time reference.

Once these parameters have been set, the insurer selects a "sampling unit." Sampling units are obtained by randomly selecting a sample of claims from within the aforementioned parameters established by the insurer. After selection, the insurer will request all documentation relating to the sampling unit. Each of these sample claims is then carefully reviewed for discrepancies and improper billing practices. The third-party payer then calculates an amount of overpayment for each sampling unit reviewed. Overpayment calculations represent the difference between the amount actually paid to the provider and the amount that the insurer contends should have been paid.

Once the overpayment totals are determined for the sample claims, the insurer utilizes extrapolation techniques to set an estimated total overpayment. Specifically, the aggregate amount of overpayments involved in the sampled cases is totaled, and an average overpayment is calculated by determining the percentage of error involved in the aggregate overpayment as compared to the total amount paid for the claims involved in the sampling. This average is then extrapolated across the provider's universe of claims and an estimated total amount of overpayment is determined.

The facts in *Rockland Medilabs, Inc. v. Perales* provide a poignant lesson of how the sampling and audit procedure is employed in actual practice.[5] In that case, the state Medicaid carrier

---

[4] Sampling Guidelines, Medicare Carriers Manual, Part 3 (HCFA-Pub. 14-3); hcfa.hhs.gov/pubforms/ 14%5fcar/3b7602ap01.htm.

[5] 719 F.Supp. 1191, 1194-1195 (S.D.N.Y. 1989).

performed a random sample audit of a laboratory provider's billings for a five month "subject period."

> The provider's total Medicaid billings during the subject period amounted to $1,370,099 comprising some 21,912 visits for services rendered to 14,762 patients. A random sample of 100 billings comprising 151 individual visits totaling $9,090 in Medicaid payments was examined. Of that sample, [the Medicaid carrier] found 16 improper billings amounting to $3,237 in allegedly fraudulent charges, or some 35% of the random sample. Extrapolating from those figures, [the carrier] ultimately determined that [the provider] had overcharged Medicaid some $477,933 during the subject period.[6]

An example of an actual notice of overpayment based upon a statistically valid random sampling and extrapolation involving an emergency medicine practice at a suburban hospital is appended as Exhibit XXIX. In that case, a sample of 200 claims for CPT Code 99285 submitted to Medicare were reviewed. It was determined that 46% of all these Level 5 claims were inappropriate and thus constituted overpayments. This 46% error rate was applied to the total universe of paid claims for this CPT Code for a two-year period ($456,251) to arrive at a projected overpayment of $209,876.

Large overpayment demands requested as a result of such audits have led a number of providers to challenge the use of statistical sampling and extrapolation. Specifically, providers have argued that these procedures are arbitrary, capricious, discriminatory and/or otherwise violative of due process. Courts have generally rejected these arguments, however, and upheld the use of these statistical techniques. For example, the District of Columbia Court of Appeals upheld the validity of Medicare's use of statistical sampling procedures in the seminal case of *Chaves County Home Health Services, Inc. v. Sullivan* ("*Chaves*").[7] In upholding the use of sampling against challenges that Medicare should have conducted a case-by-case claims review, the *Chaves* court stated:

> Absent an explicit provision in the statute that requires individualized claims adjudication for overpayment assessments against providers, the private interest at stake is easily outweighed by the government interest in minimizing administrative burdens; in light of the fairly low risk of error so long as the extrapolation is made from a representative sample and is statistically significant, the government interest predominates.[8]

The fact that the use of statistical sampling has been upheld in the health care audit context should not, however, prevent providers from challenging these audits.

---

[6] *Id.*

[7] 931 F.2d 914 (D.C. Cir. 1991), *cert. denied*, 112 S.Ct. 1160 (1992).

[8] 931 F.2d at 922.

9.3 CHALLENGING STATISTICAL SAMPLING

Medicare carriers are generally steadfast in their support of statistical sampling. Indeed, a letter received by a physician from the Texas Medicare carrier stated as follows:

> The audit is a statistically valid random sample of [assigned claims paid during a given time period]. A statistically valid random sample is a mathematically sound method by which an accurate determination of specific items or problems may be made on the basis of careful determination of a portion of the claims under scrutiny. It is a method widely used by: 1) industry in quality control; 2) audit agencies in the performance of audits; 3) public relation firms in determining public opinion; etc. It is acceptable in courts of law in the presentation of evidence. The particular method we used was developed by the U.S. Department of Commerce and refined for the specific purposes of the Medicare Program by the Department of Health and Human Services Inspector General's Office. The sampling process is carefully performed, and the random sampling and mathematical calculations are accurate on the information you have provided.[9]

Such self-serving statements, however, must not be taken at face value. Indeed, while the courts have consistently upheld the general use of sampling, particular audits have been deemed inappropriate as a result of unacceptable sampling techniques. For example, in an early case, the court took exception to the size of the sample used and found that, in the circumstances of the case, the extrapolation of the sample results to the provider's entire claims universe constituted a violation of due process.[10]

It is prudent, therefore, for healthcare providers and their counsel confronted with the results of audits to closely examine the circumstances of the audit and sampling techniques. In fact, providers' rights to challenge statistical samples have been upheld and recognized by the courts, by HCFA and, in some instances, have been established by state statutes.[11] For example, in the HCFA ruling regarding the appropriateness of statistical sampling, HCFA stated that:

> Sampling does not deprive a provider of its rights to challenge the sample, nor of its rights to procedural due process. Sampling only creates a presumption of validity as to the amount of an overpayment which may be used as the basis for recoupment.

---

[9] Letter from Senior Supervisor, Post Payment Medical Review, Medicare Part B Blue Cross and Blue Shield of Texas, Inc., dated September 20, 1990.

[10] Daytona Beach General Hospital, Inc. v. Weinberger, 435 F.Supp. 891 (M.D.Fla. 1977).

[11] Some state Medicaid regulations specifically state that the provider may challenge the correctness of the random sample methodology and that the provider is to be given full access to the findings that were made. *See, e.g.*, 470 Ind.Adm.Code 5-1-3.6(b)(2(A).

> The burden then shifts to the provider to take the next step. The provider could attack the statistical validity of the sample, or it could challenge the correctness of the determination in specific cases identified by the sample... In either case, the provider is given a full opportunity to demonstrate that the overpayment determination is wrong. If certain individual cases within the sample are determined to be decided erroneously, the amount of overpayment projected to the universe of claims can be modified. If the statistical basis upon which the projection was based is successfully challenged, the overpayment determination can be corrected.[12]

Additionally, courts reviewing the use of statistical sampling studies have consistently expressed concern that providers have an adequate opportunity to examine and rebut samplings conducted by insurers.[13]

Although providers have the right to challenge statistical samples, what are the appropriate bases for such challenges? The following brief list sets out a number of factors upon which statistical samples can be challenged:

> Statistical Significance: Each statistical sample must be of a large enough number of claims to generate statistically valid results. Contrary to what providers may assume, the size of the sample is influenced significantly by the size of the overpayment demand.

> Universe Stratification: Stratification involves insurers splitting the universe population into sub-populations for the purposes of conducting a sampling. The use or lack of stratification can lead to improper statistical results. Providers should analyze the appropriateness of the insurers stratification techniques and challenge these techniques when appropriate.

> Outliers: Unrepresentative sample claims, known as outliers, can significantly bias the results of a statistical sample. Providers should review the sampled claims to determine whether any such outliers exist.

> Extrapolation Techniques: The manner in which insurers extrapolate sampling results may be inappropriate. Extrapolation failing to take sampling errors and other variables into account may result in overinflated overpayment demands.

---

[12] HCFC Ruling No. HCFAR-86-1 (Feb. 20, 1986).

[13] OMAC v. Health Div., 96 Or.App. 528, 534, 774 P.2d 1113, 1117 (1989); Quality Clinical Lab v. Dept. of Social Services, 141 Mich.App. 597, 367 N.W.2d 390, 393 (1985); Illinois Physicians Union v. Miller, 675 F.2d 151 (7th Cir. 1982).

Providers should request information regarding how an insurer's extrapolation was conducted.

Documentation: Insurers conducting statistical studies must maintain detailed documentation throughout the sampling process so that providers can evaluate and challenge the validity of the sampling techniques. Lack of such documentation can be the basis for invalidation of a sampling. See Medicare Carriers Manual §4.1

Other Non-Sampling Errors: Occasionally the actual process of collecting data and the calculations performed are flawed. Any such flaws can significantly affect the results of a sampling and can be challenged.

9.4 PRACTICAL SUGGESTIONS FOR CONFRONTING A STATISTICAL SAMPLING STUDY

When confronting the results of a statistical sampling, the healthcare provider and counsel must evaluate the study to determine if either the factual findings derived from the sampled cases are in error or the statistical sampling methodology was flawed.

9.4.1 Re-Examination of the Audited Cases

First, it is essential that each of the sampled cases be re-examined to determine if the results reached by the carrier are correct. Under the Carriers Manual, all findings with respect to each case involved in the sample must be documented as to why the original claim was changed and how the overpayment was determined.[14] These findings should be obtained and examined by counsel. For example, if it is alleged that the medical records did not disclose the medical necessity of the services rendered, the physician can provide written justification for the services. If it is alleged that an improper billing code was used, the physician again can justify the use of the billing code based upon the overall condition of the patient or inadequate billing instructions from the insurer. In some instances, either the billing instructions or billing codes changed during the time period encompassed by the audit. A sample of an appeal to a carrier for fair hearing is appended as Exhibit XXX.

9.4.2 Having A Medical Consultant Review the Medical Findings

Through counsel, the provider should also retain a medical consultant for the purpose of rebutting the findings made by the insurer. Experience with Medicare and other insurers has shown that the insurer will exclude from the sampling well-documented case evaluations that demonstrate the propriety of the services rendered. In a surprising number of cases, the insurer's medical consultant recommended payment for the services be denied simply because his personal medical

---

[14] Medicare Carriers Manual, §7155.

philosophy differed from that of the provider under review. If the provider can persuade Medicare that a number of the claims involved in the actual sampling were in fact correctly submitted for payment, the resulting percentage of error on which the extrapolation is based will also be reduced, resulting in a much-reduced projected claim for reimbursement from what the insurer initially sought.

9.4.3 Retaining An Expert Statistician

Additionally, it is vital to retain an experienced statistician to examine the methodology on which the statistical sampling and the resulting projection was conducted. Statisticians are generally experienced at challenging the statistical sampling methodologies employed by insurers. As discussed above, a statistician will understand the process of challenging samplings on the basis of statistical validity, improper stratification, improper presence of outliers, improper extrapolation techniques, insufficient documentation, and other improper non-sampling errors.

9.5 HCFA CONSENT SETTLEMENT PROCEDURES

Because of the administrative problems inherent in constructing and conducting a statistically valid sampling study, HCFA has made a policy decision to obtain consent settlements based upon a "probable" extrapolated overpayment rather than engaging in a full-fledged sampling study. Medicare carriers are authorized to enter into consent settlements in overpayment cases based not on a "statistically valid random sample" of claims but instead on a smaller "mini-sample." The stated goal of this program is to successfully recoup an estimated overpayment based on a limited audit in an expeditious manner. It is designed to remove the uncertainty inherent in the fair hearing process involving overpayment claims where both the validity of the sampling study and the correctness of the overpayment determination can be challenged. Within the Medicare Carriers Manual HCFA states, "We believe a consent settlement process is an appropriate tool to modify a physician's billing process while limiting the carrier's cost in monitoring physician practice patterns."[15]

The rationale for promulgating this "consent procedure" is to streamline the recoupment process, and to reduce the administrative costs of conducting statistically valid random samplings, while educating the physician as to problems with the billing.

The "consent settlement" process is entirely voluntary on the part of the provider. It affords the provider with an opportunity to resolve the disputed issues without further inquiry by the carrier. However, if the provider does not agree to the "consent settlement" process, the physician is advised that a full statistical sampling will be conducted.

---

[15] Medicare Carriers Manual §7511.3.

HCFA requires the carrier to describe three options available to the provider during this consent settlement procedure.[16] Option One is for the provider to accept the projected overpayment. The provider agrees there was a problem in the billing and to correct the billing procedure in the future. In addition, the provider agrees to refund the entire projected overpayment amount and to waive any right to appeal the sampled individual overpayments. In return, the carrier agrees not to audit the physician's claims for any procedure codes again for the period considered in the audit (unless fraud is involved).

Option Two is for the physician to accept the capped potential projected overpayment, but be allowed to submit additional medical documentation relevant to the individual claims that made up the mini-sample. The carrier, in turn, would review this material to determine if an adjustment should be made in the projected sampling results. By agreeing to this option, however, the physician must agree to accept any revised determination made about these claims and to waive any right to appeal. The only concession granted the physician is that the revised potential overpayment amount will not exceed the initial capped amount. Once again, the carrier agrees not to audit any additional claims involved during the relevant period of time.

Option Three is an election to proceed to a statistically valid random sample for the same universe and time period involved in the audit. By choosing this option, the provider retains all its procedural due process rights to a fair hearing and an appeal to an administrative law judge.

9.6 CONCLUSION

With the increasing emphasis on cost containment for health services, providers are undergoing audits on a frequent basis. Familiarization with the audit process and the methodologies employed in sampling studies will enable healthcare provider and their attorneys to develop effective strategies for limiting exposure to overpayment demands.

---

[16] *See* Exhibit XXXI.

10. AFFIRMATIVE DEFENSE TECHNIQUES

Whenever healthcare providers are the subject of any fraud and abuse investigation, the inevitable question of what should and must be done will always arise. The answer to this question may often be elusive, impossible, and/or difficult to determine; or it may be just the opposite—easily identified and simple to execute. Whatever the answer, only through the compilation of all relevant facts and data can an effective legal strategy be determined.

Healthcare fraud investigations necessarily involve voluminous amounts of documents (claim forms, cost reports, supporting data, medical records, EOMBs, remittance advices, checks, business records, compliance reports, etc.). The volume of documents and number of witnesses involved can increase dramatically as an investigation expands in scope, time period, and/or number of alleged criminal acts. Giving credence to the saying "information is the key to success," healthcare providers under investigation should expect their counsel to utilize some particular method of gathering and organizing the facts in a manner allowing for ease of factual analysis and delegation of tasks.

The strategies, techniques, and methods discussed in this chapter offer one system (and certainly not an exclusive one) for tracking an ongoing healthcare fraud investigation, with a view towards maximizing the opportunities to address all issues in a thorough and organized fashion. The system discussed is flexible and easily adapted to address individual case concerns as they arise throughout the course of the typical healthcare fraud investigation.

10.1 ASSESSING THE INFORMATION AVAILABLE

An assessment of the client's legal exposure will affect counsel's strategy of how to handle the case. The only way to assess one's potential liability and the defense strategy's likelihood of success is to first accumulate and analyze all the available and relevant facts and information. In other words, *do not* expect immediate answers or results, and *do* expect that you and your defense team will spend expend significant amounts of time gathering facts, data, documents, testimony, and other relevant information.

The factual underpinnings of any case can be divided into two distinct categories: information conveyed by means of testimony, and information conveyed by documents. The following are issues that healthcare providers can expect to encounter when dealing with these aspects of the case.

10.1.1 Testimonial Evidence

Healthcare providers can expect that counsel will immediately want a list of any person who might have knowledge concerning the subject matter under investigation. This list should include the individual's full name, title position, address, telephone number, and a description of why that person might have knowledge of the subject matter. It would not be unusual that many of these individuals might be employees, patients, or other providers. If this is the case, counsel will also want to know what duties the employee was assigned, the dates of employment, and the positions occupied.[1] It would not be unusual for many of these individuals to have already been interviewed by the government at an early stage in the investigation. If this is the case, it will be important to re-interview these individuals as soon as possible.

Usually the most accessible witnesses are current employees, and attorneys often start the interview process with them. In general, interviews of the relevant employees should occur as soon as possible. Apart from the need to understand the nature of the investigation and the underlying facts, it is generally better to question any potential witness before government investigators have the chance. That said, any healthcare provider under investigation should also understand that, in the vast majority of cases, government investigators will usually be the first to conduct interviews with the most damaging witnesses. Once the government has contacted a potential witness, the witness has a tendency to refuse to discuss the matter with anyone else, particularly anyone associated with the perceived "target" of the investigation. It is not unusual for government agents to suggest to employees that the employer may not be looking out for their best interests and will often tell the employees that they are not obligated to submit to an interview by counsel for the employer.

Early on, all witnesses should be assigned a priority number or value to establish the order of interviews. Interviewing key employees early in an investigation may dampen the effect of some of the government tactics, as well as provide the attorney with enough information to begin assessing the client's exposure and the issues to be confronted.

10.1.1.1 *Conduct follow up interviews and obtain* affidavits

If possible, after the government has interviewed a witness or summonsed the witness to a grand jury, that witness should be debriefed with an eye towards obtaining the testimony in an affidavit, if the testimony or portions of it are at all helpful. The witness should be extensively examined about the questions asked, the answers provided, relevant or material areas that were not addressed or fully explored, and any suggestions or particular interview tactics employed by the government agents. There is no prohibition against counsel speaking to persons who were interviewed by the government or who testified before a grand jury.[2] In the authors' experience, interview reports cannot be used as effectively as signed affidavits. The goal is to *lock in* the witness's testimony by obtaining an affidavit at an early stage, before memory becomes hazy, sentiments change, or the government offers him or her an incentive to be less than cooperative. Joint defense agreements often have the tendency of maximizing defense counsels' access to relevant

---

[1] The amount of detail will vary depending upon the case and particular circumstances surrounding each potential witness.

[2] *In re Oral Testimony of a Witness Subpoenaed to Civil Investigative Demand No. 98-19*, 182 F.R.D. 196, at 20 (E.D.V.A July 29, 1998).

witnesses and documents.[3]

As discussed below, a methodical approach to the interviews can alert counsel to the particular issues on which the government is focusing, as well as the issues or facts *not* being examined by the government. Obviously, all information gathered will be of some importance in planning strategy, and will assist in the development of an effective defense strategy.

10.1.1.2 *Track all witness interviews conducted by the government*

A healthcare attorney can quickly and effectively focus on the defense to prepare by focusing on who is being interviewed, and the type of information is being sought.

If billing and clerical personnel are being interviewed by government investigators, it is safe to assume that the investigation is focused on potentially fraudulent billing practices. On the other hand, if salepersons and third-party vendors are the subject of interviews, the case may involve potential anti-kickback or Stark violations.[4] Additionally, if patients are being interviewed about the frequency and type of treatment received, the case may involve questions of not only false billing practices but of issues pertaining to overutilization and medical necessity. Similarly, by analyzing the questions that are asked of the witnesses, counsel can also get an understanding of the particular matter that the government has examined, such as anti-kickback issue, fraudulent billing issue, and prescribing practices. The information gathered should frequently be subject to analysis and re-analysis.

The following three charts include a suggested step-by-step approach to systematically analyzing the information obtained through witness interviews and determining the tasks to be completed.

---

[3] *See* Chapter 7.5.

[4] 42 U.S.C.§1320a-7b(b) (Anti-Kickback Act); 42 U.S.C. § 1395nn. (Stark Law).

Chart A1

A chart like this simply assists the attorney to narrow and compartmentalize the various issues raised by the government through the comments of various witnesses:

LISTING OF ISSUES REVIEWED
BY GOVERNMENT INVESTIGATOR
WITH CITATIONS TO INDIVIDUALS INTERVIEWED

Affidavits Reviewed: Jenney, Smith, Jones, Turgeon, Devlin,
Individuals Interviewed with no affidavit obtained: Amaral, White

No.	ISSUE RAISED BY GOVERNMENT	CITATION TO INDIVIDUAL INTERVIEWED (date of interview)
1.	Dr. Piver is "churning over" the patients in office to other doctors for unnecessary testing	*Jenney*, 7/29/95; *Turgeon*, 8/6/95;
2.	Dr. Piver is charging an inordinate amount of rent to his colleagues in exchange for referrals.	*Amaral*, 7/30/95, *White*, 8/8/95
3.	Dr. Piver is handing prescriptions out to drug addicts	*Jenney*, 7/29/95; *Jones*, 8/6/95; *Turgeon*, 8/6/95
4.	Dr. Piver is responsible for 5 deaths in the New London area.	*Jenney*, 7/29/95; *Smith*, 8/6/95; *Turgeon*, 8/6/95; *Jones*, 8/11/95 (37 deaths)
5.	Dr. Piver billed for 87 individuals in one day and sees more patients in a day than is possible under the insurance program regulations.	*Jenney*, 7/29/95; *Turgeon*, 8/6/95; *Devlin*, 8/11/95 (60 per day)
6.	Dr. Piver prescribes drugs in improper amounts, duration, and type. He has made a lot money and is very greedy.	*Jenney*, 7/29/95; *Amaral*, 7/30/95
7.	Dr. Piver is harming patients who go to him for help; he gives them drugs.	*Jenney*, 7/29/95; *Turgeon*, 8/6/95
8.	Dr. Piver adds on tests, procedures, and diagnosis to other physicians charts and bills for services not rendered in the manner billed.	*Jennison*, 7/29/95; *Turgeon*, 8/6/95
9.	Dr. Piver owns the laboratory to which he refers patients.	*Smith*, 7/30/95; *White*, 8/8/95

Chart A2

With a view towards affirmatively combating the government's allegations, the next step is to determine the tasks to be accomplished and begin accumulating the rebuttal evidence:

AFFIRMATIVE DEFENSE TASKS TO BE ACCOMPLISHED
ACCORDING TO ISSUE RAISED

No.	ISSUE RAISED BY GOVERNMENT	SUGGESTED MEANS AND METHODS OF ADDRESSING ISSUE RAISED
1.	Dr. Piver is "churning over" the patients in office to other doctors for unnecessary testing.	1. Determine from Dr. Piver when and under what circumstances referrals were made in the past seven years. 2. List of all MDs, psychs, and agencies he refers to. 3. Justify all referrals in accordance with Medicaid and Medicare regulations and contracts. 4. Obtain copies of all Dr. Piver's contracts. 5. Obtain lists of all patients referred for testing (work yearly starting with most recent year). 6. Obtain affidavits from health professionals in office that referrals meet standard of care criteria (all health care professionals to whom he refers).
2.	Dr. Piver is charging an inordinate amount of rent to his colleagues in exchange for referrals.	1. Determine rent. 2. Determine additional services provided outside of space rental. 3. Determine FMV for rent and all additional services. 4. Retain accounting firm.
3.	Dr. Piver is handing prescriptions out to drug addicts.	1. Determine under what circumstances this happens. Which patients are drug addicts. Which patients have most problems with police and may be "visible." 2. What regulations or guidelines apply. 3. Justify with regulations, guidelines, medical literature, medical records, and expert affidavits.
4.	Dr. Piver is responsible for 5 deaths in the New London area.	1. Review previous law firm file addressing this issue. Use all information developed in that case. 2. Determine which deaths have not been addressed. Obtain permission from families for autopsy reports or obtain newspaper clippings on alleged "cause of death." 3. Address all deaths with written response for submission to grand jury as exculpatory evidence.

No.	ISSUE RAISED BY GOVERNMENT	SUGGESTED MEANS AND METHODS OF ADDRESSING ISSUE RAISED
5.	Dr. Piver billed for 87 individuals in one day and sees more patients in a day than is possible under the insurance program regulations.	1. Ask Dr. Piver to reprint computer summaries of his billings and to present this office with all EOBs. Note: Government may only have EOBs relating to Medicare/caid and will not have the additional information relative to private paying patients. 2. Determine which days are the high days and what codes were billed on those days. Justify through regulations appropriate billing.
6.	Dr. Piver prescribes drugs in improper amounts, duration, and type. Dr. Piver has made a lot money and is very greedy.	1. Determine drugs prescribed and proper amounts and duration. Create list showing accepted amounts and duration and compare to Dr. Piver's practice. Address appropriateness of type of drug in reference to general medical conditions of patients. 2. Address this as an inappropriate issue in a letter to the government.
7.	Dr. Piver is harming patients who go to him for help; he gives them drugs.	1. Address the use of drugs to treat drug addicts. Use affidavits from other psychiatrists and medical literature.
8.	Dr. Piver adds on tests, procedures, and diagnosis to other physicians charts and bills for services not rendered in the manner billed.	1. Ask other physicians in office to review charts and determine if anything was added on and if so, under what circumstances. 2. Interview all office personnel about this issue. 3. Determine the codes at issue and address each code and circumstances surrounding the billing.

Chart A3

One of the most effective ways to track an investigation is chronologically and by issue. As the government refines its investigation, a chronological chart will alert the healthcare attorney to the issues on which the government plans to focus.

LISTING OF INDIVIDUALS INTERVIEWED IN CHRONOLOGICAL ORDER

No.	Date	Name (Address & tel. #)	Position	Issues Reviewed with Investigator	Affidavit Supplied
1.	June 4, 1995	Dr. Dram Riker	Partner	Issues, 1, 2, 3, and 8	No. Has an attorney. *See* notes from counsel.
2.	June 6, 1995 Tuesday	Dr. Peter Jones	Partner	Issues, 1, 2, 3, and 8	No. Has an attorney. *See* notes from counsel.
3.	July 3, 1995 Wednesday	Dr. Marianne Beaker	part-time family practitioner	Issues # 1,2, 3, 7, and 8	Yes. July 15, 1995.
4.		Dr. Sol Della Russo	family practitioner		
5.	July 29, 1995 Tuesday	Ann Jenney 29 Circuit Drive, New London, CT (000) 679-4000	Secretary (17 yrs.)	Issues # 1, 2, 3, 4, 5, 6, 7, and 8	Yes. Aug. 4, 1995
6.	July 30, 1995 Wednesday	Maria Smith 66 Sunset Hill New London, CT (008) 674-8000	Patient (1.5 yrs.)	Issues # 8 and 9	Yes. August 14, 1995
7.	August 6, 1995 Wednesday	Elizabeth Renee 49 Claflin Street New London, CT (508) 673-0000	Patient (13 yrs.)	Issues # 3, 4, 7, 8, and 9	
8.	August 6, 1995 Wednesday	Donna P. Turgeon 1123 Robeson Street, New London, CT (000) 672-7777	Secretary (4 yrs.)	Issues # 1, 2, 3, 4, 5, 8, 11, 15, and 16	Yes. August 12, 1995

10.1.2 Documentary Evidence

Over the last few years, tracking voluminous documents has become a speciality in its own right as computer software programs dramatically change how attorneys gather, retain, and keep track of this documentary information. In the authors' experience, these programs are quite economical and can quickly place the defense team on a par with the government when it comes to tracking and analyzing the documents involved in the case. At the outset, any healthcare provider whose records are requested should expect to be required to provide the originals to the government and retain one complete set for the provider and one complete set for the defense counsel or team.

In recent years, many of the more sophisticated healthcare prosecutorial agencies have begun scanning every document gathered into electronic format and tracking them with the use of one or more of the various database software programs available to the general public. These programs allow the documents to be quickly accessed with a bar code and infinitely categorized according to the issue explored. Copies of a CD-ROM containing the documents in electronic format can be quickly and inexpensively duplicated upon request. However, regardless of the method used to track documents and other data, healthcare attorneys will, in almost all cases, seek to accomplish the following:

10.1.2.1   *Track issues raised by the government's document requests/subpoenas*

Healthcare providers under investigation can expect their attorneys to do more than merely inventory documents produced to the government. To add practical value to any document production, experienced attorneys will usually track the focus of the government's investigation by inventorying documents by reference to witness as well as by reference to issue raised.

10.1.2.2   *Quantify the information developed*

Although time consuming, quantifying information is one of the easiest and most effective methods of reducing the data contained on voluminous documents to identifiable and workable concepts. Exhibit XXXII consists of one chart used in the investigation of a physician for allegedly illegally prescribing a particular class of drugs to patients.[5] The chart references all of the available data pertaining to the standard of care applicable to the drugs in question. Below the chart in the appendix are the factual points favorable to the healthcare provider, based upon quantifying the information contained in the chart. This information can be used effectively in negotiations and/or at trial.

---

[5] *See* Exhibit XXXII.

10.1.2.3 *Address all issues raised by the government*

Once counsel has gathered, organized, and analyzed all of the relevant information, he or she will be in a position to adequately assess the strengths and weaknesses of the case. More importantly, counsel will also be a position to assess the strengths and weaknesses of the government's case. Typically, it will only be at this point that it will be reasonable for the healthcare provider client to expect an accurate and detailed assessment of the case from his attorney or defense team.

10.2 IMPLEMENTING AN OFFENSE

An attorney's role is not limited to simply gathering and analyzing information during the course of a healthcare investigation. There are a number of ways that attorneys "go on the offensive" at the investigative or grand jury phase or prior to the government filing a civil FCA suit or criminal indictment. Due to the enormous consequences that can befall a health care provider in the event of a criminal prosecution or civil false claims action, it may be a mistake for counsel to hold his or her cards "too close to the vest," as is often done in the more "garden variety" type of fraud case, and more particularly in most violent crime cases.

10.2.1 Providing the Government with Exculpatory Evidence

A prosecutor is normally under no duty to search for and disclose to the grand jury evidence favorable to the target of an investigation or which negates guilt.[6] Nonetheless, "it is the policy of the Department of Justice . . . that when a prosecutor conducting a grand jury inquiry is personally aware of substantial evidence that directly negates the guilt of a subject of the investigation, the prosecutor must present or otherwise disclose such evidence to the grand jury before seeking an indictment against such a person."[7]

It is important for counsel for a healthcare provider to marshal any exculpatory evidence favorable to the client during the investigation because, on a practical basis, it is unlikely that a prosecutor will deny a request to present exculpatory evidence. At the same time, counsel must balance the risks of disclosing favorable evidence to the prosecution if it appears unlikely the evidence will have an effect on the decision to prosecute the case.

---

[6] United States v. Wilson, 789 F.2d 509, 517 (1st Cir. 1986); United States v. Ciambrone, 601 F.2d 616, 622-623 (2d Cir.1979); United States v. Civella, 666 F.2d 1122, 1127 (8th Cir.1981); United States v. Page, 808 F.2d 723, 727-28 (10th Cir.), *cert. denied*, 482 U.S. 918, 107 S.Ct. 3195, 96 L.Ed.2d 683 (1987). *See also* United States v. Williams, 112 S.Ct. 17635 (1992) (Federal courts do not have power to dismiss otherwise valid indictment where the prosecutor failed to introduce substantial exculpatory evidence to a grand jury).

[7] United States Attorney's Manual, Department of Justice, October 1997.

10.2.2 Position Statements with Memorandum of Law

Once the facts and law applicable to the case have been analyzed, a reasonable argument may occasionally be made that neither the evidence nor the law support a criminal prosecution or civil false claim action. In these cases, the attorney or defense team may consider formulating a position statement for potential submission to the prosecutor articulating reasons why the case should not be brought and why, if a prosecution or civil action is commenced, the government cannot possibly win.[8] Counsel should think about attacking the government's theory of the case in two ways:

10.2.2.1   *Legally*

- What essential elements of the case the government will be unable to prove.
- What legal issues make this an unattractive case to litigate.

10.2.2.2   *Factually*

- Focus on areas either not examined or sufficiently examined by government.
- Present additional evidence that casts doubt on the government's theory of the case.

10.2.3 Declaratory Judgment Action

There are instances where it may be appropriate to file a declaratory judgment action seeking a declaration that the healthcare provider's conduct is in compliance with the applicable laws, rules, and regulations of the program under review. Bringing such an action might counter an investigation, or at least affect the pace of the investigation or discovery. Additionally, if the case survives a motion to dismiss, counsel will be able to obtain additional insight on the concurrent investigation through the civil discovery procedures.

Indeed, during the course of a healthcare investigation, counsel has no ability to obtain documents from third parties or interview witnesses without their consent. In the context of a declaratory judgment action, however, the normal discovery rules of civil procedure apply, allowing counsel to depose witnesses and summons documents from third parties.

The legal basis for bringing a declaratory judgment action can be found in 28 U.S.C. §2201 and Fed.R.Civ.P. 57: "In a case of actual controversy...any court of the United States...may declare the rights and other legal relations of any interested party."[9] The purpose of a declaratory judgment

---

[8] *See* Exhibit XXXIII.

[9] *See generally* Public Affairs Associates v. Rickover, 369 U.S. 111, 112, 82 S.Ct. 580, 581, 7 L.Ed.2d 604 (1962) (per curiam); Interdynamics, Inc. v. Wolf, 698 F.2d 157, 167 (3rd Cir.1982); President v. Vance, 627 F.2d 353, 364 n.76 (D.C.Cir.1980); Alsager v. District Court, 518 F.2d 1160, 1163-64 (8th Cir.1975); Provident Tradesmens Bank & Trust Co. v. Patterson, 390 U.S. 102, 126-28, 88 S.Ct. 733, 746-747, 19 L.Ed.2d 936 (1968); 10A C. Wright, A. Miller & M. Kane, FEDERAL PRACTICE AND PROCEDURE: CIVIL § 2759, at 645-51 (2d ed. 1983).

action is remedial in nature: to remove uncertainty and to grant relief with respect to matters where there is an actual controversy between the parties. At the same time, an entity or person under investigation is not entitled to enjoin a pending or threatened criminal prosecution. In cases involving threatened criminal prosecution, the court will not grant relief unless it is clear that, unless relief is granted, a substantial right of the plaintiff will be impaired to a material degree; that any remedy at law is inadequate; and that injunctive relief can be applied with practical success and without imposing an impossible burden on the courts.

Therefore, it can be anticipated that the government will raise a number of defenses to any declaratory judgment that could affect the investigation, including lack of an actual case or controversy, lack of standing, and interference with an ongoing criminal prosecution.

Healthcare providers must be prepared in advance to address each of these issues if the case is to survive a motion to dismiss and be an effective tool towards finding a workable tool for the healthcare client under investigation.[10]

---

[10] *See* Exhibit XXXIV.

11. VOLUNTARY DISCLOSURES AND SETTLEMENT OPTIONS

Although healthcare providers expect to face audits by third-party payers, in today's healthcare environment all providers are also expected to police themselves for billing flaws and discrepancies. Voluntary disclosure and cooperation with the government regarding issues potentially resulting in one's own criminal liability, financial debt, or exclusion from Medicare/Medicaid represent an enormously intimidating prospect. However, after the initial fears caused by such suggestions subside, it is often determined that making voluntary disclosures and/or entering into settlements with the government can provide significant benefits. This chapter examines how these options can enable healthcare providers to maintain some semblance of control when facing government action and, in certain cases, allow providers to forestall government action altogether.

11.1 VOLUNTARY DISCLOSURE

Both Medicare and Medicaid regulations make any healthcare provider responsible for any overpayments made by the program. Occasionally, a provider may discover that the government mistakenly paid it multiple times for submitted claims, or that it unintentionally submitted a number of incorrectly coded claims. In other cases, a provider may even uncover the fact that members of its organization submitted fraudulent claims to the government. When such discoveries occur, the provider must consider making a voluntary disclosure to the government.

Although not without risks, reporting overpayments discovered through internal review can lead to reductions in exposure to civil and criminal fines and penalties, and allow the disclosing provider to maintain some control over how information is disseminated. Further promoting voluntary disclosure, in June 1998 the OIG issued a Provider Self-Disclosure Protocol[1] in which the OIG stated its belief that "health care providers have an ethical and legal duty to ensure the integrity

11.1.1 Making the Decision to Disclose

The decision to voluntarily disclose information to the government involves a number of considerations. Providers must weigh the legal consequences that can be avoided by making a disclosure with the strategic benefits disclosure can provide with the potential harm that could result from disclosure.

---

[1] *See* 63 Fed. Reg. 58399.

11.1.1.1 *Legal Duty to Disclose Discovered Overpayments*

An initial question a provider must ask is whether a legal obligation exists to disclose a discovered overpayment. The Social Security Act makes it a felony for persons to "conceal or fail to disclose" certain overpayments when that person has "an intent fraudulently to secure" the overpayment[s].[2] Similarly, 18 U.S.C. § 4 makes illegal the affirmative concealment and non-disclosure of a federal felony offense. Under these laws, active concealment of government overpayments can result in criminal liability. This law is ambiguous at best as to whether it requires a healthcare provider to report every instance of an overpayment; nevertheless, it is the government's position that this provision obligates providers to make a voluntary disclosure and refund upon becoming aware that the provider is "retaining" funds that should not have been paid initially.

However, the scope of lessor actions that will trigger potential criminal liability is somewhat unclear. Although the mere failure to disclose or return an overpayment is generally not enough to violate these laws, the nature of the particular overpayment (i.e., whether the overpayment stemmed from a scheme implemented by employees of the provider or a mistake of the government) and the provider's actions after the overpayment was discovered (i.e., whether the provider attempted to conceal the overpayment in any way) can make such non-disclosure illegal. The somewhat ambiguous nature of these laws leads the authors to recommend that providers consult with legal counsel specializing in healthcare fraud and abuse issues when an internal review uncovers an overpayment. Avoiding increased exposure to liability upon the discovery of an overpayment should be a provider's primary initial goal.

11.1.1.2 *The Strategic Benefits of Disclosure*

Making a voluntary disclosure to the government can carry with it certain strategic benefits. First and foremost is the potential of avoiding criminal prosecution. The government has two basic choices when it uncovers fraud and abuse. The government can, and generally does, seek civil recoupment and penalties against persons or entities discovered to have committed fraud. Second, the government can bring criminal charges against a provider under criminal provisions such as the criminal FCA,[3] which can result in significant jail terms and fines. The scope of the enforcement options depends in part on the government's opinion of a provider's intentions and character. Voluntary disclosure can raise the government's opinion of a provider and lead to a reduction in penalties sought.

The decision to seek criminal sanctions, as well as the decision to bring charges under laws carrying severe civil penalties (e.g., the civil FCA, which carries mandatory per violation fines), is a

---

[2] *See* 42 U.S.C. § 1320(a-7b(a)(3); Social Security Act § 1128B(a)(3).

[3] *See* 18 U.S.C. § 287

discretionary choice of the government. Consequently, when a provider makes a voluntary disclosure, the government may accept it as an act of goodwill and, in return, either decline to seek prosecution or to at least reduce the scope of the penalties sought. In the civil context, the federal FCA provides that a voluntary disclosure will reduce any damages to twice the amount of damages instead of the potential three times.[4] However, to be granted the advantage of this provision, the disclosure must be made to the U.S. Attorney within thirty days after the provider first becomes aware of the violation.[5]

Moreover, even where the government chooses to bring criminal charges, voluntary disclosure can act as a mitigating factor under the federal sentencing guidelines, and help to reduce any ultimate criminal fines and sentences. When making a disclosure, providers must be cautious, however, not to injure their credibility with the government. This can occur if a provider fails to reveal all of its findings to the government, and the government later discovers that the provider knew of other undisclosed overpayments. In such cases, it is quite likely that the government will view the initial disclosure as an attempt to hide overpayments and go after the provider with full force.

Another significant benefit from making a voluntary disclosure is the increased ability of the provider to control the scope and pace of the information released to the government. When overpayments are discovered and fraud is suspected, it is not uncommon for government investigators to barge into offices waiving subpoenas and search warrants in an attempt to seize any and all relevant information. This is a very imposing and unsettling process that is best to be avoided if possible. Generally, when a self-disclosure is made, the provider submits relevant information to the government and then establishes a plan with the government under which the government can perform its investigation in an orderly and organized process. This usually results in significantly less disruption to an organization's business. Additionally, if the government desires to interview any employees, time is generally available to inform the employees about events taking place and prepare them for the process of being interviewed.

Similarly, a provider making a self-disclosure has the opportunity to control some of the information that is reported to the public. Typically, voluntary conversations with government agencies are not matters of public record. On the other hand, nothing will result in adverse publicity faster than a newspaper article involving search warrants, subpoenas, prejudgment seizures of assets, or payment suspensions. Consequently, voluntary disclosure can save providers from having to make defensive explanations to patients, customers, insurers, creditors, and the public.

A number of other significant benefits may arise from making a voluntary disclosure. As previously stated, the government may accept a disclosure as evidence of a provider's character and goodwill. Consequently, if future issues arise requiring disclosures to the government, past honest dealings may lead to more favorable discussions and negotiations with government representatives.

---

[4] 31 U.S.C. § 3729a(7).

[5] *See Id.*

Also, in the event a settlement agreement is negotiated with the government regarding the overpayments, a provider's voluntary disclosure may be used to negotiate for the imposition of more lenient standards.

11.1.1.3 *Potential Negative Consequences of Disclosure*

All disclosures come with risks that may not arise if no disclosure is made. Initially, although the above discussions address avoiding criminal penalties and severe fines, it should be noted that not every overpayment involves these threats. Many potential overpayments result from reasonable interpretation of ambiguous government payment rules. Consequently, some apparent overpayments may not actually represent overpayments. A provider should be careful that when making a voluntary disclosure it does not admit to being overpaid when the claims in question can be defended.

Another factor to consider is the fact that, upon making a disclosure, the potential exists that the government will perform a close examination or investigation of the business. Consequently, a provider making a self-disclosure should perform a detailed internal review of its claim development and submission process and be well aware of any potential risk areas within its organization.

Furthermore, a definite risk exists that the government may not waive its right to bring criminal charges against a provider making a disclosure. There is no guarantee that, simply because a provider approaches the government, the government might not still deem the provider's acts worthy of criminal prosecution.

Finally, lest any providers believe that voluntary disclosure represents a "get out of jail free card," it should be noted that providers making disclosures should expect that the government will, at a minimum, seek the recoupment of any overpayments disclosed. Depending on the size of the overpayment, this can result in a significant burden to the provider. Making this an even riskier prospect is the fact that without voluntary disclosure, there exists the possibility that the government may never discover the disclosed overpayment.

11.1.1.4 *The Risks of Not Disclosing*

Along with the potential benefits and risks of making a disclosure, every provider must also consider the potential detriment that could arise from failing to make a disclosure. The primary risk in not disclosing a discovered overpayment is clear: Someone else could discover the overpayment. Whether an overpayment is discovered by the government or a potential qui tam relator, there is always the potential of an overpayment being discovered prior to making a self-disclosure. Once discovered by a third party, it is too late to backtrack and attempt to claim that it was the intent of the provider to disclose the information. Consequently, any potential "goodwill" benefits to be gained by voluntary disclosure will be lost.

11.1.2 How and To Whom to Disclose

11.1.2.1 *Carrier/Intermediary Disclosures*

Upon a discovery of an overpayment that involved no intentional wrongdoing, a provider making a voluntary disclosure should do so to its appropriate carrier or intermediary. It is generally unnecessary to invite the attention of OIG investigators or the U.S. Attorney unless the provider has determined that the overpayments resulted from potential violations of criminal or civil statutes. Once again, prior to making any disclosure, it is crucial that a provider conduct an internal review and become acutely aware of any potential risk areas.

Examples of two voluntary disclosures involving employee dishonesty are appended as Exhibit XXXV.

11.1.2.2 *Voluntary Disclosure Protocol*

When overpayments discovered internally by providers implicate violations of federal criminal or civil statutes, the OIG has set out a system for self-disclosure that may lead to government leniency if utilized.[6] It is important to emphasize that this Provider Self-Disclosure Protocol ("the Protocol") is designed only for situations where a provider believes a potential violation of law may have occurred. In a recent Open Letter to the Health Care Community, while urging providers to self-disclose improper conduct, the Inspector General emphasized that matters that involve overpayments or errors that do not indicate violations of the law should be brought directly to the attention of the Fiscal Intermediary, Medicare carrier, or other entity responsible for claims processing and payment.[7]

Providers should be aware that making a repayment to the Fiscal Intermediary or Carrier does not remove the possibility that the matter will be referred to the OIG for investigation if the refund is substantial in amount or appears to be the result of systemic billing errors. The government has indicated, however, that use of the protocol will "generally benefit" those that choose to use it.

Under this Protocol, providers are expected to make an initial disclosure, which generally sets forth the scope and nature of the overpayment being disclosed, the relevant identification information regarding the provider including entity affiliations, and certifications regarding the truthfulness of the disclosure. Additionally, the provider must attest to whether it has knowledge of any government or government contractor investigations regarding the issues being disclosed.

In addition to this initial disclosure, a provider is expected to perform an independent review of its organization and to report the results of the review in detail to the government. As to the scope of the review to be performed, the OIG goes so far as to recommend that providers engage in either a claim-by-claim review or a statistical sampling of its billing history. To assist providers and insurers

---

[6] *See* 63 Fed. Reg. 58399. this Protocol can also be found on the OIG Web site at www.dhhs.gov/progorg/oig/modcomp/oigdis.pdf.

[7] *See* Letter dated March 9, 2000, at www.hhs.gov.oig/modcomp/openletter.htm.

in the practice of self-review, the OIG has established a statistical device entitled "RAT-STATS", essentially a computer program that performs statistical sampling. A provider should obtain the services of billing consultants and statisticians to assist with a statistical self-assessment.

The Protocol further requires that reports regarding these reviews contain narratives from the provider that detail the potential causes of the overpayment, estimate the financial scope of the overpayment, and identify employees having knowledge of or participating in activities associated with the overpayment. Additionally, such reports are to discuss which government agencies are impacted, any disciplinary actions taken against those involved, and what actions the provider has taken to prevent future overpayments.

After a provider has filed its initial disclosure and completed and submitted its internal review, the OIG will take steps to verify the details submitted in those reports and disclosure. The OIG may conduct interviews, examine billing records, and engage in other activities to determine the veracity of the disclosures. Once the OIG verifies the details disclosed by the provider, payment options will be discussed. In general, it is recommended that when a disclosure is being made the provider begin to consider the financial impact of the expected recoupment. If possible, this includes putting aside money in an escrow account to be used for repayment.

11.2 SETTLEMENT AGREEMENTS

The decision to settle with the government regarding civil or criminal issues must be based on the facts of the provider's particular situation. Factors such as the scope of the acts or overpayments involved, the provider's relationship with government representatives, the size of the organization, and the political atmosphere influence the decision whether a settlement is the best course of action. In addition to these factors, when making the decision to settle, providers and their counsel should also weigh the various provisions that can be incorporated into settlement agreements to make post-settlement life bearable.

11.2.1 Plea Agreement (Criminal Settlement)

The primary goal in defending any investigation is avoiding a conviction and the subsequent fines, penalties, and exclusion from the Medicare program. Although it is impossible to accurately predict whether and to what extent the government will be flexible with the level of penalties it seeks, providers and their counsel should discuss and set target goals regarding the level of fines and penalties that it would find acceptable. Often, an acceptance of larger financial penalties can allow a healthcare provider to reduce the level of initially sought-after jail time for its managers and employees. Additionally, the government may be amenable to payment according to a payment schedule that may allow the provider to stay financially viable. In general, providers should note that federal sentencing guidelines recognize "acceptance of responsibility" as a mitigating factor that can result in lower potential penalties.

Other than reducing or avoiding potential jail terms and financial penalties, a crucial goal for many providers during the settlement process is to avoid exclusion from Medicare/Medicaid. Under 42 U.S.C. §1320 a-7a(1), conviction of certain crimes results in mandatory exclusion regardless of whether the conviction stems from a plea agreement or a plea of *nolo contendere*. Additionally, under 42 U.S.C. §1320 a-7b, the government has certain discretion to exclude providers from the Medicare or Medicaid programs for violations of the Social Security Act. Upon entering negotiations, a number of strategies may be employed to ensure that exclusion does not occur.

One such strategy that may be available, depending upon the size of the provider, is to have a subsidiary of the organization plead guilty. In the past, the government has agreed to allow the subsidiary to transfer its assets to another arm of the organization, plead guilty, and accept exclusion for that subsidiary only. Any agreement along these lines should expressly state that the government (and OIG in particular) agrees that the parent organization and its remaining subsidiaries will not be excluded by reason of the charged subsidiary's conduct.

A second strategy to avoid exclusion is to negotiate a plea to a criminal charge that the government agrees does not require exclusion. For instance, the government (including OIG) has accepted a guilty plea to "misprision of a felony," which means failing to disclose a known felony, in a case involving allegations of overbilling and misrepresentations to the Medicare intermediary, and agreed that the organization and individual who pled guilty would not be excluded.[8]

When negotiating a settlement, a provider should also contemplate any legal status that may implicate its ability to continue operations if not protected. For example, if the defendant pleading guilty is a tax-exempt hospital or organization, it will be crucial that the provider obtain a written assurance (preferably in the plea agreement) from the Internal Revenue Service that the plea will not serve as a basis for the Service to cause the organization to forfeit its tax-exempt status.

11.2.2 Civil Settlement

A similar approach taken by providers facing criminal settlements should be employed by providers facing civil settlements. Providers facing civil settlements should set goals regarding the financial penalties that would be acceptable, and consider the various options of payment that will enable the provider to effectively maintain its business operations.[9]

Similar to the criminal conviction scenario, the government's permissive authority to exclude providers from Medicare/Medicaid extends to violations of certain civil statutes. Consequently, providers should contemplate potential strategies to avoid exclusion. Any agreement with the

---

[8] 18 U.S.C. §4. A copy of a sample plea agreement is attached as Exhibit XXXVI.

[9] A copy of a sample civil settlement agreement is attached as Exhibit XXXVII.

government allowing the provider to avoid exclusion should be incorporated into the civil settlement agreement.

Once again, any critical status-based issues, such as tax-exempt status, must be considered and protected. This can be achieved either by incorporating language into the agreement itself, or through obtaining a letter from the appropriate government agency assuring that the provider's status will not be challenged or revoked as a result of the settlement agreement.

Specifically, with regard to settlement agreements involving the federal civil FCA,[10] issues regarding any qui tam suit and relators must be addressed. If a qui tam lawsuit had been filed, counsel must include language in the Settlement Agreement dismissing with prejudice the qui tam suit. Counsel should also attempt to obtain a release from the qui tam relator for any "whistleblower" claims. Generally, however, the government has refused to require a relator to release such claims if he or she refuses.

11.2.2.1 Corporate Integrity Agreements

Upon entering into settlements with the government, the government often requires that a corporate integrity agreement (CIA) be entered into to help assure future compliance by providers. Generally, a CIA details specific requirements that a provider must follow, and specifies potential fines or penalties for failure to remain in compliance with the agreement.[11]

CIAs universally require that a compliance program be put into place to monitor the provider's billing activities. Additionally, a CIA generally mandates the development of a code of conduct and training requirements for employees. Significantly, CIAs also contain reporting requirements that require providers to notify the government of any overpayments or investigations and to report on the status of the implementation of any programs required by the CIA.

As with settlement agreements, negotiation may allow a provider to narrow the scope and requirements of a CIA. The severity of the provider's indiscretions, the size of any past overpayments, and the type of overpayment will generally determine the level of flexibility that the government will allow. Providers can typically negotiate the timeframe for implementation and the duration of the CIA, which usually will last a minimum of five years. Furthermore, if a provider already has a CIA in place, the provider may be able to use its current compliance plan to reduce the requirements of the CIA.

---

[10] *See* 31 U.S.C. § 3729.

[11] A copy of a sample CIA is attached as Exhibit XXXVII.

EXHIBIT I.
Example of OIG Special Fraud Alert

OFFICE OF INSPECTOR GENERAL

Special Fraud Alert

RENTAL OF SPACE IN PHYSICIAN OFFICES BY PERSONS OR ENTITIES TO WHICH PHYSICIANS REFER

February 2000

The Office of Inspector General (OIG) was established at the Department of Health and Human Services by Congress in 1976 to identify and eliminate fraud, abuse and waste in the Department's programs and to promote efficiency and economy in departmental operations. The OIG carries out this mission through a nationwide program of audits, investigations and inspections.

To reduce fraud and abuse in the Federal health care programs, including Medicare and Medicaid, the OIG actively investigates fraudulent schemes that are used to obtain money from these programs and, when appropriate, issues Special Fraud Alerts that identify practices in the health care industry that are particularly vulnerable to abuse.

This Special Fraud Alert focuses on the rental of space in physicians' offices by persons or entities that provide health care items or services (suppliers)[1] to patients that are referred either directly or indirectly by their physician-landlords. In this Special Fraud Alert, we describe some of the potentially illegal practices the OIG has identified in such rental relationships.

Questionable Rental Arrangements For Space in Physician Offices

A number of suppliers that provide health care items or services rent space in the offices of physicians or other practitioners. Typically, most of the items or services provided in the rented space are for patients, referred or sent, either directly or indirectly, to the supplier by the physician-landlord. In particular, we are aware of rental arrangements between physician-landlords and:

- comprehensive outpatient rehabilitation facilities (CORFs) that provide physical and occupational therapy and speech-language pathology services in physicians' and other practitioners' offices;

- mobile diagnostic equipment suppliers that perform diagnostic related tests in physicians' offices; and

- suppliers of durable medical equipment, prosthetics, orthotics and supplies (DMEPOS) that set up "consignment closets" for their supplies in physicians' offices.

The OIG is concerned that in such arrangements, the rental payments may be disguised kickbacks to the physician-landlords to induce referrals. We have received numerous credible reports that in many cases, suppliers, whose businesses depend on physicians' referrals, offer and pay "rents" -- either voluntarily or in response to physicians' requests -- that are either unnecessary or in excess of the fair market value for the space to access the physicians' potential referrals.

The Anti-Kickback Law Prohibits Any Payments to Induce Referrals

Kickbacks can distort medical decision-making, cause overutilization, increase costs and result in unfair competition by freezing out competitors who are unwilling to pay kickbacks. Kickbacks can also adversely affect the quality of patient care by encouraging physicians to order services or recommend supplies based on profit rather than the patients' best medical interests.

Section 1128B(b) of the Social Security Act (the Act) prohibits knowingly and willfully soliciting, receiving, offering or paying anything of value to induce referrals of items or services payable by a Federal health care program. Both parties to an impermissible kickback transaction are liable. Violation of the statute constitutes a felony punishable by a maximum fine of $25,000, imprisonment up to five years, or both. The OIG may also initiate administrative proceedings to exclude persons from Federal health care programs or to impose civil money penalties for fraud, kickbacks and other prohibited activities under sections 1128(b)(7) and 1128A(a)(7) of the Act.[2]

Suspect Rental Arrangements For Space in Physician Offices

The questionable features of suspect rental arrangements for space in physicians' offices may be reflected in three areas:

- the appropriateness of rental agreements;
- the rental amounts; and
- time and space considerations.

Below, we examine these suspect areas, which separately or together may result in an arrangement that violates the anti-kickback statute, in order to help identify questionable rental arrangements between physicians and the suppliers to which they refer patients. This list is not exhaustive, but rather gives examples of indicators of potentially unlawful activity.

Appropriateness of Rental Agreements. The threshold inquiry when examining rental payments is whether payment for rent is appropriate at all. Payments of "rent" for space that traditionally has been provided for free or for a nominal charge as an accommodation between the parties for the benefit of the physicians' patients, such as consignment closets for DMEPOS, may be disguised kickbacks. In general, payments for rent of consignment closets in physicians' offices are suspect.[3]

Rental Amounts. Rental amounts should be at fair market value, be fixed in advance and not take into account, directly or indirectly, the volume or value of referrals or other business generated between the parties. Fair market value rental payments should not exceed the amount paid for comparable property. Moreover, where a physician rents space, the rate paid by the supplier should not exceed the rate paid by the physicians in the primary lease for their office space, except in rare circumstances. Examples of suspect arrangements include:

- rental amounts in excess of amounts paid for comparable property rented in arms-length transactions between persons not in a position to refer business;

- rental amounts for subleases that exceed the rental amounts per square foot in the primary lease;

- rental amounts that are subject to modification more often than annually;

- rental amounts that vary with the number of patients or referrals;

- rental arrangements that set a fixed rental fee per hour, but do not fix the number of hours or the schedule of usage in advance (i.e., "as needed" arrangements);

- rental amounts that are only paid if there are a certain number of Federal health care program beneficiaries referred each month; and

- rental amounts that are conditioned upon the supplier's receipt of payments from a Federal health care program.

Time and Space Considerations. Suppliers should only rent premises of a size and for a time that is reasonable and necessary for a commercially reasonable business purpose of the supplier. Rental of space that is in excess of suppliers' needs creates a presumption that the payments may be a pretext for giving money to physicians for their referrals. Examples of suspect arrangements include:

- rental amounts for space that is unnecessary or not used. For instance, a CORF requires one examination room and rents physician office space one afternoon a week when the physician is not in the office. The CORF calculates its rental payment on the square footage for the entire office, since it is the only occupant during that time, even though the CORF only needs one examination room;

- rental amounts for time when the rented space is not in use by the supplier. For example, an ultrasound supplier has enough business to support the use of one examination room for four hours each week, but rents the space for an amount equivalent to eight hours per week;

- non-exclusive occupancy of the rented portion of space. For example, a physical therapist does not rent space in a physician's office, but rather moves from examination room to examination room treating patients after they have been seen by the physician. Since no particular space is rented, we will closely scrutinize the proration of time and space used to calculate the therapist's "rent".

In addition, rental amount calculations should prorate rent based on the amount of space and duration of time the premises are used. The basis for any proration should be documented and updated as necessary. Depending on the circumstances, the supplier's rent can consist of three components: (1) exclusive office space; (2) interior office common space; and (3) building common space.

1. Apportionment of exclusive office space - The supplier's rent should be calculated based on the ratio of the time the space is in use by the supplier to the total amount of time the physician's office is in use. In addition, the rent should be calculated based on the ratio of the amount of space that is used exclusively by the supplier to the total amount of space in the physician's office. For example, where a supplier rents an examination room for four hours one afternoon per week in a physician's office that has four examination rooms of equal size and is open eight hours a day, five days per week, the supplier's prorated annual rent would be calculated as follows:

Physician Office Rent Per Day	% of Physician Office Space Rented by Supplier	% of Each Day Rented by Supplier	No. of Days Rented by Supplier Per Year	
$\frac{\text{annual rent of primary lease}}{\text{no. of work days per year}}$ X	$\frac{\text{sq. ft. exclusively occupied by supplier}}{\text{total office sq. ft.}}$ X	$\frac{\text{4 hours}}{\text{8 hours}}$ X	52 days (i.e., 1 day per week) =	Supplier's annual rent for exclusive space

2. <u>Apportionment of interior office common space</u> - When permitted by applicable regulations, rental payments may also cover the interior office common space in physicians' offices that are shared by the physicians and any subtenants, such as waiting rooms. If suppliers use such common areas for their patients, it may be appropriate for the suppliers to pay a prorated portion of the charge for such space. The charge for the common space must be apportioned among <u>all</u> physicians and subtenants that use the interior office common space based on the amount of non-common space they occupy and the duration of such occupation. Payment for the use of office common space should not exceed the supplier's pro rata share of the charge for such space based upon the ratio of the space used exclusively by the supplier to the total amount of space (other than common space) occupied by all persons using such common space.

3. <u>Apportionment of building common space</u> - Where the physician pays a separate charge for areas of a building that are shared by all tenants, such as building lobbies, it may be appropriate for the supplier to pay a prorated portion of such charge. As with interior office common space, the cost of the building common space must be apportioned among <u>all</u> physicians and subtenants based on the amount of non-common space they occupy and the duration of such occupation. For instance, in the example in number one above, the supplier's share of the additional levy for building common space could not be split 50/50.

The Space Rental Safe Harbor Can Protect Legitimate Arrangements

We strongly recommend that parties to rental agreements between physicians and suppliers to whom the physicians refer or for which physicians otherwise generate business make every effort to comply with the space rental safe harbor to the anti-kickback statute. (See 42 CFR 1001.952(b), as amended by 64 FR 63518 (November 19, 1999)). When an arrangement meets all of the criteria of a safe harbor, the arrangement is immune from prosecution under the anti-kickback statute. The following are the safe harbor criteria, all of which must be met:

- The agreement is set out in writing and signed by the parties.

- The agreement covers all of the premises rented by the parties for the term of the agreement and specifies the premises covered by the agreement.

- If the agreement is intended to provide the lessee with access to the premises for periodic intervals of time rather than on a full-time basis for the term of the rental agreement, the rental agreement specifies exactly the schedule of such intervals, their precise length, and the exact rent for such intervals.

- The term of the rental agreement is for not less than one year.

- The aggregate rental charge is set in advance, is consistent with fair market value in arms-length transactions, and is not determined in a manner that takes into account the volume or value of any referrals or business otherwise generated between the parties for which payment may be made in whole or in part under Medicare or a State health care program.

- The aggregate space rented does not exceed that which is reasonably necessary to accomplish the commercially reasonable business purpose of the rental.

Arrangements for office equipment or personal services of physicians' office staff can also be structured to comply with the equipment rental safe harbor and personal services and management contracts safe harbor. (See 42 CFR 1001.952(c) and (d), as amended by 64 FR 63518 (November 19, 1999)). Specific equipment used should be identified and documented and payment limited to the prorated portion of its use. Similarly, any services provided should be documented and payment should be limited to the time actually spent performing such services.

What To Do If You Have Information About Fraud and Abuse Against Medicare or Medicaid Programs

If you have information about physicians, DMEPOS suppliers, CORFs or other suppliers engaging in any of the activities described above, contact any of the regional offices of the Office of Investigations of the Office of Inspector General, U.S. Department of Health and Human Services, at the following locations:

Field Offices	States Served	Telephone
Boston	MA, VT, NH, ME, RI, CT	617-565-2664
New York	NY, NJ, PR, VI	212-264-1691
Philadelphia	PA, MD, DE, WV, VA, DC	215-861-4586
Atlanta	GA, KY, NC, SC, FL, TN, AL, MS	404-562-7603
Chicago	IL, MN, WI, MI, IN, OH, IA,	312-353-2740
Dallas	TX, NM, OK, AR, LA, CO, UT, WY, MT, ND, SD, NE, KS, MO	214-767-8406
Los Angeles	AZ, NV, So. CA	714-246-8302
San Francisco	No. CA, AK, HI, OR, ID, WA	415-437-7961

1. Persons or entities may be either suppliers or providers. For purposes of this Special Fraud Alert, we will refer to such persons as suppliers.

2. Some of the arrangements identified as suspect in this Special Fraud Alert may also implicate the Ethics in Patient Referrals Act, also known as the Stark law (section 1877 of the Act). The interpretation of the Stark law is under the jurisdiction of the Health Care Financing Administration (HCFA).

3. This Special Fraud Alert does not address the appropriateness of consignment closet arrangements under HCFA's DMEPOS supplier standards. The interpretation of the DMEPOS supplier standards is a matter under HCFA's jurisdiction.

EXHIBIT II.
Example of OIG Annual Work Plan

Department of Health and Human Services

Office of Inspector General

WORK PLAN

FISCAL YEAR 2000

June Gibbs Brown
Inspector General

Department of Health and Human Services

Office of Inspector General Projects

HEALTH CARE FINANCING ADMINISTRATION
Table of Contents

HOSPITALS

One-Day Hospital Stays	1
Same-Day Discharge and Readmission to Same Hospital	1
Payments for Related Hospital and Skilled Nursing Stays	1
Skilled Nursing Facility Coverage After Unnecessary Hospital Stays	1
Prospective Payment System Transfers	2
Prospective Payment System Transfers Between Chain Members	2
Prospective Payment System Transfers: Administrative Recovery	2
Prospective Payment System Transfers During Hospital Mergers	3
Uncollected Beneficiary Deductibles and Coinsurance	3
Updating Diagnosis-Related Group Codes	3
Medicare Payment for Diagnosis-Related Group 14	4
Diagnosis-Related Group Payment Limits	4
Outlier Payments for Expanded Services	4
Changes in the Inpatient Case Mix Index for Medicare	4
Diagnosis-Related Group Payment Window	5
Hospitals Exempt From the Prospective Payment System	5
Outpatient Hospital Psychiatric Claims	5
Outpatient Hospital Revenue Centers Without Common Procedure Codes	6
Billing Routine Services on a "Stat" Basis	6
Payments for Capital Items	6
Graduate Medical Education Payments	7
Hospital Closures: 1998	7

HHS/OIG Fiscal Year 2000 Work Plan - Health Care Financing Administration

HOME HEALTH
    Home Health Compliance Programs 7
    Physician Involvement in Approving Home Health Care 7
    Screening of Home Health Beneficiaries 8
    Payments Based on Location of Service 8
    Reasonableness of Current Payments 8

NURSING HOME CARE
    Nursing Home Resident Assessments 9
    Role of the Nursing Home Medical Director 9
    Quality Assessment and Assurance Committees 9
    Nurse Aide Training 10
    Family Experience With Nursing Home Care 10
    Nursing Home Vaccination Rates: State Initiatives 10
    Implementing the Skilled Nursing Facility Prospective Payment System 10
    Beneficiary Access to Skilled Nursing Facility Care 11
    Financial Screening and Distinct Part Rules 11
    Physician Routine Nursing Home Visits 11
    Therapy Services in Skilled Nursing Facilities 11
    Ancillary Medical Supplies 12

PHYSICIANS
    Physicians at Teaching Hospitals 12
    Automated Encoding Systems for Billing 12
    Reassignment of Physician Benefits 12
    Podiatrists' Medicare Billings 13
    Podiatry Services 13
    Myocardial Perfusion Imaging 13
    Private Physician Contracting 14
    Advance Beneficiary Notices 14

MEDICAL EQUIPMENT AND SUPPLIES
    Operations of Durable Medical Equipment Carriers 14
    Duplicate Billings for Medical Equipment and Supplies 15
    Balance Billing for Medical Equipment and Supplies 15
    Appropriateness of Home Medical Equipment and Supplies 15
    Medicare Payments for Orthotics 16
    Blood Glucose Test Strips 16

END STAGE RENAL DISEASE
    External Oversight of Dialysis Facilities 16
    Separately Billable Services 16
    Method II Billing for End Stage Renal Disease 17
    Medical Appropriateness of Tests and Other Services 17
    Questionable Dialysis Claims 17
    Duplicate Payments for Office Visits to Nephrologists 18

DRUG REIMBURSEMENT
    Effect of Average Wholesale Price Discount on Medicare Prescription Drugs 18
    Medicare Outpatient Prescription Drugs 18
    Medicare Payments for "Not Otherwise Classified" 19

OTHER MEDICARE SERVICES
    Outpatient Rehabilitation Facilities 19
    Comprehensive Outpatient Rehabilitation Facilities 19
    Vulnerable Medicare Beneficiaries 20
    Clinical Laboratory Proficiency Testing 20
    Excess Payments for Ambulance Services 20
    Hyperbaric Oxygen Treatment 21

MEDICARE MANAGED CARE
    New Adjusted Community Rate Proposal Process 21
    General and Administrative Costs 21
    Cost-Based Managed Care Plans 22
    Enhanced Managed Care Payments 22
    HMO Profits 22
    Investment Income Earned by Risk-Based HMOs 22
    Physician Incentive Plans 23
    National Marketing Guidelines 23
    Usefulness of Medicare+Choice Performance Measures 23
    Educating Beneficiaries About Medicare+Choice 24
    Managed Care Health Plan Data 24
    Managed Care Additional Benefits 24
    Enrollment Incentives/Disincentives 25
    Enrollee Access to Emergency Services 25
    Chiropractic Services 25

    Medicare Managed Care Prescription Drug Benefit 25
    Managed Care Organization Closings 26

MEDICAID MANAGED CARE
    Medicaid Dually Eligible Fee-for-Service Payments 26
    Emergency Services to Enrollees of Medicaid Managed Care 26

MEDICAID - CHILDREN'S HEALTH INSURANCE PROGRAM
    States' Outreach Efforts to Medicaid Eligibles 27
    Performance Measures 27
    Involvement of Federally Funded Health Centers in Children's Health 28

OTHER MEDICAID SERVICES
    Hospital-Specific Disproportionate Share Payment Limits 28
    Payments for Services to Dually Eligible Beneficiaries 28
    State Survey and Certification Costs 29
    Credentialing Medicaid Providers 29
    HCFA Oversight of Institutions for the Mentally Retarded 29
    Medicaid Payments to Institutions for the Mentally Retarded 29
    Medicaid Outpatient Prescription Drug Pricing 30

MEDICARE CONTRACTOR OPERATIONS
    Comparison of Payment Safeguard Activities 30
    Identifying and Collecting Overpayments 30
    Collecting Medicare Secondary Payer Overpayments 31
    Medicare Provider Numbers and Unique Physician Identification Numbers 31
    Billing for Resident Services 31
    Implementation of Therapy Caps 32
    Contractors' Year 2000 Remediation Costs 32
    Preaward Review of Medicare Integrity Program Contract Proposals 32
    Contract Close-Out Audits of Peer Review Organizations 33
    Contractors' Administrative Costs 33
    Unfunded Pensions 33
    Pension Segmentation/Costs Claimed 33
    Pension Termination 34

GENERAL ADMINISTRATION
    Improper Medicare Fee-for-Service Payments 34
    Year 2000 Computer Renovation Plans 34

    Analysis of HCFA Data 35
    OIG-Excluded Persons 35
    Medicare Secondary Payer 35
    Joint Work With Other Federal and State Agencies 36

INVESTIGATIONS
    Medicare Part A 37
    Medicare Part B 37
    Medicare Part C 37
    Medicaid 38
    Pneumonia Diagnosis-Related Group Upcoding Project 38
    Prospective Payment System Transfer Project 38

LEGAL COUNSEL
    Compliance Program Guidance 38
    Corporate Integrity Agreements 39
    Advisory Opinions and Fraud Alerts 39
    Anti-Kickback Safe Harbors 39
    Patient Anti-Dumping Statute Enforcement 40
    Program Exclusions 40
    Civil Monetary Penalties 40

EXHIBIT III.
Example of OIG Written Request for Records

DEPARTMENT OF HEALTH & HUMAN SERVICES **OFFICE OF INSPECTOR GENERAL**

Washington, D.C. 20201

JUL 07 1999

REQUEST FOR INFORMATION
OR ASSISTANCE

Our Reference: OI File No. 1-99-
Your Reference:

To: Paul Shaw, Esquire
      Schwartz, Shaw & Griffith
      30 Federal Street
      Fourth Floor
      Boston, Massachusetts 02110-2508

The Inspector General of the Department of Health and Human Services, pursuant to the authority contained in 5 USC Appendix 3 et seq., requests that you furnish information or assistance as follows:

   All patient records identified in the   investigation be made available to
   agents for their review at

Pertinent sections of the United States Code are set forth on the reverse hereof. The request is made for law enforcement purposes and in connection with an official investigation being conducted by the Department.

CAUTION: Representatives of the Office of Inspector General are required to show their official identification when personally requesting information or assistance.

Requested by: _____, Special Agent
                    Name and Title

DHHS/OIG/OI
P.O. Box 8767
Boston, MA 02114
Office

OI-2 (10/92)

Pursuant to the authority contained in 5 USC Appendix 3 et seq., the Inspector General (or his delegate) is authorized to:

(1) have access to all records, reports, audits, reviews, documents, papers, recommendations, or other material available to the applicable Department which relate to programs and operations with respect to which the Inspector General has responsibilities under this Act (section 6(a)(1));

(2) request such information or assistance as may be necessary for carrying out the duties and responsibilities provided by this Act from any Federal, State, or local government agency or unit thereof (section 6(a)(3));

(3) require by subpoena the production of all information documents, reports, answers, records, accounts, papers, and other data and documentary evidence necessary in the performance of the functions assigned by this Act, which subpoena, in the case of contumacy or refusal to obey, shall be enforceable by order of any appropriate United States District Court (section 6(a)(4))--

other provisions state:

(1) Upon request of the Inspector General for information or assistance under section 6(a)(3), the head of any Federal agency involved shall, insofar as is practicable and not in contravention of any existing statutory restriction, or regulation of the Federal agency from which the information is requested, furnish to the Inspector General, or to an authorized designee, such information or assistance.

(2) Whenever information or assistance requested under subsection 6 (a)(1) or 6 (a)(3) is, in the judgement of the Inspector General unreasonably refused or not provided, the Inspector General shall report the circumstances to the head of the establishment involved without delay.

OI-2 (10/92)

EXHIBIT IV.
Example of OIG Subpoena Duces Tecum

UNITED STATES OF AMERICA

DEPARTMENT OF HEALTH AND HUMAN SERVICES
OFFICE OF INSPECTOR GENERAL

SUBPOENA DUCES TECUM

TO

CANCELLED

YOU ARE HEREBY COMMANDED TO APPEAR BEFORE _____,
an official of the Office of Inspector General, at _____
in the City of _____ and State of _____
on the _____ day of _____, 19 ___, at ___ o'clock, ___ m of
that day, in connection with _____
_____
_____
_____ ;
and you are hereby required to bring with you and produce at said time and place the following:

which are necessary in the performance of the responsibility of the Inspector General under Public Law 95-452 [5 USC App. 3 Section 6(a)(4)], as amended by Public Law 100-504, to conduct and supervise audits and investigations and to promote economy, efficiency and effectiveness in the administration of and to prevent and detect fraud and abuse in the programs and operations of the Department of Health and Human Services.

IN TESTIMONY WHEREOF

_____ the undersigned official of the Office of Inspector General of said DEPARTMENT OF HEALTH AND HUMAN SERVICES, has hereunto set h____ hand this _____ day of _____ 19 ___.

_____

**UNITED STATES OF AMERICA
DEPARTMENT OF HEALTH AND HUMAN SERVICES
OFFICE OF INSPECTOR GENERAL**

SUBPOENA DUCES TECUM

~~CANCELLED~~

~~CANCELLED~~

Upon contumacy or refusal to obey, this subpoena shall be enforceable by order of the appropriate United States District Court.

~~CANCELLED~~

RETURN OF SERVICE

I, being a person over 18 years of age, hereby certify that a copy of this subpoena was duly served on the person named herein by means of—

1. personal delivery to an individual, to wit:

   _____
   (Name)
   _____
   (Title)
   _____
   (Address)

   ~~CANCELLED~~

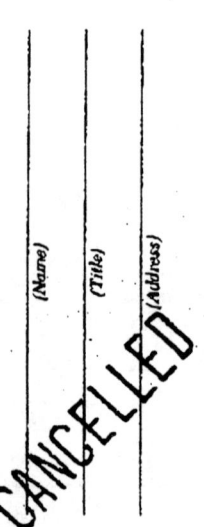

2. personal delivery to an address, to wit:

   _____
   (Description of premises)
   _____
   (Address)

3. registered or certified mailing to:

   _____
   (Name)
   _____
   (Address)

at ____ ( ) a.m. ( ) p.m. on
19 ____ .

~~CANCELLED~~

_____
(Signature)
_____
(Title)

~~CANCELLED~~

OIG-1 (4/88)

EXHIBIT V.
Example of DOJ Subpoena Duces Tecum

UNITED STATES OF AMERICA
DEPARTMENT OF JUSTICE

SUBPOENA DUCES TECUM

TO: KEEPER OF THE RECORDS

YOU ARE HEREBY COMMANDED TO APPEAR BEFORE Sandra S. Bower, Assistant United States Attorney, United States Attorney's Office, District of Massachusetts

an official of the U.S. Department of Justice, and you are hereby required to bring with you and produce the following records, which are necessary in the performance of the responsibility of the U.S. Department of Justice to investigate Federal health care offenses, defined in 18 U.S.C. § 24(a) to mean violations of, or conspiracies to violate: 18 U.S.C. §§669, 1035, 1347, or 1518; and 18 U.S.C. §§ 287, 371, 664, 666, 1001, 1027, 1341, 1343, or 1954 if the violation or conspiracy relates to a health care benefit program (defined in 18 U.S.C. § 24(b)):

See Attachment. In lieu of appearing, you may make arrangements for the delivery of the records by contacting Special Agent Scott Schettinger with the Federal Bureau of Investigation at (617)223-6288.

PLACE AND TIME FOR APPEARANCE:

At United States Attorney's Office, Suite 9200, United States Courthouse, One Courthouse Way, Boston, MA, 02210
on the 1st day of December, 1999, at 2 o'clock P. M.

Failure to comply with the requirements of this subpoena will render you liable to proceedings in the district court of the United States to enforce obedience to the requirements of this subpoena, and to punish default or disobedience.

Issued under authority of Sec. 248 of the Health Insurance Portability & Accountability Act of 1996, Public Law No. 104-91 (18 U.S.C. § 3486)

IN TESTIMONY WHEREOF

Michael K. Loucks, Health Care Fraud Chief, the undersigned official of the U.S. DEPARTMENT OF JUSTICE, has hereunto set his/her hand this 22 day of _____, 1999.

(SIGNATURE)

FORM CRM-180
MAR. 97

UNITED STATES OF AMERICA
DEPARTMENT OF JUSTICE

Upon contumacy or refusal to obey, this subpoena shall be enforceable by order of the appropriate United States District Court.

SUBPOENA DUCES TECUM

RETURN OF SERVICE

I, being a person over 18 years of age, hereby certify that a copy of this subpoena was duly served on the person named herein by means of --

1. personal delivery to an individual, to wit:

   _____
   (Name)

   _____
   (Title)

   _____
   (Address)

2. personal delivery to an address, to wit:

   _____
   (Description of premises)

   _____
   (Address)

3. registered or certified mailing to:

   _____
   (Name)

   _____
   (Address)

   at ____ ( ) a.m.
      ____ ( ) p.m. on

   _____
   (Signature)

   _____
   (Title)

ATTACHMENT

All records, including patient files, treatment notes, documents reflecting service provided, dates of service, relating to claims submitted, and all claims submitted, to Metropolitan Property and Casualty Insurance Company and to Liberty Mutual Insurance Company for the period January 1, 1995, to the present.

EXHIBIT VI.
Example of Search Warrant

United States District Court

_____ DISTRICT OF _____ CONNECTICUT _____

In the Matter of the Search of
(Name, address or Brief description of person, property or premises to be searched)

New Britain, Connecticut

(See Attachment A)

SEARCH WARRANT

CASE NUMBER:

To: **Special Agent Edward M. Adams, Jr.** and any Authorized Officer of the United States

Affidavit(s) having been made before me by **Agent Edward Adams** who has reason to believe that on the person of or on the property or premises known as (name, description and/or location)

New Britain, Connecticut, as more particularly described in Attachment A

in the _____ District of _____ CONNECTICUT _____ there is now concealed a certain person or property, namely (describe the person or property to be seized)

See Attachment B

I am satisfied that the affidavit(s) and any recorded testimony establish probable cause to believe that the person or property so described is now concealed on the person or premises above-described and establish grounds for the issuance of this warrant.

YOU ARE HEREBY COMMANDED to search on or before _____ October 24, 1998 _____

(not to exceed 10 days) the person or place named above for the person or property specified, serving this warrant and making the search (in the daytime - 6:00 A.M. to 10:00 P.M.) and if the person or property be found there to seize same, leaving copy of this warrant and receipt for the person or property taken, and prepare a written inventory of the person or property seized and promptly return this warrant to U.S. Magistrate Judge William I. Garfinkel as required by law.

October 14, 1998 3:00 pm
Date and Time Issued

at Bridgeport, Connecticut
City and State

_____
Signature of Judicial Officer

Hon. William I. Garfinkel, U.S. Magistrate Judge
Name and Title of Judicial Officer

ATTACHMENT A

PREMISES TO BE SEARCHED

_____, Inc. occupies a portion of a two-story red brick building located at _____ Street, New Britain, CT. The first floor of the building has street-level store fronts and there is a blue and white sign, which reads _____ hanging over the space occupied by _____. The building is located on the east side of _____ Street between _____ Avenue and _____ Avenue.

ATTACHMENT B

ITEMS TO BE SEIZED

For the period January 1, 1994 to the present: books, records, documents, materials, computer hardware and software and computer associated data relating to the financial and accounting operations of ⸺ ⸺., including, but not limited to, computer processing units (CPUs), disks and tapes on which computer files might be stored, all software and hardware instruction manuals, general journals, subsidiary ledgers, cash receipts, disbursement journals and sales journals, bank statements, deposit tickets, canceled checks, and check registers for all bank accounts, and receipts and invoices for expenditures; state, federal and employment tax returns; all records or files relating to customers who are insured by Medicaid; all certificates of medical necessity and prescriptions relating to customers who are insured by Medicaid; all documents, including, but not limited to, notes, memoranda, and correspondence, relating to customers who are insured by Medicaid; all documents, including, but not limited to, notes, memoranda, charts, summaries, price lists, and correspondence, relating to fees charged to and/or the billing of services rendered or goods delivered to customers who are insured by Medicaid; all purchase orders, invoices, or contract files pertaining to the purchase of durable medical equipment; all documents, including, but not limited to, all business agreements, contracts or other records, relating to vendors supplying durable medical equipment to M&N Medical, Inc.; all documents relating to payments made to vendors supplying durable medical equipment to ⸺ ⸺; all documents relating to durable medical equipment prices charged to non-Medicaid insured individuals by ⸺ ⸺.; all documents relating to Medicaid insurance billing regulations, policies, or procedures; all documents, including notes, memoranda and correspondence, relating to employee duties and responsibilities; all delivery tickets relating to the delivery of durable medical equipment to customers who are insured by Medicaid; all documents relating to ⸺ ⸺ inventory of goods; all documents relating to the delivery of goods from vendors by common carrier; all employment contracts; all calendars, appointment books, diaries, or other records relating to the delivery of durable medical equipment to customers; and, all calendars, appointment books, or diaries reflecting entries relating to ⸺ ⸺, or ⸺ ⸺ in the possession, custody or control of ⸺ ⸺.

EXHIBIT VII.
Example of HIPAA Subpoena Served at Conclusion of Search

UNITED STATES OF AMERICA
DEPARTMENT OF JUSTICE

SUBPOENA DUCES TECUM

TO: Custodian of Records

New Britain, CT

ATTN:

YOU ARE HEREBY COMMANDED TO APPEAR BEFORE Assistant United States Attorney James J. Finnerty, an official of the U.S. Department of Justice, and you are hereby required to bring with you and produce the following:

SEE ATTACHED

which are necessary in the performance of the responsibility of the U.S. Department of Justice to investigate Federal health care offenses, defined in 18 U.S.C. § 24(a) to mean violations of, or conspiracies to violate: 18 U.S.C. §§669, 1035, 1347, or 1518; and 18 U.S.C. §§ 287, 371, 664, 666, 1001, 1027, 1341, 1343, or 1954 if the violation or conspiracy relates to a health care benefit program (defined in 18 U.S.C. § 24(b)).

PLACE AND TIME FOR APPEARANCE:

At United States Attorney's Office, 915 Lafayette Blvd., Bridgeport, CT on the 3rd day of November, 1998, at 9:00 o'clock A.M.

Failure to comply with the requirements of this subpoena will render you liable to proceedings in the district court of the United States to enforce obedience to the requirements of this subpoena, and to punish default or disobedience.

Issued under authority of Sec. 248 of the Health Insurance Portability & Accountability Act of 1996, Public Law No. 104-91
(18 U.S.C. § 3486)

IN TESTIMONY WHEREOF
James J. Finnerty, the undersigned official of the U.S.
DEPARTMENT OF JUSTICE, has hereunto set his
hand this 14th day of October 1998.

JAMES J. FINNERTY
ASSISTANT UNITED STATES ATTORNEY

FORM CRM-180
MAR. 97

ATTACHMENT

For the period January 1, 1994 to the present: books, records, documents, and materials relating to the financial and accounting operations of   , including, but not limited to, general journals, subsidiary ledgers, cash receipts, disbursement journals and sales journals, bank statements, deposit tickets, canceled checks, and check registers for all bank accounts, and receipts and invoices for expenditures; state, federal and employment tax returns; all records or files relating to customers who are insured by Medicaid; all certificates of medical necessity and prescriptions relating to customers who are insured by Medicaid; all documents, including, but not limited to, notes, memoranda, and correspondence, relating to customers who are insured by Medicaid; all documents, including, but not limited to, notes, memoranda, charts, summaries, price lists, and correspondence, relating to fees charged to and/or the billing of services rendered or goods delivered to customers who are insured by Medicaid; all purchase orders, invoices, or contract files pertaining to the purchase of durable medical equipment; all documents, including, but not limited to, all business agreements, contracts or other records, relating to vendors supplying durable medical equipment to   ; all documents relating to payments made to vendors supplying durable medical equipment to   Inc.; all documents relating to durable medical equipment prices charged to non-Medicaid insured individuals by   ; all documents relating to Medicaid insurance billing regulations, policies, or procedures; all documents, including notes, memoranda and correspondence, relating to employee duties and responsibilities; all delivery tickets; all documents relating to the delivery of durable medical equipment to customers who are insured by Medicaid; all documents relating to   inventory of goods; all documents relating to the delivery of goods from vendors by common carrier; all employment contracts; all calendars, appointment books, diaries, or other records relating to the delivery of durable medical equipment to customers; and, all calendars, appointment books, or diaries in the possession, custody or control of

EXHIBIT VIII.
Example of Grand Jury Subpoena

United States District Court

_____ DISTRICT OF __MASSACHUSETTS__

TO:

Keeper of the Records

SUBPOENA TO TESTIFY BEFORE GRAND JURY

SUBPOENA FOR:
☐ PERSON ☒ DOCUMENT(S) OR OBJECT(S)

YOU ARE HEREBY COMMANDED to appear and testify before the Grand Jury of the United States District Court at the place, date, and time specified below.

PLACE	COURTROOM
Receptionist - 9th Floor United States Attorney's Office Suite 9200 1 Courthouse Way Boston, MA 02210	Grand Jury
	DATE AND TIME Thursday, June 17, 1999 10:00 A.M.

YOU ARE ALSO COMMANDED to bring with you the following document(s) or object(s):

SEE ATTACHMENT

In lieu of appearing before the Grand Jury at the date and time shown above, you may comply with this subpoena by, at your option, causing the materials described to be delivered to the agent serving this subpoena or by causing such materials to be mailed to the Assistant U.S. Attorney at the address shown below. If you have any questions contact Denis Drum, Special Agent, Federal Bureau of Investigation, One Center Plaza, Suite 600, Boston, MA 02108 (617) 223-6463.

☐ Please see additional information on reverse. Witness travel & reimbursement instructions are attached. Call Witness Coordinator Amy Jones at (617)748-3153, if you have any questions. For after business hour emergencies, call (617)748-3100.

This subpoena shall remain in effect until you are granted leave to depart by the court or by an officer acting on behalf of the court.

CLERK
TONY A_____

(BY) DEPUTY CLERK

DATE
May 13, 1999

This subpoena is issued on application of the United States of America

DONALD K. STERN
United States Attorney

NAME, ADDRESS AND PHONE NUMBER OF ASSISTANT U.S. ATTORNEY
MICHAEL K. LOUCKS
Assistant U.S. Attorney
1 Courthouse Way - Suite 9200
Boston, MA 02210
(617) 748-3100

AO 110 (Rev. 5/85) Subpoena to Testify Before Grand Jury

RETURN OF SERVICE (1)

RECEIVED BY SERVER	DATE	PLACE
SERVED	DATE	PLACE

SERVED ON (NAME)

SERVED BY	TITLE

STATEMENT OF SERVICE FEES

TRAVEL	SERVICES	TOTAL

DECLARATION OF SERVER (2)

I declare under penalty of perjury under the laws of the United States of America that the foregoing information contained in the Return of Service and Statement of Service Fees is true and correct.

Executed on _____   _____
                    Date   Signature of Server

                                          _____
                                                  Address of Server

ADDITIONAL INFORMATION

---

(1) As to who may serve a subpoena and the manner of its service see Rule 17(d), Federal Rules of Criminal Procedure, or Rule 45(c), Federal Rules of Civil Procedure.

(2) "Fees and mileage need not be tendered to the witness upon service of a subpoena issued on behalf of the United States or an officer or agency thereof (Rule 45(c), Federal Rules of Civil Procedure; Rule 17(d), Federal Rules of Criminal Procedure) or on behalf of certain indigent parties and criminal defendants who are unable to pay such costs (28 USC 1825, Rule 17(b) Federal Rules of Criminal Procedure)".

Attachment to Subpoena

This subpoena covers documents for the time period 1/1/92 to the present.

This subpoena calls for production of original records.

"You" refers to the persons or entity to whom the subpoena is addressed as well as any person working for or employed by that entity in any capacity (as a doctor, as a bookkeeper, as an office manager, etc.)

The term documents as used in this subpoena includes all items of any kind for the storage or retention of information, including all manner of documents, videotapes, audiotapes, other electronic storage media (disks, disk drives).

To the extent that any document is withheld on a claim of privilege, that fact must be identified in writing.

1. All documents regarding or related in any way to the purchase by you of either _____ r ___ex, including all invoices, monthly statements, checks, or correspondence.

2. All documents regarding or related in any way to any _____ or _____ that you have received for which you made no payment, including any free samples, so-called extra kits, free products, un-reimbursed product, or extra product supplied as a part of a volume purchase.

3. All sample receipt cards for the items described in paragraph 2.

4. All correspondence or other documents that you have received from _____ Inc. or any employee of that company.

5. All documents regarding or related in any way to any consulting or other services you received from any consultant or any person in any line of business for which services _____ Inc. made any payment in whole or in part for such services.

6. All documents regarding or related to in any way to anything of value that you have received from _____ Inc. or any employee of that company, including but not limited to, so-called Educational Grants, money, TVs, VCRs, trips, so-called Tap into the Future programs, research grants.

EXHIBIT IX.
Example of Letter Confirming Document Production Agreements

INITIAL LETTER TO U.S. ATTORNEY

Schwartz, Shaw and Griffith

Attorneys at law

Robert A. Griffith	Gregory J. Aceto
Paul W. Shaw	Jonathan B. Bruno
Harvey A. Schwartz	James F. O'Brien
	William C. Taussig
	Jerome B. Tichner
	Robin J. Dimieri, Esq., P.C., Of Counsel

August 24, 1999

Michael C. Loucks, Assistant U.S. Attorney
Health Care Fraud Chief
United States Attorney's Office
United States Courthouse
One Courthouse Way
Boston, MA 02210

Re: Subpoena duces tecum issued to the Custodian of Records of the XYZ Healthcare Corporation pursuant to 18 U.S.C. §3486.

Dear Mr. Loucks:

This will confirm that the law firm of Schwartz, Shaw and Griffith represents the XYZ Healthcare Corporation in connection with the subpoena duces tecum issued on August 19, 1999. During our telephone conference, I stated that it was unlikely that XYZ could comply with the subpoena by Thursday, September 9, 1999. Based on this representation, you agreed to extend the compliance date. With regard to Paragraph 5 of the subpoena, you also agreed that XYZ does not have to produce regular payroll checks issued to persons who fell within the definition of "Sales Representative" but only commission and bonus checks for the period of 1995 to date.

I will be in contact with you once I meet with XYZ's management and support staff to determine when these records can be produced. If you have any questions in the interim, please do not hesitate to contact me.

Very truly yours,

Paul W. Shaw

PWS:og

cc: General Counsel
 XYZ Healthcare Corporation

F:\PAUL\PF\AHLABook\forms\usa-initial.ltr.wpd

30 Federal Street
Boston, Massachusetts 02110-2508

617 338 7277 Fax 617 338 1923
E mail: office@ssglaw.com
www.ssglaw.com

EXHIBIT X.
Example of Letter Identifying Independent Custodian of Records

SUPPLEMENTAL LETTER TO U.S. ATTORNEY

Schwartz, Shaw and Griffith

Attorneys at law

Robert A. Griffith
Paul W. Shaw
Harvey A. Schwartz
Gregory J. Aceto
Jonathan B. Bruno
James F. O'Brien
William C. Taussig
Jerome B. Tichner

Robin J. Dimieri, Esq., P.C.,
Of Counsel

September 9, 1999

Michael C. Loucks, Assistant U.S. Attorney
Health Care Fraud Chief
United States Attorney's Office
United States Courthouse
One Courthouse Way
Boston, MA 02210

Re: Subpoena duces tecum issued to the Custodian of Records of the XYZ Healthcare Corporation pursuant to 18 U.S.C. §3486.

Dear Mr. Loucks:

This will confirm my conversation with you of September 8, 1999. Robert Recordkeeper, the individual designated by the XYZ Healthcare Corporation as the Custodian of Records for the purpose of complying the above-referenced subpoena, is in the process of obtaining the various documents responsive to the subpoena. I expect to provide your office with a number of documents relating to the past four years by Thursday, September 30, 1999. The additional records for 1990 through 1995 may take several more weeks to obtain and review due to their being in storage.

Paragraph 3 of the subpoena seeks the production of "all records, including any internal memoranda, correspondence, notes or documents of any nature, relating to the XYZ Healthcare Corporation's compensation structure for any sales personnel, sales representatives, marketing personnel or any person holding a similar position." As I informed you during our September 8, 1999 telephone conference, I have advised XYZ to withhold the production on the basis of attorney-client privilege certain correspondence between the Corporation and attorney John Doe from the law firm of Big and Bigger. I will maintain a privilege log of the documents withheld on this basis.

If you have any questions before September 30, 1999, please do not hesitate to contact me.

Very truly yours,

Robert A. Griffith

RAG/og

cc: General Counsel
XYZ Healthcare Corporation

F:\BOB\BF\AHLA\Book\forms\usa-2nd.ltr.wpd

30 Federal Street
Boston, Massachusetts 02110-2508

617 338 7277 Fax 617 338 1923
E mail: office@ssglaw.com
www.ssglaw.com

EXHIBIT XI.
Example of Memorandum to Custodian of Records

MEMORANDUM TO CUSTODIAN OF RECORDS[1]

TO: Robert Recordkeeper

FROM: _____
General Counsel/Senior officer

RE: Document Review Responsibilities

DATE: September 1, 1999

     You have agreed to act as corporate document custodian for the limited purpose of XYZ Healthcare Corporation's response to requests for information from the United States Attorney (the "Requester"). A description of those requests, as well as a memorandum I have sent to relevant department heads, are attached.

     Your responsibilities are as follows:

1. Work with each department head who received the attached memorandum to ensure that copies of the memo are distributed to employees within his/her department who may have documents responsive to the Requester's requests.

2. Compile a list of employees to whom my memo is circulated.

3. Follow up with those employees believed to have responsive documents to assure compliance.

4. Obtain certifications from such employees of their search and forwarding of responsive documents.

5. Forward all responsive documents to the company's attorneys for their review and submission to the Requester.

If you have any questions regarding these matters, please contact me or our outside counsel, Robert A. Griffith and Paul W. Shaw (617-338-7277), representing us in this matter.

F:\PAUL\PF\AHLABook\forms\custodian-apptmt

---

[1] This form is reprinted from the the AHLA *"Best Practices Handbook In Advising Clinets on Fraud & Abuse Issues,"* (1999).

EXHIBIT XII.
Example of Instructions to Document Searchers

INSTRUCTIONS TO DOCUMENT SEARCHERS[1]

CONFIDENTIAL

TO: Distribution List

FROM: _____
General Counsel/Senior Officer

RE: Request for Information from the United States Attorney's Office

DATE: September 1, 1999

Enclosed as Attachment A is a description of categories of documents and records requested by the United States Attorney's Office (the "Requester"). Please read the description carefully and forward copies of this memo, with its attachments, to those employees in your department who may have documents that fall within one of the categories of documents sought by the Requester.

Your employees (and you, if you have responsive documents) should deliver the originals and existing copies of all documents sought by the Requester to Robert Recordkeeper, the person acting as custodian of records, at [location of custodian's office] as they are located. If there is any doubt about whether any item or object or document is sought by the Requester, it should be provided as part of the collection process. E-mail and computer files should also be searched for responsive data. You and your employees should be careful not to destroy or discard any documents sought by the Requester. All responsive documents should be delivered no later than September 15, 1999. If, for any reason, you or your employees cannot respond by or before that time, you should notify Robert Recordkeeper.

In order to demonstrate full compliance with the Requester's request, it is important that we be able to document fully the collection process. You and your employees should keep a written record of the search technique utilized. After the searches have been completed, the Certification included as Attachment B should be signed and sent to Robert Recordkeeper.

The documents forwarded to Robert Recordkeeper will be returned to you and your employees. However, if you anticipate that you or your employees may need the document, or information from the document, in the near future, a copy of the document should be made for you to retain before the original is submitted.

Please note that negative responses are required on the attached certification form if no documents are located.

If you have any questions regarding the scope of the Requester's request or the instructions in this memorandum, please contact me as soon as possible.

cc: Robert Recordkeeper, Custodian of Records

---

[1] This form is reprinted from the the AHLA *"Best Practices Handbook In Advising Clinets on Fraud & Abuse Issues,"* (1999).

ATTACHMENT A

CATEGORIES OF DOCUMENTS SOUGHT BY THE UNITED STATES ATTORNEY

Request 1.

Request 2.

Request 3.

Request 4.

Request 5.

Request 6.

Request 7.

Request 8.

ATTACHMENT B

CERTIFICATION

I have received the memorandum from _____ [general counsel], dated September 15, 1999, which seeks documents requested by the United States Attorney's Office. I have reviewed all files within my possession, custody or control, and hereby state that:

_____ I have found no responsive documents.

_____ I am forwarding all responsive documents with this certification.

_____ I have previously forwarded all responsive documents.

_____ I have previously forwarded some responsive documents and am attaching additional documents.

I UNDERSTAND THAT THE DOCUMENTS IN QUESTION ARE BEING SOUGHT BY THE GOVERNMENT PURSUANT TO A SUBPOENA, AND THAT THERE MAY BE SERIOUS CONSEQUENCES TO THE COMPANY AND TO ME, INDIVIDUALLY, IN FAILING TO PRODUCE RESPONSIVE DOCUMENTS.

_____   _____
Date   (Signature)

                                            _____
                                            (Print Name)

                                            _____
                                            (Location)

                                            _____
                                            (Telephone No.).

Return to: Robert Recordkeeper

EXHIBIT XIII.
Example of Cover Letter Specifying Produced Documents

LETTER REGARDING THE PRODUCTION OF DOCUMENTS

Schwartz, Shaw and Griffith

Attorneys at law

Robert A. Griffith
Paul W. Shaw
Harvey A. Schwartz
Gregory J. Aceto
Jonathan B. Bruno
James F. O'Brien
William C. Taussig
Jerome B. Tichner
Robin J. Dimieri, Esq., P.C., Of Counsel

September 29, 1999

Michael C. Loucks, Assistant U.S. Attorney
Health Care Fraud Chief
United States Attorney's Office
United States Courthouse
One Courthouse Way
Boston, MA 02210

Re: Subpoena duces tecum issued to the Custodian of Records of the XYZ Healthcare Corporation pursuant to 18 U.S.C. §3486.

Dear Mr. Loucks:

Enclosed please find a memorandum submitted by the designated custodian of Records of the XYZ Healthcare Corporation that contains a detailed listing of the documents being produced by the XYZ Healthcare Corporation in response to the subpoena duces tecum dated August 19, 1999.

As stated in the memorandum, the Custodian is still in the process of duplicating and reviewing a number of files kept by the XYZ Healthcare Corporation to determine if they contain documents within the scope of the subpoena. I expect that this task will be completed within two weeks. At that time, the Custodian will supplement XYZ's response and deliver any additional responsive documents to your office.

Thank you one again for your courtesy in this matter. If you have any questions about the enclosed memorandum or materials, please do not hesitate to give me a call.

Very truly yours,

Robert A. Griffith

RAG:og

cc: General Counsel
XYZ Healthcare Corporation

Enclosures:
i. Memorandum to AUSA Loucks.
ii. Envelope entitled "Document Response No. 1."
iii. Two (2) envelopes entitled "Document Response No. 2."
iv. Three (3) envelopes entitled "Document Response No. 3."
v. One (1) envelope entitled "Document Response No. 4."
vi. Three (3) envelopes entitled "Document Response No. 5."

F:\BOB\BF\AHLA\Book\forms\usa-response.wpd

30 Federal Street
Boston, Massachusetts 02110-2508

617 338 7277 Fax 617 338 1923
E mail: office@ssglaw.com
www.ssglaw.com

EXHIBIT XIV.
Example of Memorandum Specifying Produced Documents

MEMORANDUM

TO: Michael K. Loucks, Assistant United States Attorney
United States Attorney's Office
for the District of Massachusetts
United States Courthouse
One Courthouse Way
Boston, MA 02110

FROM: Robert Recordkeeper, Designated Custodian of Records
XYZ Healthcare Corporation

CC: Robert A. Griffith
Paul W. Shaw
Schwartz, Shaw and Griffith
30 Federal Street
Boston, MA 02110

DATE: September 29, 1999

RE: Listing of Documents Produced by the XYZ Healthcare Corporation in Response to the Subpoena Duces Tecum dated August 19, 1999.

The following is a listing of the documents that are being produced in response to the subpoena duces tecum issued on August 19, 1999 to the Custodian of Records of XYZ Healthcare Corporation ("the Corporation") pursuant to 18 U.S.C. § 3486.

The subpoena states that it "covers documents for the time period January 1, 1990 to the present." As explained to FBI Special Agent Drum, the Corporation only has records available dating back to January 1, 1996. The additional records for 1990 through 1995 will take several more weeks to obtain and review due to their being in storage. As a result, the Corporation has produced all responsive documents within its possession from January 1, 1996 to the present.

Upon receipt of the records from storage, I will review and duplicate any documents within the scope of the subpoena. I expect this task will be completed within two weeks. At that time, I will supplement the Corporation's response and deliver any additional responsive documents to your office.

1. <u>"Documents sufficient to show the legal structure, corporate officers, directors, partners, trustees and/or owners of the Entity."</u>

   Enclosed in the envelope entitled, "Document Response No. 1 - Legal Structure and Corporate Officers and Directors," is a copy of the XYZ Healthcare Corporation's articles of organization, together with a listing of the various officers and directors of the Corporation. (Bate Stamped Nos. 000378-390).

2. <u>Correspondence, internal communications, and telephone messages to, from or about any work by any sales person, sales representative, independent contractor or any person holding a similar position."</u>

   a. With regard to the request for "correspondence," enclosed please find an envelope marked "Document Response No. 2 - Correspondence to/from Sales Representatives," which contains a copy of the correspondence file of letters "to/from" Sales Representatives maintained by the Sales Department from 1996 to the present. (Bate Stamped Nos. 001552-001823). Additional correspondence files from January 1, 1990 through December 31, 1995 have been obtained from storage but the duplicating process has not been completed.

   b. With regard to the request for "internal communications," enclosed please find an envelope entitled, "Document Response No. 2 - Internal Communications" that contain the only materials found to date responsive to this paragraph of the subpoena. (Bate Stamped Nos. 000324-000429).

3. <u>All records, including any internal memoranda, correspondence, notes or documents of any nature, relating to the XYZ Healthcare Corporation's compensation structure for any sales personnel, sales representatives, marketing personnel or any person holding a similar position.</u>

   Enclosed are three (3) envelopes marked "Document Response No. 3 - Compensation Structure of Sales Representatives," which contain a copy of the documents responsive to this request. (Bate Stamped Nos. 011012-011067).

4. <u>All correspondence or other documents that you have received from ABC Pharmaceuticals, Inc. or any employee of said company.</u>

   Enclosed is an envelope marked "Document Response No. 4 - Correspondence from ABC Pharmaceuticals" which contains all available responsive documents. (Bate Stamped Nos. 000231 to 000308).

5. <u>All records relating to the payment by XYZ Healthcare Corporation of any sums to any for any sales person, sales representative, marketing personnel or any person holding a similar position.</u>

   In correspondence from attorney Paul W. Shaw on August 24, 1999, you agreed XYZ Healthcare only had to produce commission and bonus checks in response to this request, and not regular payroll/draw checks. Enclosed please find three envelopes marked "Document Response No. 5 - Commission and Bonus Checks," which contain copies of all commission and bonus checks issued to any sales representative for the period of 1995 to date. (Bate Stamped Nos. 000856 to 001303).

6. <u>All documents regarding or related in any way to any consulting or other services you received from any consultant or any person in any line of business for which services ABC Pharmaceutical, Inc. made any payment in whole or in part.</u>

   There are no such documents.

EXHIBIT XV.
Example of Letter re: Notice of Potential Interview

Schwartz, Shaw and Griffith

Attorneys at law

Robert A. Griffith	Gregory J. Aceto
Paul W. Shaw	Jonathan B. Bruno
Harvey A. Schwartz	James F. O'Brien
	William C. Taussig
	Jerome B. Tichner
	Robin J. Dimieri, Esq., P.C., Of Counsel

August 24, 1999

_____, President
XYZ Healthcare Corporation
Boston, MA 02115

Re: Notifying Company Personnel of the Potential of Being Interviewed in Connection with the Department of Justice Investigation.

Dear Mr. _____:

Attached is a memorandum that we propose be sent to selected present and former employees of the XYZ Healthcare Corporation, including billing personnel. It is essential both that the corporation be aware of these points and that the employees understand their rights. Frequently, employees speak with investigators because they mistakenly believe they have no choice. In addition, it is our experience that management personnel often instruct employees not to speak with investigators. This is a mistake. It can be interpreted by the government as obstruction of justice and, at the very least, gets the corporation off to a bad start with the government. Therefore, the enclosed memorandum should be circulated within the near future, as it is likely investigators will contact selected employees.

If you have any questions, do not hesitate to call.

Very truly yours,

Paul W. Shaw

Robert A. Griffith

PWS/dp
Enclosure

F:\PAUL\PF\AHLABook\forms\advice-ltr

30 Federal Street
Boston, Massachusetts 02110-2508

617 338 7277 Fax 617 338 1923
E mail: office@ssglaw.com
www.ssglaw.com

EXHIBIT XVI.
Example of Memorandum to Staff re: Potential Investigation

XYZ HEALTHCARE CORPORATION

MEMORANDUM

TO: Distribution List

FROM: _____, President
XYZ Healthcare Corporation

THRU: Paul W. Shaw, Esq.
Robert A. Griffith, Esq.
Schwartz, Shaw and Griffith

DATE: August 24, 1999

RE: Potential Investigation by the United States Attorney's Office.

1. The United States Attorney's office is conducting a review of the company's billing practices. Investigators assigned to the United States Attorney's Office may attempt to interview company personnel both at work and at their homes. It is important that you understand your rights and obligations.

2. You have the right to be interviewed, or to decline to be interviewed. You cannot be compelled to give any statement.

3. If you are contacted by an investigator and you decide to speak to him or her, you have the right to consult an attorney <u>before</u> each and every conversation. You are also entitled to have an attorney with you during any conversations you may have with investigators.

4. The company has hired Paul W. Shaw and Robert A. Griffith of the firm Schwartz, Shaw and Griffith (Tel. No. 617-338-7277) to advise and assist us in connection with the investigation. Should you so desire, these attorneys are available to answer any questions you may have concerning the investigation. If you wish, the company will arrange to have an attorney will represent you and be present with you during any interview with a government investigator.

5. In the event you decide to be interviewed by a government investigator, you <u>must</u> provide full and truthful information in response to any questions you choose to answer.

6. Whether to speak to government investigators is your decision alone. However, in view of the broad scope of the investigation, we urge you to consult with an attorney before you agree to speak to any investigators.

7. We ask that you immediately contact either Mr. Shaw or Mr. Griffith if you are approached by anyone requesting information.

EXHIBIT XVII.
Example of Memorandum to Key Personnel re: Search Warrants

Schwartz, Shaw and Griffith

MEMORANDUM

TO: Key Personnel
XYZ Healthcare Corporation

FROM: Paul W. Shaw, Esq.
Robert A. Griffith, Esq.
Schwartz, Shaw and Griffith

RE: What To Do In Case Of A Search Warrant

Searches by government investigators have become a more frequent occurrence for health care providers subject to investigation in recent years. Although we have no reason to believe that this might happen to the XYZ Healthcare Corporation, it is useful and timely to review what should be done in the event a government agent arrives at a facility with a search warrant.

The following is merely an overview of the issues that will arise during the execution of a search warrant. If government agents do arrive at the Company with a valid search warrant or other legal process allowing immediate access to Company property, you should do the following:

1. Immediately contact attorney Robert A. Griffith or Paul W. Shaw of Schwartz, Shaw and Griffith (617-338-7277). It is critical that you notify these individuals as soon as possible.

2. Ask to see the government investigators' identification and/or business cards. You should write down the name and positions of the government investigators participating in the search.

3. The agents are required to provide you with a copy of the search warrant. Ask for a copy of the warrant and any attachments.

4. The warrant authorizes the agents to search specific premises and seize specific property. The warrant will identify the locations the agents are permitted to search. You will want to make sure the agents do not go beyond the areas identified by the warrant. If the agents attempt to search in an area not designated by the warrant,

ask them to wait so that counsel can be consulted. If they refuse to wait, do not interfere with their efforts.

5. The warrant will also include an attachment listing all of the items (or categories of items) to be seized. Ask for a copy of the attachment and make sure the agents do not seize any items not covered by the warrant. If the agents attempt to seize items not designated by the warrant, ask them to wait so that counsel can be consulted. If they refuse to wait, do not interfere with their efforts.

6. Do not "agree" that the search can be expanded beyond the specific limits or objects described in the search warrant.

7. The agents are entitled to take the original documents and items described in the warrant. While you can ask for copies of the documents before they are taken by the agents, the agents are not required to give you copies of the documents. As a result, consider asking only for copies of specific documents that are essential to your conducting business. If the agents refuse to give you copies, do not be concerned, as copies can be obtained later.

8. Do not attempt to impede, physically or otherwise, the person(s) serving and executing the warrant. The warrant authorizes the agents to use force where necessary to execute the warrant. You should instruct all personnel not to impede or obstruct the agents' efforts to execute the warrant in any way. Obstruction of the execution of a search warrant is a felony under federal law.

9. It is advised that all non-essential employees be sent home on paid leave.

10. The search warrant authorizes the agents to search and to seize property only. It does not give the agents the authority to interview employees or ask questions. Neither you nor any employees are required to answer any questions of a substantive nature, such as "tell us about your activities," "what operations are carried on at this site," etc. You may politely decline to answer these questions.

11. If the agents do interview any employees, make a note of who was interviewed and the questions that were asked by the agents.

12. The agents may serve grand jury subpoenas on employees. The grand jury subpoenas require attendance before the grand jury on a specified date for the purpose of giving testimony. *The subpoena does not require the employees to speak with the agents during the search.* If any subpoenas are served on employees, make a list of all employees who are subpoenaed. In addition, ask the employee for a copy of the subpoena, because it is likely to reflect the names of the government attorneys involved in the investigation and their phone numbers.

13. Observe the search and take notes regarding where the agents searched and what

documents or items were taken from particular locations. Also record any comments or statements made by the government agents.

14. The agents may seize legal files or other attorney-client privileged materials as part of the search. If the agents attempt to seize any attorney-client privileged materials, ask to speak with the agent in charge of the search. If the agent will not cooperate on this issue, counsel should be notified so they can attempt to contact the Assistant United States Attorney. Ultimately, if the agents decide to take privileged materials, you can not stop them and you should not try.

15. The agents are required to give you an inventory of all property taken pursuant to the warrant.

EXHIBIT XVIII.
Examples of Application for Search Warrant and Supporting Affidavit

United States District Court

DISTRICT OF RHODE ISLAND

In the Matter of the Search of
(Name, address or brief description of person or property to be searched)
Safety Deposit Box # , Washington Trust Company, 126 Franklin Street, Westerly, RI

SEARCH WARRANT

CASE NUMBER: 1:94-M-0356

TO: FBI Special Agent James Pitcavage and any Authorized Officer of the United States

Affidavit(s) having been made before me by Special Agent James Pitcavage who has reason to believe that ☐ on the premises known as (name, description and/or location)

Safety Deposit Box # , Washington Trust Company, 126 Franklin Street, Westerly, RI

in the _____ District of Rhode Island there is now concealed a certain property, namely (describe the person or property)

United States currency and documents showing ownership and control of Safety Deposit Box # further described above which is evidence of violations of Title 18, U.S.C. Sections 371, 286, 287, 1341, and 1343.

I am satisfied that the affidavit(s) establish probable cause to believe that the property so described is now concealed on the premises above-described and establish grounds for the issuance of this warrant.

YOU ARE HEREBY COMMANDED to search on or before March 11, 1994

the place named above for the property specified, serving this warrant and making the search (in the daytime — 6:00 A.M. to 10:00 P.M.) and if the property be found there to seize same, leaving a copy of this warrant and receipt for the property taken, and prepare a written inventory of the property seized and promptly return this warrant to Honorable ~~Robert W. Lovegreen~~ as required by law.

Mar 9, 1994 @ 1540
Date and Time Issued

~~ROBERT W. LOVEGREEN~~ T.M. Bendery S.
United States Magistrate Judge
Name & Title of Judicial Officer

at Providence, Rhode Island
City and State

Signature of Judicial Officer

AFFIDAVIT FOR SEARCH WARRANT

United States District Court

DISTRICT: Rhode Island

United States of America vs.
Safety Deposit Box # ?, Washington Trust Company, 126 Franklin Street, Westerly, RI

DOCKET NO.

MAGISTRATE'S CASE NO.

NAME AND ADDRESS OF JUDGE OR MAGISTRATE:
Honorable Robert W. Lovegreen
United States Magistrate Judge
United States District Court
Providence, Rhode Island 02903-1720

The undersigned being duly sworn deposes and says: That there is reason to believe that

[ ] on the person of   [X] on the premises known as

DISTRICT: Rhode Island

See attached Affidavit of Special Agent James Pitcavage

The following property (or person) is concealed:

See attached Affidavit of Special Agent James Pitcavage

Affiant alleges the following grounds for search and seizure:

See attached Affidavit of Special Agent James Pitcavage

[X] See attached affidavit which is incorporated as part of this affidavit for search warrant

Affiant states the following facts establishing the foregoing grounds for issuance of a Search Warrant

See attached Affidavit of Special Agent James Pitcavage

SIGNATURE OF AFFIANT

OFFICIAL TITLE, IF ANY
Special Agent, FBI

Sworn to before me, and subscribed in my presence:

DATE

JUDGE OR U.S. MAGISTRATE

[1] United States Judge or Judge of a State Court of Record.
[2] If a search is to be authorized "at any time in the day or night" pursuant to Federal Rules of Criminal Procedure 41(c), show reasonable cause therefor.

SENT BY:US ATTY HARTFORD ; 3- 9-94 ; 13:43 ; → 8 838 5433;# 4

AO 93 (Rev. 5/85) Search Warrant

United States District Court

DISTRICT OF CONNECTICUT

In the Matter of the Search of
(Name, address or brief description of person or property to be searched)

, Connecticut

SEARCH WARRANT

CASE NUMBER:

TO: Special Agent Dawn Landreth and any Authorized Officer of the United States

Affidavit(s) having been made before me by Dawn Landreth who has reason to
believe that ☐ on the person of or ☒ on the premises known as (name, description and/or location) Medical Center, , Connecticut. The Medical Center occupies approximately 5,000 square feet on the first floor of a three-story brick building at There is a large sign next to the driveway that says Medical Center" and another sign inside the lobby. On the left side of the lobby, there is a short flight of stairs leading up to a main hallway. The patient entrance is on the right and the entrance to the business offices is on the left. The entrance to patient area is labelled "103" and the entrance to the business offices is labelled "103A).
in the XXXXXXXXXXXX District of Connecticut there is now concealed a certain person or property, namely (describe the person or property)

Please see attachment A.

I am satisfied that the affidavit(s) and any recorded testimony establish probable cause to believe that the person or property so described is now concealed on the person or premises above-described and establish grounds for the issuance of this warrant.

YOU ARE HEREBY COMMANDED to search on or before March 17, 1994
Date
(not to exceed 10 days) the person or place named above for the person or property specified, serving this warrant and making the search (in the daytime — 6:00 A.M. to 10:00 P.M.) (at any time in the day or night as I find reasonable cause has been established) and if the person or property be found there to seize same, leaving a copy of this warrant and receipt for the person or property taken, and prepare a written inventory of the person or property seized and promptly return this warrant to Honorable Joan G. Margolis
as required by law.
U.S. Judge or Magistrate

3/7/94, 2:22 p.m.   at New Haven, Connecticut
Date and Time Issued   City and State

Hon. Joan G. Margolis, U.S. Magistrate Judge   /s/ JGM

SENT BY:US ATTY HARTFORD ; 3- 9-94 ; 13:43 ;   →   8 838 5433;# 5

AO 93 (Rev. 5/85) Search Warrant

United States District Court

DISTRICT OF CONNECTICUT

In the Matter of the Search of
(Name, address or brief description of person or property to be searched)

Namaug Medical Center, 816 Long Hill Road, Groton, CT

SEARCH WARRANT

CASE NUMBER:

TO: Special Agent Dawn Landreth _____ and any Authorized Officer of the United States

Affidavit(s) having been made before me by Dawn Landreth who has reason to
                                              Affiant
believe that ☐ on the person of or ☒ on the premises known as (name, description and/or location)
Medical Center is located within a one story, white clapboard building at _____ The medical center occupies the entire building. There is a large, white sign in the entrance to the building that says _____ Medical Center".

In the ____XXXXXXXXXXXXX____ District of __Connecticut__ there is now
concealed a certain person or property, namely (describe the person or property)

Please see attachment A.

I am satisfied that the affidavit(s) and any recorded testimony establish probable cause to believe that the person or property so described is now concealed on the person or premises above-described and establish grounds for the issuance of this warrant.

YOU ARE HEREBY COMMANDED to search on or before March 19, 1994
                                                        Date

(not to exceed 10 days) the person or place named above for the person or property specified, serving this warrant and making the search (in the daytime — 6:00 A.M. to 10:00 P.M.) (at any time in the day or night as I find reasonable cause has been established) and if the person or property be found there to seize same, leaving a copy of this warrant and receipt for the person or property taken, and prepare a written inventory of the person or property seized and promptly return this warrant to Honorable Joan G. Margolis
as required by law.   U.S. Judge or Magistrate

3/9/94   2:22 p.m.   at New Haven, Connecticut
Date and Time Issued   City and State

Hon. Joan G. Margolis, U.S. Magistrate Judge   [signature]

SENT BY:US ATTY HARTFORD ; 3- 9-94 ; 13:44 ; → 8 838 5433;# 6

AO 93 (Rev. 5/85) Search Warrant

United States District Court

DISTRICT OF __CONNECTICUT__

In the Matter of the Search of
(Name, address or brief description of person or property to be searched)

Home of Dr.

, CT

SEARCH WARRANT

CASE NUMBER:

TO: __Special Agent Dawn Landreth__ and any Authorized Officer of the United States

Affidavit(s) having been made before me by __Special Agent Dawn Landreth__ who has reason to
Affiant

believe that ☐ on the person of or ☒ on the premises known as (name, description and/or location)

_____, Connecticut is a red brick, single family home with an attached, one car garage with a white front door and a white garage door. The number "1050" is affixed to the mailbox on the front of the house.

in the __XXXXXXXXXXXXXX__ District of __CONNECTICUT__ there is now concealed a certain person or property, namely (describe the person or property)

Please see attachment A.

I am satisfied that the affidavit(s) and any recorded testimony establish probable cause to believe that the person or property so described is now concealed on the person or premises above-described and establish grounds for the issuance of this warrant.

YOU ARE HEREBY COMMANDED to search on or before __March 17, 1994__
Date

(not to exceed 10 days) the person or place named above for the person or property specified, serving this warrant and making the search (in the daytime — 6:00 A.M. to 10:00 P.M.) ~~(at any time in the day or night as I find reasonable cause has been established)~~ and if the person or property be found there to seize same, leaving a copy of this warrant and receipt for the person or property taken, and prepare a written inventory of the person or property seized and promptly return this warrant to __Honorable Joan G. Margolis__
U.S. Judge or Magistrate
as required by law.

__3/9/94, 2:23 p.m.__   at New Haven, Connecticut
Date and Time Issued   City and State

Hon. Joan G. Margolis, U.S. Magistrate Judge
Name and Title of Judicial Officer   Signature of Judicial Officer

IN THE DISTRICT COURT OF THE UNITED STATES

FOR THE DISTRICT OF RHODE ISLAND

A F F I D A V I T

I, JAMES PITCAVAGE, being duly sworn, do hereby depose and say:

1. I am a Special Agent of the Federal Bureau of Investigation, and have been so employed for approximately two years.

2. I am aware that there is presently a joint investigation in progress in the District of Connecticut involving the Federal Bureau of Investigation, the Office of Inspector General, Department of Health and Human Services and the Department of Defense, Office of Inspector General, Defense Criminal Investigative Service, focusing on Dr.   ,
         ,   , Connecticut and the
    ,   ,   and   ,

3. I understand that during the course of the investigation, the case agents developed information that Dr. has committed violations of Title 18, United States Code, Section 371 (conspiracy), Title 18, United States Code, Section 286 (conspiracy to defraud the United States), Title 18, United States Code, Section 287 (filing false claims), Title 18, United States Code, Section 1341 (mail fraud) and Title 18, United States Code, Section 1343 (wire fraud).

4. The investigation focuses on allegations that Dr. has engaged in the systematic submission of false and fraudulent bills to Medicare, Blue Cross Blue Shield, M.D. Health Plan, CHAMPUS, Electric Boat health insurance program, Electric Boat workers' compensation program, and Camp Weicker.

5. On March 7, 1994, the United States Attorney's Office in Connecticut obtained three search warrants to search the home of Dr. and the two for evidence of violations of the federal criminal code. Copies of the three search warrants and the affidavit in support thereof are attached hereto and made a part of this affidavit. These documents have all been sealed.

6. I have been advised by Special Agent Jeffery Paula of the Department of Health and Human Services, one of the case agents in this investigation, that during the search of Dr. home at , ., Agent Paula discovered approximately $125,201 in cash in a safe in the laundry room. Additionally, Agent Paula found $10,500 in hundred dollar bills on Dr. person during the search.

7. Dr. advised Agent Paula that he was carrying $10,500 because he intended to go to the bank that day.

8. During the search of Dr. house, Agent Paula reviewed and seized certain financial records including bank deposit tickets and savings account passbooks which reflect that Dr. has engaged in numerous financial transactions in which he deposited currency in amounts of $9,900. Based on Agent Paula's

training and experience, he is aware that financial transactions involving $10,000 or more in United States currency trigger the filing of a Currency Transaction Report (CTR). Accordingly, he asked Dr. whether he was aware of existence of the CTR regulations. Dr. told Agent Paula that he was aware that any transaction involving $10,000 or more of United States currency required that a CTR be filed by the financial institution in question.

9. During the search of Dr. home, Agent Paula discovered and seized two safe deposit box keys for safe deposit boxes at the Washington Trust Company, 126 Franklin Street, Westerly, Rhode Island and at Fleet Bank (formerly CBT), 1 Union Plaza, New London, Connecticut. The key for the Washington Trust box was inscribed with the number " " and was found in close proximity to the $125,201 in cash. I understand that agents who are participating in this joint investigation learned that the Washington Trust safe deposit box which is rented by Dr. is listed under account number . I also understand that the key to the CBT/Fleet safe deposit box did not bear a number which appears to be related to the safe deposit box number. This key was found in Dr. briefcase. I have been advised by law enforcement agents in Connecticut who are participating in this investigation that the Fleet Bank safe deposit box which is rented by Dr. is box number

10. I have been advised that CW-2, the Supervisor of Nameaug's billing office, said that Dr. takes cash

3

out of the daily deposits of the   two or three times per week. She also advised that as a result of Dr.   removal of cash from   daily deposits,   a   employee who prepares the financial records at   , that she must re-write and falsify   daily balance sheets to erase and remove any record of Nameaug's receipt of this cash.

11.   ve also been advised that   was interviewed on March 8, 1994 during the search of the   and she confirmed that Dr.   regularly removes cash from   daily receivables. She also confirmed that she has been instructed by Dr.   to alter the daily balance sheet to make it appear as if this cash had never been received by   .

12. Based on my training and experience, I know that people frequently keep the fruits of criminal activity in safe deposit boxes for purposes of concealing it from law enforcement authorities. I also know that people who handle large amounts of cash frequently store it in safe deposit boxes in order to conceal it from the Internal Revenue Service.

13. Based on the foregoing, there is probable cause to believe and I do believe that safe deposit box   located at the Washington Trust Company, 126 Franklin Street, Westerly, Rhode Island, contains fruits of the criminal conduct which is the subject of this on-going investigation. Additionally, based on the foregoing, there is probable cause to believe and I do believe

that the safe deposit box contains evidence of Dr. violations of the Internal Revenue Code. Accordingly, I hereby request authority to seize any United States currency and documents showing ownership and control of said safety deposit box found in Safety Deposit Box ∫ located at the Washington Trust Company, 126 Franklin Street, Westerly, Rhode Island.

JAMES PITCAVAGE
SPECIAL AGENT

Subscribed and sworn to before me
this ___ day of March, 1994,
at Providence, Rhode Island.

ROBERT W. LOVEGREEN
UNITED STATES MAGISTRATE JUDGE

STATE OF CONNECTICUT   :
                          : ss: New Haven, March 7, 1994.
COUNTY OF NEW HAVEN   :

AFFIDAVIT

I, DAWN LANDRETH, being duly sworn, do depose and say:

1. I am a Special Agent of the Federal Bureau of Investigation, United States Department of Justice, currently assigned to the FBI's New Haven Division, and have been so employed for approximately four (4) years. My duties are to investigate violations of the federal criminal laws. My investigative experience includes foreign counterintelligence investigations, bank robbery and fugitive investigations, and investigations of white collar crime.

2. As a criminal investigator with the FBI, I have participated in and/or conducted numerous investigations of criminal violations of the United States Code and I have assisted in the execution of numerous search warrants.

3. I am currently participating in a joint investigation with Special Agents from the Office of Inspector General, Department of Health and Human Services (hereinafter "HHS"), and the Department of Defense, Office of Inspector General, Defense Criminal Investigative Service (hereinafter "DCIS"), of Dr.   (hereinafter "Dr.   ") for violating Title 18, United States Code, Section 371 (conspiracy); Title 18, United States Code, Section 286 (conspiracy to defraud the United States); Title 18, United States Code, Section 287

(filing false claims); Title 18, United States Code, Section 1341 (mail fraud), and Title 18, United States Code, Section 1343 (wire fraud).

4. I base this affidavit upon my personal knowledge, on my experience as a criminal investigator, on facts I learned in the course of this investigation, on information provided to me by other FBI agents and by HHS and DCIS agents who are participating in this joint investigation. Additionally, I have conducted interviews, reviewed reports prepared by Special Agents of HHS and DOD, reports of surveillance conducted by the FBI, toll record information and Blue Cross Blue Shield's (hereinafter "BCBS") investigative audit and documentation reflecting complaints made by former   patients. I have also debriefed cooperating witnesses who have personal knowledge of the information provided. Finally, I reviewed information obtained through the monitoring of a closed circuit television camera which intercepted visual, non-verbal activity in the personal office of Dr.   at the   in

5. I submit this affidavit in support of three applications for warrants authorizing the search of (1) the   ,   ,   Connecticut (hereinafter   "); (2) the   ,   ,   , Connecticut (hereinafter "   "); and (3) the home of Dr.   ,   ,   , Connecticut. Based on my training and experience and on my participation in this

investigation, I have probable cause to believe and I do believe that in these three locations, there is evidence of violations of federal law including Title 18, United States Code, Section 371 (conspiracy); Title 18, United States Code, Section 286 (conspiracy to defraud the United States); Title 18, United States Code, Section 287 (filing false claims); Title 18, United States Code, Section 1341 (mail fraud), and Title 18, United States Code, Section 1343 (wire fraud).

BACKGROUND

6. Dr. _____, age 39, is the president, owner and operator of _____ and _____. As _____ owner, Dr. _____ directs and oversees all medical and administrative activity at both medical centers.

7. _____ occupies approximately 5,000 square feet on the first floor of a three-story brick building at _____. There is a large sign next to the driveway of the building that says " _____ Medical Center" and another sign inside the lobby. On the left side of the lobby, there is a short flight of stairs leading up to a main hallway. The patient entrance is on the right side of the hallway and the entrance to the business offices is on the left side of the hall. The entrance to the patient area is labelled " _____ " and the entrance to the business offices is labelled " _____ ". Dr. _____ has a private office with a computer terminal inside the patient area

(through door " ") located through the main lobby near the coat closet.

8.   is located within a one story, white clapboard building at   . The medical center occupies the entire building. There is a large, white sign at the entrance to the building that says '   Medical Center".

9.   , is a red brick, single family home with an attached, one car garage with a white front door and a white garage door. The number "   " is affixed to the mailbox on the front of the house.

10. In the course of this joint investigation, I obtained information from the HHS case agent with whom I am working that Medicare is a federal program established under Title XVIII of the Social Security Act to pay certain health care expenses for individuals who are 65 years of age or older and for eligible individuals who are under 65 and who are disabled. The United States Department of Health and Human Services is responsible for administering the Medicare program.

11. I also learned that the Health Care Finance Administration (hereinafter "HCFA"), an agency of HHS, is the governmental body responsible for administering the Medicare program. In the State of Connecticut, the Travelers Insurance Company (hereinafter "Travelers") is under contract with HCFA to administer the Medicare program. As such, Travelers handles the receipt, processing and payment of Medicare claims which are

submitted by physicians and health care providers for medical services rendered to Medicare beneficiaries in Connecticut.

12. In or about May of 1986, Dr.   applied for and became an approved Medicare provider under applicable federal laws and regulations thereby allowing him to submit claims to Medicare for reimbursement for medical services he provided to Medicare beneficiaries. In or about May of 1986,   applied for and became an approved Medicare provider under applicable federal laws and regulations thereby allowing it to submit claims to Medicare for reimbursement for medical services provided by any   physician to Medicare beneficiaries.

13. I have been advised that from approximately September of 1990 through December of 1993,   submitted Medicare claims electronically by transmitting data from their computer at   to Travelers. Since December of 1993, Dr.   has submitted Medicare claims electronically by transmitting data from a computer at   to Promed Systems Incorporated, a medical software company located in New Haven (hereinafter "Promed"). Thereafter, Promed transmits the claims electronically to a computer at Travelers.

14. The Civilian Health and Medical Program of the Uniformed Services (hereinafter "CHAMPUS") is a health benefits program for active duty and retired members of the Army, Navy, Marine Corps, Air Force, Coast Guard, Public Health Service and National Oceanic and Atmospheric Administration and their dependents. CHAMPUS is funded by the United States Department of

Defense and administered by the Uniform Services Benefit Programs Inc., a fiscal intermediary located in Columbus, Indiana which receives, processes and pays CHAMPUS claims. Physicians and health care providers who participate in the CHAMPUS program must agree to accept CHAMPUS' allowable charge as their full fee for the care provided.

15. On or about October 1, 1983, Dr.   and   applied for and became approved CHAMPUS providers under applicable federal laws and regulations thereby allowing it to submit claims for reimbursement for medical services provided by   to CHAMPUS patients.

16. During the course of my investigation, I learned that General Dynamics' Electric Boat Division (hereinafter "EB") located in Groton, Connecticut is a U.S. Department of Defense ("DOD") contractor. EB is self-insured and finances its own health care and Workers' Compensation claims. EB contracts with the National Employees Company, New London, Connecticut to administer, process and reimburse any Workers' Compensation claims that are filed by EB's employees. EB administers its own health care program for its employees and their dependents. EB is ultimately reimbursed by the DOD for all payments made under its Workers' Compensation program.

17. To the best of my knowledge and belief, BCBS, M.D. Health Plan and other private insurance companies are not federally funded or federally regulated. As such, it is my understanding that the FBI has jurisdiction over the submission

of fraudulent claims to such private insurance companies if, in the course of the scheme, materials have been wire transferred or sent through the United States Postal Service.

COOPERATING WITNESS-1

18. A cooperating witness (hereinafter "CW-1") has been providing information to the FBI since July 1, 1993 regarding the alleged illegal billing practices of Dr   . CW-1 was employed as the General Manager for the   from June 1991 through October of 1992, and worked directly for Dr.   . Additionally, while serving as   General Manager, CW-1 resided at Dr.   home at   ,   , during the work week and traveled home to Winthrop, Massachusetts on weekends.

19. CW-1 advised me that while he was living at Dr.   home, he observed Dr.   routinely changing patient chart sheets and manipulating records to reflect medical tests and procedures that were never actually conducted. He also observed Dr.   inflating medical bills by charging for lengthier and more extensive services than were actually provided. CW-1 indicated that Dr.   regularly brought patient files home and used a computer equipped with a modem which allowed him to access the computer database at   to manipulate and upcode patient billing records. He also witnessed Dr.   use of floppy disks and smaller diskettes while working at home on a computer.

20. CW-1 explained that when a patient comes to one of the   offices, he is treated by a doctor who circles the appropriate codes on a charge slip which reflect the medical services provided. At the conclusion of the examination, the charge slip is delivered by the treating physician to the receptionist. The receptionist enters the codes circled on the charge slip into the computer. Sometime thereafter, the bill is either electronically transmitted to the appropriate insurance company or a hard copy is printed and mailed to the appropriate insurance company.

21. CW-1 recalled that Dr.   instructed the employees to destroy the patient charge slips following entry of the information into the computer.

22. CW-1 stated that some patients are required to pay approximately 20 percent of the total bill at the time of their appointment. These patients are advised that   will directly bill their insurance company for the remaining 80 percent.

23. CW-1 explained that Dr.   would routinely access the   computer's billing system database either from a computer terminal in one of the   clinics or from a computer and computer modem at his residence at 1050 Ocean Avenue, New London, to change or upcode the original billing information in the computer. Specifically, CW-1 stated that Dr. Parrot altered the billing information by adding in medical tests

8

and procedures that were never conducted and by billing for more extensive examinations than were actually performed.

24. CW-1 recalled that a number of staff physicians confronted Dr. about upcoded bills which contained false information but when such a question was raised, the physician was either let go or resigned. As a result, CW-1 said that Dr. frequently had difficulty staffing the clinics.

DR.

25. On March 2, 1993, DCIS agents with whom I am working in this joint investigation interviewed Dr. (hereinafter " "), a staff physician at Groton from approximately July of 1990 until August of 1992. stated that during the summer of 1992, he began to suspect that Dr. was submitting fraudulent claims for reimbursement to health insurance companies, to Medicare and to CHAMPUS.

26. At the request of the interviewing agents, Dr. reviewed medical records he completed following his treatment of certain patients in January through July of 1992 who were covered by CHAMPUS. compared those records to the bills that were submitted by to CHAMPUS. Following this comparison, Dr. identified twelve instances where CHAMPUS was billed for treatment that he never provided to the patient in question. Additionally, Dr.

found that a certain number of the claims reflected more extensive treatment than he actually provided.

DR.

27. On or about October 18, 1992, Dr. contacted the FBI and stated that he was previously employed as a physician at the   . During his employment there, he became suspicious about the accuracy of bills that were submitted to insurance companies. After hearing numerous patient complaints and discussing the billing system with other employees, Dr.   concluded that charges were being added to bills which were not originally indicated by the attending physician. Dr.   advised that he suspected Dr.   was responsible for manipulating the billing records in this manner. Dr.   also believed certain tests and procedures which were expensive but not medically necessary were conducted on   patients in order to earn more profits for the clinic.

COOPERATING WITNESS-2

28. Over the past eight months, I have had almost daily contact with a second cooperating witness who is currently employed as the Supervisor of   billing office (hereinafter "CW-2"). As a result of her position, CW-2 is responsible for and familiar with   billing procedures. CW-2 has been employed at   for approximately three years

10

and during that period, she has had regular, frequent contact with Dr.   .

29. CW-2 told me that all medical bills are sent either electronically or by mail from   to Medicare or to private insurance carriers.   has an arrangement which allows it to transmit bills electronically to BCBS and Medicare. Bills which are directed to other insurance companies are generally sent through the mail and bills to EB are generally hand-delivered.

30. CW-2 advised me that the   clinics are presently equipped with an IBM computer system with five separate terminals all connected to a central hard drive. Three of the five terminals are located at   , one in Dr.   personal office, one on CW-2's desk and a third on the desk of another billing clerk,   . Two terminals are located at   All of the computers contain Promed software which is a computer program that generates patient bills.

31. CW-2 advised me that Dr.   frequently uses the computer terminal in his office to log onto   central billing database and alter or upcode patient records after hours or on Sundays when the clinic is closed.

32. CW-2 further explained that before anyone logs on to one of   computer terminals, he or she must give a password to get onto the system. CW-2 further advised that, to the best of her knowledge, every   employee who uses the

computer has a unique password. Accordingly, employees do not log onto the computer using someone else's password.

33. CW-2 advised that one of her daily duties as billing supervisor is to print a hard copy of the clinic's transaction register (hereinafter "TR") every morning. CW-2 explained that the TR is a summary of all computer activity that took place at   during the previous day. It reflects computer entries from every computer terminal at the   clinics and from any portable or lap-top computer which is connected by a modem to the central computer at   . According to CW-2, the TR allows her to identify which employee used the computer at any given date and time and what entries were made.

34. According to CW-2, the TRs she has reviewed reflect the original billing information entered into the computer by the   receptionist and any changes subsequently made to a bill by Dr.   . CW-2 explained that she recognizes computer manipulations made by Dr.   because on the TRs, the computer identifies him as "   ", " .   ", "Billing" or "Hello   ". Based on her review of the TRs, CW-2 has observed hundreds of computer entries made by Dr.   in which he altered or upcoded the original billing information which was entered into the computer. Specifically, CW-2 said that Dr.   manipulates the computerized billing records for patients by fictitiously adding codes which reflect medical tests and procedures that were never conducted. CW-2 explained that

Dr. makes these changes on the computer after a patient has been treated at the clinic but before the bills are submitted to the appropriate insurance company. CW-2 said that the majority of Dr. fraudulent claims are submitted to BCBS, M.D. Health Plan, Medicare and EB.

35. CW-2 advised me that Dr. also regularly upcodes and manipulates Worker's Compensation bills in the same manner that he upcodes bills which are submitted to other insurance companies. She specifically recalled that Dr. has upcoded Worker's Compensation bills which are submitted to EB.

36. Based on CW-2's review of the TR from Thursday September 23, 1993, Dr. spent several hours in the evening of September 22, 1993, changing, upcoding, and manipulating the billing records for patients.

37. CW-2 advised me that on Sunday, September 26, 1993, Dr. Parrot had manipulated patient billing records from his office at . Based on her review of the TR she printed on Monday, September 27, 1993, she determined that Dr. changed or upcoded dozens of Medicare bills.

38. CW-2 advised me that in the regular course of her duties, she reviewed a TR from Sunday, October 17, 1993 which indicated that Dr. had upcoded patient billing records on that date. CW-2 confirmed that Dr. was in the clinic on that date to see a patient.

39. CW-2 recalled that on December 1, 1993, Dr. confided that he had stayed at   until 1:00 a.m. on November 30, 1993, "working" on numerous EB claims. CW-2 said that she understood Dr.   to mean that he had upcoded the EB claims that night.

40. CW-2 told me that on more than one occasion, Dr.   has instructed her to manipulate patient billing records on the computer because, he said, he was too busy to do it himself or because he was out of the office on vacation.

41. To the best of my knowledge and based in part on information provided by CW-2, Dr.   instructed another employee at the   ,   , to engage in the computerized manipulation of the BCBS billing records from December 13 and December 16, 1993 because he was going to be out of town for several days. CW-2 advised me that Pam Morrell used her own computer terminal and not Dr.   computer terminal to manipulate these bills.

42. CW-2 further advised me that she personally observed Pam Morrell working on the computer at her desk and manipulating the BCBS billing records Dr.   had given to her. Shortly thereafter, the TR confirmed that an employee identified on the computer as "   " had manipulated or upcoded numerous BCBS bills.

43. CW-2 advised she frequently receives telephone calls from patients who are inquiring about their medical bills. According to CW-2, several patients have expressed an opinion

that Dr.   is defrauding their insurance company. CW-2 further advised that Dr.   has received several letters from the Connecticut Department of Consumer Protection which indicated that they had received complaints from   patients regarding Dr.   medical bills.

44. CW-2 stated that occasionally, a   patient will pay a medical bill in full at the time service is rendered. On those occasions, Dr.   frequently submits a bill to the patient's insurance company as if the patient had not already paid it. Thereafter, when the insurance company pays there will be a credit balance in the patient's account which is reflected on the TR as "unallocated cash". CW-2 explained Dr.   keeps the double payment and does not notify either the patients or the insurance companies of this practice.

45. CW-2 explained that computer backup tapes which contain billing information for   patients are routinely made and maintained in the billing office at   .

46. CW-2 told me that there are two safes at   , one in the personal office of Krista   , a   employee who manages the financial accounts and a second behind the desk in Dr.   personal office.

COOPERATING WITNESS-3

47. On several occasions during the past month, I have interviewed a cooperating witness (hereinafter "CW-3") who is currently employed as the Workers' Compensation Billing

Coordinator at   (CW-3 was originally hired on March 15, 1993 as   receptionist). CW-3 is specifically responsible for reviewing and overseeing   corporate accounts and Worker's Compensation claims.

48. CW-3 indicated that during her employment at   , she has noticed inconsistencies in the bills that   submits to various Worker's Compensation carriers.

49. CW-3 specifically advised that Dr.   has instructed her to change the billing codes on many Worker's Compensation claims prior to submitting them for payment. CW-3 recalled that Dr.   said he wanted the claims "marked up" in order to earn more money.

50. CW-3 was also aware that Dr.   upcodes or manipulates bills which are submitted to BCBS, M.D. Health Plan, EB, and Medicare. CW-3 explained that, in her experience, Dr.   personally reviews all computerized billing records before they are transmitted, mailed or hand-delivered to the relevant insurance companies to provide him the opportunity to bill for tests or other procedures which were never provided and to otherwise inflate the bills.

51. As a result of Dr.   fraudulent billing practices, CW-3 has given notice to Dr.   that she is presently seeking employment elsewhere.

ROBERT P. SORBARA (BCBS)

52. Over the past eight months, I have been working with Robert P. Sorbara, Senior Financial Investigator, Department of Payment Integrity, BCBS. Sorbara has provided me with information, documents and a copy of an investigative audit that BCBS conducted on or about October 21, 1991 regarding bills which were submitted by Dr.

53. On August 13, 1993, Sorbara advised me that an investigative audit was conducted by BCBS which covered payments made to   from September 1, 1989 through August 31, 1991. BCBS concluded that Dr.   received approximately $18,369.67 in improper payments as a result of upcoding, falsifying diagnoses, and billing for services that were never actually rendered. The audit report also suggested that Dr.   has conducted tests on patients that were "not medically necessary."

54. On June 29, 1993, BCBS sent a letter to Dr.   advising him that he was no longer considered a participating provider by BCBS. As a result, when a BCBS patient is treated by Dr.   , BCBS pays the patient directly instead of reimbursing

55. Sorbara advised me that on or about October 1, 1993, he conducted a pre-payment review of certain claims submitted by   to BCBS. This review revealed that a large number of   bills were submitted with the representation that Dr.   a staff physician at   , had treated the patients in question.

56. Sorbara told me that he believes following BCBS' removal of ▬ from their approved provider list, Dr. ▬ submitted bills to BCBS under Dr. ▬ name in order to receive payment directly from BCBS.

57. Sorbara further explained that on January 17, 1994, ▬ submitted to BCBS a number of claims for reimbursement which allegedly reflected treatment provided by Dr. ▬. However, Sorbara discovered that these claims were identical to claims previously submitted by ▬ under another physician's name.

KATHERINE IARUSSO AND LEAHA CRAWFORD (MEDICARE)

58. I was advised by the HHS agent with whom I am working in this joint investigation that he has spoken with Katherine Iarusso and Leaha Crawford of the Medicare Fraud and Abuse Section of Travelers. Iarusso and Crawford reported that from approximately August of 1992 through February of 1994, they reviewed certain Medicare claims that ▬ submitted to Travelers for reimbursement. In addition, they contacted individual Medicare patients to ascertain whether the medical bills accurately reflected the medical services provided. As a result of this inquiry, Iarusso and Crawford concluded that ▬ had submitted bills to Travelers for patient services that were never provided. They also concluded that ▬ submitted inflated bills to Travelers for a higher level of service than was actually provided.

PHYSICAL SURVEILLANCE

59. From approximately September 1, 1993 through approximately November 30, 1993, the FBI has conducted physical surveillance of Dr.   . This surveillance has revealed that Dr.   frequently travels to and enters   on Sundays when the clinic is closed.

60. On Sunday, September 19, 1993, surveillance revealed that Dr.   arrived at   at 3:55 p.m. and approximately one hour later, Dr.   was observed leaving.

61. On Sunday, September 26, 1993, Dr.   was observed entering   at approximately 2:50 p.m. and leaving at 5:10 p.m.

62. On Sunday, October 3, 1993, surveillance revealed that Dr.   entered   at approximately 1:19 p.m. and departed at 3:24 p.m.

63. On Sunday October 17, 1993, surveillance revealed that Dr.   arrived at   at approximately 1:20 p.m. and departed at 2:15 p.m. He returned there at 2:50 p.m. Dr.   was still inside when the surveillance was discontinued at 5:15 p.m.

64. I conducted surveillance of Dr.   on Sunday, January 9, 1994 and observed him entering   at approximately 1:15 p.m and departing at 7:45 p.m. CW-2 advised me that in the normal course of her duties, she reviewed the TR

from January 9, 1994 and determined that Dr. ____ had manipulated BCBS patient bills on that date.

TITLE III SURVEILLANCE

65. On December 10, 1993, United States District Judge Peter C. Dorsey issued an order authorizing the interception of visual, non-verbal conduct and activities of Dr. ____ inside his personal office at ____ for 30 days. On January 10, 1994, the order was extended for an additional 30 days.

66. On or about December 11, 1993, Special Agents of the FBI entered the personal office of Dr. ____ at ____ and installed a closed circuit television camera.

67. Since December 11, 1993 when the closed circuit camera was activated, Dr. ____ was observed in his office at ____ working on his computer on Monday December 13, 1993 and Thursday December 16, 1993 "batching" or organizing insurance claims for submission to BCBS. Dr. ____ was also observed in his office working on his computer on the following dates and times: on Thursday December 23, 1993 at various times in the late afternoon and evening; on Monday December 27, 1993 from approximately 5:56 p.m. through 6:29 p.m.; on Monday January 3, 1994 from approximately 5:56 p.m. until 6:08 p.m. and from approximately 7:52 p.m. until 9:39 p.m.; on Tuesday January 4, 1994 from approximately 9:30 p.m. until 10:30 p.m.; and on Thursday January 6, 1994 from approximately 5:05 p.m. until 8:33

p.m.; on Sunday January 9, 1994 from approximately 3:05 p.m. through 7:45 p.m.; on Tuesday January 11, 1994 from approximately 5:05 p.m. through 11:06 p.m.; on Saturday January 15, 1994 from approximately 2:05 p.m. through 5:41 p.m.; and on Sunday January 16, 1994 from approximately 12:18 p.m. through 6:15 p.m. The closed circuit television camera was turned off on or about Friday January 21, 1994 and has remained off since that date.

68. CW-2 advised me that in the regular course of her duties at   , she reviewed the TRs from January 9, 1994 and January 16, 1994 and they revealed that Dr.   accessed   computer and manipulated BCBS and Medicare patient billing records on those dates.

69. During the Title III surveillance described above, Dr.   was observed on nine occasions between January 3, 1994 and January 20, 1994 in his office working on a white, lap-top computer. On Monday January 3, 1994, Thursday January 6, 1994, Friday January 14, 1994 and Saturday January 15, 1994, Dr.   was observed putting the white, lap-top computer, papers, files and computer disks into his briefcase and leaving the office.

CAMP WEICKER

70. In the course of this investigation, I learned that Camp Weicker is a state military facility located in Niantic, Connecticut where the Connecticut National Guard administers and runs the Challenge Program. The Challenge Program is partially funded by the DOD and is intended to provide

education, leadership, discipline and physical fitness training to Connecticut residents, age 16 to 18, who have dropped out of high school. Admission is voluntary and a five month stay is required.

71. Through my investigation, I learned that on or about July 6, 1993, Dr. ~~~~ applied for and became an approved health care provider to Camp Weicker. As such, Dr. ~~~~ provides health care services to Camp Weicker students as needed. According to the contract between Dr. ~~~~ and Camp Weicker, ~~ is paid $30.00 per office visit.

72. CW-2 advised me that when Camp Weicker students have private health insurance coverage, Dr. ~~~~ bills their insurance company and upcodes or inflates the bill. Thereafter, he reimburses Camp Weicker for $30.00 regardless of the amount he received from the private carrier.

73. CW-2 explained that the Camp Weicker bills are generated at ~~~~. She has reviewed TRs regarding the Camp Weicker bills from December 23, 1993 through approximately January 10, 1994 and concluded that they were frequently manipulated by Dr. ~~~~. Additionally, on or about February 15, 1994, CW-2 advised me that Dr. ~~~~ had recently spent a great deal of time in his personal office at ~~~~ in the evenings and on weekends "working on" the Camp Weicker claims.

74. I have consulted an FBI computer specialist who informed me that to properly retrieve and analyze all

electronically stored data, to insure accuracy and completeness of such data and to prevent the loss of data either from accidental or programmed destruction, both on site and laboratory analysis by a qualified computer specialist is required. To effect such accuracy and completeness also requires the seizure of all computer equipment and peripherals, the software to operate them and any related instruction manuals.

75. Based on my experience, knowledge and training as a Special Agent with the FBI, I have found that individuals and businesses typically maintain books and records at their offices. I have further found that it is a common practice in the business community to maintain journals, ledgers, computer equipment, floppy disks and diskettes and other records and equipment showing the receipt and disposition of funds. I have also found in my experience analyzing business records that the flow of funds into and out of a business can be tracked by tracing a paper trail. The paper trail is created by manual and computerized entries into business records and by the documents received or prepared to support a transaction. Based on my training and experience, I believe that any existing books and records relating to the handling of cash and reimbursement payments from insurance companies to ~eauc will be maintained at ~9 , , , Connecticut and Groton, Road, Groton, Connecticut and at Dr. home at , , , Connecticut.

76. Based on my training and experience as a special agent for the FBI, I know that businesses and individuals create records for illegal payments, to disguise them as legitimate, so that they can be explained or justified at a later date. I have further found that businesses and individuals will often report the receipt of illegal payments falsely and will falsely characterize illegal payments in order to conceal their true nature.

77. Based on the foregoing, there is probable cause to believe and I do believe that the items listed on Attachment A are now located at (1) the   Medical Center,   ,   , Connecticut; (2) the   Medical Center, 816 Lon   Road, G   , Connecticut; and (3) the home of Dr.   es   t,   Jce   venue,   , Connecticut. Based on the foregoing, there is probable cause to believe and I do believe that these items are evidence of violations of Title 18, United States Code, Section 371 (conspiracy); Title 18, United States Code, Section 286 (conspiracy to defraud the United States); Title 18, United States Code, Section 287 (filing false

claims); Title 18, United States Code, Section 1341 (mail fraud), and Title 18, United States Code, Section 1343 (wire fraud).

/S/ Dawn Landreth
DAWN LANDRETH
SPECIAL AGENT
FEDERAL BUREAU OF INVESTIGATION

Subscribed and sworn to before me this 7Th day of March, 1994, at Hartford, Connecticut.

/S/ Joan Glazer Margolis
JOAN GLAZER MARGOLIS
UNITED STATES MAGISTRATE JUDGE

EXHIBIT XIX.
Example of Search Warrant

United States District Court

DISTRICT OF CONNECTICUT

In the Matter of the Search of
(Name, address or Brief description of person, property or premises to be searched)

New Haven, Connecticut

SEARCH WARRANT

CASE NUMBER:

To: Special Agent Kevin W. Bishop, HHS-OIG, and any Authorized Officer of the United States

Affidavit(s) having been made before me by Kevin W. Bishop, who has reason to believe that on the property or premises known as (name, description and/or location)

See Attachment A.

in the _____ District of Connecticut _____ there is now concealed a certain person or property, namely (describe the person or property to be seized)

See Attachments B and C.

I am satisfied that the affidavit(s) and any recorded testimony establish probable cause to believe that the person or property so described is now concealed on the person or premises above-described and establish grounds for the issuance of this warrant.

YOU ARE HEREBY COMMANDED to search on or before July 1, 1999,

the person or place named above for the person or property specified, serving this warrant and making the search, in the daytime - 6:00 A.M. to 10:00 P.M., and if the person or property be found there to seize same, leaving copy of this warrant and receipt for the person or property taken, and prepare a written inventory of the person or property seized and promptly return this warrant to as required by law.

6/2/99 10:10 a.-
Date and Time Issued

at New Haven, CT
City and State

Honorable Joan G. Margolis, U.S. Magistrate Judge
Name and Title of Judicial Officer

Signature of Judicial Officer

ATTACHMENT A

Description of 646 George St., New Haven Connecticut

The medical office operated by .   is located in a three story white colored colonial style building at 646 George St., New Haven, Connecticut, which is on the corner of   . and   . There is a parking lot in the rear of the building on Greenwood St.   There is a sign attached to two columns near the front door which reads '   The glass on the front door has a gold number (painted on it, as well as a sign that reads '   . In the rear of the building, there is a sign near the rear door which reads "WARNING: This parking lot is monitored by surveillance camera". There is a blue ADT security system sign on the brown rear door. New Haven, Connecticut City Tax Assessor records reflect the property is owned by

ATTACHMENT B
ITEMS TO BE SEIZED

For the period January 1, 1993 to the present: books, records, documents, materials, computer hardware and software and computer associated data relating to the financial and accounting operations of   , including, but not limited to, central processing units (CPUs), disks and tapes on which computer files might be stored, all software and hardware instruction manuals, general journals, subsidiary ledgers, cash receipts, disbursement journals and sales journals, bank statements, deposit tickets, canceled checks, and check registers for all bank accounts, and receipts and invoices for expenditures; state, federal, and employment tax returns; documents related to insurance or Medicare billing, regulations or procedures, including correspondence relating to any patient to or from any insurance company or Medicare; documents, including notes and memoranda, relating to employee duties and responsibilities; employment contracts; calendars, appointment books, diaries, day sheets, or other records relating to patient appointments; and calendars, appointment books, or diaries in the possession, custody, or control of

For all patients listed in ATTACHMENT C, for the period January 1, 1993 to the present: all patient medical records, in whatever media stored; documents, including, but not limited to, notes, memoranda, correspondence, superbills, patient billing statements, insurer billing statements and Explanations of Benefits (also known as "EOBs"), relating to the billing of services rendered to such patients.

EXHIBIT XX.
Example of Receipt for Property Seized

FD-597 (Rev 8-11-94)

UNITED STATES DEPARTMENT OF JUSTICE
FEDERAL BUREAU OF INVESTIGATION
Receipt for Property Received/Returned/Released/Seized

File # 209 NH 38555

On (date) 6/23/99

item(s) listed below were:
- ☐ Received From
- ☐ Returned To
- ☐ Released To
- ☒ Seized

(Name) _____

(Street Address) _____

(City) _____

Description of Item(s):
- X INSURANCE CERTIFICATES (Top of file cabinet-right) KILLEN (JM)
- X PRIVATE INSURANCE APPLICATIONS (JM) file cabinet - right
- X PROVIDER AGREEMENTS (JM) file cabinet - right
- X PROVIDER APPLICATIONS (JM) file cabinet - right
- X STATE OF CT DEPT OF SOCIAL SERVICES APPLIC. file cabinet - right
- X BANK TRANSACTION RECEIPTS (JM) file cabinet - right
- X PARTNERSHIP AGREEMENT (JM) file cabinet - rt.
- X MEDICARE POLICY (JM) file cabinet right
  - ADDED Page 1 - COMPUTER BACK-UP FBI ROOM N
  - 2 - MADONNA sign from Room B

Received By: _____ Received
(Signature)

FD-697 (Rev 8-11-94)

UNITED STATES DEPARTMENT OF JUSTICE
FEDERAL BUREAU OF INVESTIGATION
Receipt for Property Received/Returned/Released/Seized

File # 209A-NH-38959

On (date) 6/23/99

item(s) listed below were:
- [ ] Received From
- [ ] Returned To
- [ ] Released To
- [x] Seized

(Name) _____

(Street Address) _____

(City) _____

Description of Item(s): Room H1
Employee hours, phone list
X Medicare guidelines memos
X Fl. _____
Daily paperwork beginning 12/1/98

Received By: _____ (Signature)
Received From: _____ (Signature)

FD-597 (Rev 8-11-94)

UNITED STATES DEPARTMENT OF JUSTICE
FEDERAL BUREAU OF INVESTIGATION
Receipt for Property Received/Returned/Released/Seized

File # 209A NH 38959

On (date) 6-23-99

item(s) listed below were:
- [ ] Received From
- [ ] Returned To
- [ ] Released To
- [x] Seized

(Name) _____

(Street Address) _____

(City) _____

Description of Item(s): Location: Room K-1 Wall shelves: Medicare billing news letters and other billing information for Medicare

K-2 metal desk below shelves: Medicare billing info and internal office correspondences concerning Medicare billing

Desk Reception window Sandy's desk
Day Book 1999
checks paid — BS
mail receipt book
remittances
property policy amounts
correspondence File

Received By: _____ (Signature)

Received Fr

FD-597 (Rev 8-11-94)

Page 18 of ___

UNITED STATES DEPARTMENT OF JUSTICE
FEDERAL BUREAU OF INVESTIGATION
Receipt for Property Received/Returned

File # 209A-NH-38959

On (date) 6/23/99

(Name) _____
(Street Address) _____
(City) _____

Description of Item(s): MEDICARE FEES - (MILLENIUM) RIGHT SIDE DESK
MD HEALTHPLAN FEES - (jm) RIGHT SIDE DESK
STATEMENT OF PAYMENTS (2) - Top of Radiator (jm)
MEDICARE WAIVER OF LIABILITY - Top Left Desk (jm)
HCFA FORMS - Top Left Desk (jm)
MEDICARE REMITTANCE NOTICES - Top left of Desk (jm)
NEW MEDICARE REGULATIONS - Top right Computer table (jm)
LIST OF ASSIGNED CLAIMS - Top right computer table (jm)
MEDICARE CODING INFORMATION + BILLING INFO - Top left Computer desk (jm)
"PAYABLE" PROCEDURES LIST - Top right Computer desk (jm)
PATIENT LIST WITH PROCEDURE + FEE - Top right Computer desk (jm)
LINED PAPER LISTING PROCEDURE QUESTIONS - Top right Computer desk (jm)
MEDICARE KEYSTROKE - Top right Computer desk (jm)
MEDICARE GUIDELINES FOR FOOT CARE - Top right computer desk (jm)
MEDICARE FEES 1/1/98 - Top right computer desk (jm)
MEDICARE PROVIDER NEWS - Top right computer desk (jm)
MEDICARE NEW GUIDELINES 1/1/98 - Top right computer desk (jm)
1999 MEDICARE FEE SCHEDULE - Top right computer desk (jm)
MEDICARE ASSIGNED CLAIMS - Lower right computer desk (jm)
BILLING FILES

Received By: _____ (Signature)   Received From: _____ (Signature)

EXHIBIT XXI.
Example of Memorandum Outlining Potential Conflict of Interest

POTENTIAL CONFLICT OF INTEREST
DISCLOSURE MEMORANDUM AND WAIVER

In re: Investigation by the United States Attorney's Office into Downtown Medical Healthcare Associates, Inc., David Smith, M.D., Joseph Doe, M.D. and Mary Roe, M.D.

A potential conflict of interest exists in any situation where a single law firm represents more than one party to a matter and particularly so when the multiple parties are all targets of an investigation. This memorandum discusses the pros and cons of such joint representation and includes an acknowledgment of the potential for conflict of interest and a waiver statement.

It is often in the best interests of investigatory targets to be represented by a single law firm. Such representation assures equal access to information and a consistent defense. Additionally, such representation often provides for the most productive allocation of defense costs by eliminating duplication in fees.

Problems with joint representation of multiple clients can arise in several areas:

(1) Government prosecutors do not like joint representation of targets because it makes it more difficult to employ a divide and conquer strategy of offering leniency to one target in return for assistance in prosecuting the others. In such situations the prosecutor may seek to have the court order the targets to obtain separate representation. It is not unknown for a prosecutor to offer leniency to one of several jointly-represented targets primarily for the purpose of requiring the targets to retain separate counsel.

The court will then determine whether the clients are aware of the potential conflict of interest and have been adequately informed of their rights to retain separate counsel.

The court will assess whether the clients are making a knowing waiver of their rights. In some cases courts have held that it is impossible for jointly represented clients to be informed by their single counsel of the advantages and disadvantages of continuing to be jointly represented and have ordered the clients to obtain individual counsel. More frequently, the court makes an individual assessment of the situation and often permits the clients to make their own decision of what is in their best interests.

(2) If an attorney feels he cannot conscientiously represent several clients simultaneously, he must cease such representation. This situation is controlled by two rules of the Supreme Judicial Court of Massachusetts, as follows:

Disciplinary Rule 5-105 (B)

> A lawyer shall not continue multiple employment if the exercise of his independent professional judgment on behalf of a client will or is likely to be adversely affected by his representation of another client, or if it would be likely to involve him in representing differing interests, except to the extent permitted by DR 5-105(C).

Disciplinary Rule 5-105 (C)

> In the situations covered by DR 5-105 ... (B), a lawyer may represent multiple clients if it is obvious that he can adequately represent the interests of each and if each consents to the representation after full disclosure of the possible effect of such representation on the exercise of his independent professional judgment on behalf of each.

Violation of these rules subjects the attorney to disciplinary proceedings. A genuine conflict of interest exists when there is a joint representation and an attorney can not use his best efforts to exonerate one defendant/client for fear of implicating another defendant/client. An impermissible conflict may also arise when an attorney's own interests or those of a third party affect his independent judgment.

(3) A third area of potential conflict of interest arises when a corporation and its employees are targets of an investigation and the corporation pays the legal fees of the employees. It could be said that the attorney's loyalties will be divided between his client, the employee, and the party paying the attorney, the corporation. In such a situation the attorney owes his loyalty to the client. This is governed by a third disciplinary rule:

Disciplinary Rule 5-107

(A) Except with the consent of his client after full disclosure, a lawyer shall not:
(1) Accept compensation for his legal services from one other than his client.
(2) Accept from one other than his client anything of value related to his representation of or his employment by his client.

(B) A lawyer shall not permit a person who recommends, employs or pays him to render legal services for another to direct or regulate his professional judgment in rendering such legal services.

In the case of a corporation paying its employees' legal fees, the attorney may accept such payment only with the permission of the employee. The attorney may not allow the corporation's payment of the employees' fees to influence his representation of the employee.

(4) A fourth potential for conflict of interest is where an attorney represents several targets of an investigation, all of whom are indicted and tried. If one of the defendants chooses to cooperate with the government and testify against the others, the attorney would be placed in the position of having to cross-examine a former client. The attorney may not ethically utilize information he received from the former client in confidence during that cross-examination. This ethical restriction thus could prevent the client from receiving complete representation from that attorney.

The potential for conflict of interest exists in these areas and may arise at any point during the joint representation of multiple clients. Each client must weigh the benefits to be gained from joint representation and fee payment against the potentials for conflict of interest. The attorney or law firm must determine whether the conflict prevents them from adequately representing the interests of each client. Only after both the individual clients and the law firm have independently decided that joint representation is permissible and mutually beneficial may a representation agreement be entered into. Such joint representation must cease if at any point either the client or the law firm determine that adequate representation of each individual client is no longer possible.

                                              SCHWARTZ, SHAW and GRIFFITH
                                              30 Federal Street
                                              Boston, MA 02110
                                              (617) 338-7277

December 8, 1999

EXHIBIT XXII.
Example of Waiver of Potential Conflict of Interest

WAIVER OF POTENTIAL CONFLICT OF INTEREST

In re: Investigation by the United States Attorney's Office into Downtown Medical Healthcare Associates, Inc., David Smith, M.D., Joseph Doe, M.D. and Mary Roe, M.D.

    I have carefully read the attached Potential Conflict of Interest Disclosure memorandum. I have had the opportunity to consult with independent counsel concerning the matters discussed in the disclosure memorandum. After considering the matter thoroughly I have decided that it is in my best interest at present to retain the law firm of Schwartz, Shaw and Griffith, of 30 Federal Street, Boston, Massachusetts 02110 to represent me in all matters concerning an investigation by the United States government and its various investigative agencies. I understand that the same law firm is also representing Downtown Medical Healthcare Associates, Inc., Joseph Doe, M.D. and Mary Roe, M.D.

    I understand that if at any time I feel the law firm can no longer adequately represent my interests I am free to retain independent counsel of my choosing and discharge the law firm. I also understand that if at any time the law firm determines that it can no longer adequately represent my interests it will so inform me and withdraw from representing me further.

    In the light of the above understandings I hereby waive any potential for conflict of interest on the part of the law firm.

_____
David M. Smith, M.D.

December 8, 1999

WAIVER OF POTENTIAL CONFLICT OF INTEREST

In re: Investigation by the United States Attorney's Office into Downtown Medical Healthcare Associates, Inc., David Smith, M.D., Joseph Doe, M.D. and Mary Roe, M.D.

I have carefully read the attached Potential Conflict of Interest Disclosure memorandum. I have had the opportunity to consult with independent counsel concerning the matters discussed in the disclosure memorandum. After considering the matter thoroughly I have decided that it is in my best interest at present to retain the law firm of Schwartz, Shaw and Griffith, of 30 Federal Street, Boston, Massachusetts 02110 to represent me in all matters concerning an investigation by the United States government and its various investigative agencies. I understand that the same law firm is also representing Downtown Medical Healthcare Associates, Inc., David Smith, M.D. and Mary Roe, M.D.

I understand that if at any time I feel the law firm can no longer adequately represent my interests I am free to retain independent counsel of my choosing and discharge the law firm. I also understand that if at any time the law firm determines that it can no longer adequately represent my interests it will so inform me and withdraw from representing me further.

In the light of the above understandings I hereby waive any potential for conflict of interest on the part of the law firm.

_____
Joseph Doe, M.D.

December 8, 1999

WAIVER OF POTENTIAL CONFLICT OF INTEREST

In re: Investigation by the United States Attorney's Office into Downtown Medical Healthcare Associates, Inc., David Smith, M.D., Joseph Doe, M.D. and Mary Roe, M.D.

I have carefully read the attached Potential Conflict of Interest Disclosure memorandum. I have had the opportunity to consult with independent counsel concerning the matters discussed in the disclosure memorandum. After considering the matter thoroughly I have decided that it is in my best interest at present to retain the law firm of Schwartz, Shaw and Griffith, of 30 Federal Street, Boston, Massachusetts 02110 to represent me in all matters concerning an investigation by the United States government and its various investigative agencies. I understand that the same law firm is also representing Downtown Medical Healthcare Associates, Inc., David Smith, M.D. and Joseph Doe, M.D.

I understand that if at any time I feel the law firm can no longer adequately represent my interests I am free to retain independent counsel of my choosing and discharge the law firm. I also understand that if at any time the law firm determines that it can no longer adequately represent my interests it will so inform me and withdraw from representing me further.

In the light of the above understandings I hereby waive any potential for conflict of interest on the part of the law firm.

_____
Mary Roe, M.D.

December 8, 1999

WAIVER OF POTENTIAL CONFLICT OF INTEREST

In re: Investigation by the United States Attorney's Office into Downtown Medical Healthcare Associates, Inc., David Smith, M.D., Joseph Doe, M.D. and Mary Roe, M.D.

On behalf of Downtown Medical Healthcare Associates, Inc., I have carefully read the attached Potential Conflict of Interest Disclosure memorandum and have had the opportunity to consult with independent counsel concerning the matters discussed in the disclosure memorandum. After considering the matter thoroughly the corporation has decided that it is in its best interest at present to retain the law firm of Schwartz, Shaw and Griffith, of 30 Federal Street, Boston, MA 02110 to represent it in all matters concerning an investigation by the United States Attorney and related investigative agencies. I understand that the same law firm is representing David Smith, M.D., Joseph Doe, M.D. and Mary Roe, M.D.

I understand that if at any time the corporation feels the law firm can no longer adequately represent its interests, it is free to retain independent counsel and discharge the law firm. I also understand that if at any time the law firm determines that it can no longer adequately represent the corporation's interests it will so inform its shareholder(s) and withdraw from representing it further.

In the light of the above understandings the corporation hereby waives any potential for conflict of interest on the part of the law firm.

_____
Joseph R. Doe, President, on behalf of
Downtown Medical Healthcare Associates, Inc.,

December 8, 1999

EXHIBIT XXIII.
Example of Engagement Letter for Auditor

Schwartz, Shaw and Griffith

Attorneys at law

Robert A. Griffith
Paul W. Shaw
Harvey A. Schwartz
Gregory J. Aceto
Jonathan B. Bruno
James F. O'Brien
William C. Taussig
Jerome B. Tichner
Robin J. Dimieri, Esq., P.C., Of Counsel

December 8, 1999

Douglas J. McGregor, CPA
Director of Healthcare Services
Feeley & Driscoll, P.C.
100 North Washington Street
Boston MA 02114

Re: City Hospital Surgical Foundation

Dear Mr. McGregor:

As you know, City Hospital Surgical Foundation ("the Foundation") has retained Schwartz, Shaw and Griffith ("SS&G"). We submit this engagement letter confirming your provision of certain accounting and audit services to SS&G in connection with our rendering legal advice to the Foundation.

I. **OBJECTIVE**

The objective of this engagement is to assess the Foundation's level of compliance with applicable laws and regulations. Your principal role will be to assist SS&G in responding to the investigation being conducted by the United States Attorney's Office into certain billing, coding and documentation requirements, and more specifically to design and implement a statistical sampling and extrapolation study to determine the scope of any payments received by the Foundation for certain ____ procedures performed by the Foundation's staff. Your engagement should not include a detailed inspection of every Foundation transaction and you are specifically not being relied on to disclose all errors or irregularities that may exist at the Foundation. However, you will inform SS&G of any such matters that come to your attention, unless they are clearly inconsequential.

II. **PROJECT STAFFING**

You have agreed to staff this engagement with professionals knowledgeable about the operation of healthcare providers and the development of statistical sampling studies. Such individuals should be supported by staff members you deem appropriate.

30 Federal Street
Boston, Massachusetts 02110-2508

617 338 7277   Fax 617 338 1923
E mail: office@ssglaw.com
www.ssglaw.com

Schwartz, Shaw and Griffith

Attorneys at law

III. <u>DOCUMENTATION AND RECORD KEEPING</u>

The Foundation will provide you with all the information required to develop and implement a sampling study, and they are solely responsible for the accuracy and completeness of this information. If the Foundation is unable to provide any requested information, we will discuss any necessary changes in the scope of your engagement.

IV. <u>APPLICATION OF THE ATTORNEY WORK-PRODUCT PRIVILEGE TO THIS ENGAGEMENT</u>

In connection with your engagement, all communications between you and SS&G, as well as any communication with any attorney, agent or employee acting on the Foundation's behalf, shall be regarded as confidential and made solely for the purpose of assisting us in rendering legal advice to the Foundation with respect to the investigation being conducted. You will not disclose to anyone, without our prior written permission, the nature or content of any oral or written communication with SS&G in the course of this engagement. The foregoing, of course, is subject to the operation of law in any court of competent jurisdiction. If, however, you are served with a subpoena, search warrant or any other compulsory legal process that may require the disclosure of information or documents protected by the attorney-client privilege or attorney work-product privilege, you will: (1) inform any governmental agent that your only engagement regarding the scope of this project was with SS&G, not the Foundation (2) inform the government agent(s) that any removal of documents protected by these privileges constitutes an illegal search and seizure, and (3) immediately advise me or one of my partners of the service of process. If I am not immediately available, you should attempt to contact Robert A. Griffith.

All records and other documents obtained in the course of this engagement, regardless of their nature or their source, are the property of SS&G and shall be held by you solely for our conveniences and subject to our unqualified right to direct you with respect to possession, destruction and control thereof.

As part of your agreement to provide professional services in this matter, you will immediately notify SS&G of the happening of any of the following events: (1) the exhibition or surrender of any documents or records prepared by or submitted to you or someone under your direction, in a manner not expressly authorized by SS&G; (2) any request by anyone to examine, inspect, or copy such documents or records; and (3) any attempt to serve, or the actual service of, any court order, subpoena, search warrant or summons upon you which requires the production of any such documentation or records. Subject to payment for your fees and expenses, you will immediately return all documents and work papers to SS&G at our request.

V. ACCESS BY HHS AND CONTROLLER GENERAL

Federal law requires that a contract, if its cost or value over a 12 month period is $10,000 or more, between a provider and a contractor for service, must contain a clause allowing the Secretary of the Department of Health and Human Services ("HHS") and the United States Controller General (or their representatives) to have access to the contractor's books, documents, and records which are necessary to verify the nature and extent of the cost of services furnished under the contract. This clause must be included in the Foundation's contract in order for the cost of services to be allowed for Medicare and Medicaid reimbursement purposes. Furthermore, the contract must allow access to contracts of a similar nature between the contractor and related organizations of the contractor. Please understand that you are the subcontractor in this engagement and further understand that as a subcontractor you may need to provide access to your records. Accordingly, you agree to grant access to your records subject to the limitations in our engagement with the Foundation. Therefore, you will not allow the HHS Secretary and the United States Controller General (or their representatives) to have access to your books, documents, and records unless SS&G expressly permits you to do so in writing. However, this paragraph shall be subject to the confidentiality and other applicable privilege provisions of this Agreement.

VI. NON-DISCLOSURE OBLIGATIONS

In order for you to carry out your responsibilities, it may be necessary for SS&G to disclose to you our legal theories, as well as other privileged information and attorney work product, and for the Foundation, its employees, representatives or agents to disclose to you other confidential information. Accordingly, you agree that during and after the period of your engagement you will not disclose any privileged or confidential information, attorney work product, opinions, facts, data or other information disclosed to you in connection with this engagement to any person or entity to whom disclosure has not been previously authorized (in writing) by SS&G, or identify any theories disclosed to you in connection with your engagement as those of SS&G.

All of your communications in connection with your responsibilities hereunder shall be addressed to Paul W. Shaw, Esq. and SS&G. All documents and other materials generated or prepared by or for you in connection with your activities shall be marked "Privileged and Confidential in Accordance with the Schwartz, Shaw and Griffith Engagement." All such documents and materials shall be segregated and maintained by you in secure files. You may disclose such documents and materials to persons employed by you provided that they agree to be bound by and to abide by the confidentially provisions of this Agreement.

If any person or entity to whom disclosure has not been previously authorized in writing by SS&G requests, subpoenas, or otherwise seeks to obtain any theories, opinions, facts, data, information, testimony, documents or other materials within your possession, custody or control which have been disclosed or provided to you or generated or prepared by or for you in connection with this engagement or which related or refer in

Page 4
December 8, 1999

any way to your work pursuant to this Agreement, you shall immediately inform SS&G before taking any action or making any decision in connection with such request or subpoena and, at the request of SS&G, take such measures as SS&G may deem necessary or appropriate to resist disclosure of such theories, opinions, facts, data, information, testimony, documents or other materials. Should any legal action to defend against, or to seek protection against, disclosure prove necessary, SS&G would expect to handle such matter, without cost to you.

VII. **FEES**

It is understood and agreed that your fees are not contingent upon the outcome of this matter and that, to the extent consistent with other terms of your engagement, you will be paid for services rendered whether arising from my request or otherwise necessary as a result of your efforts in the project. We agree that your fees will be invoiced to SS&G. You understand and agree, however, that the Foundation, and not SS&G, is directly responsible for the payment of any fees arising from your provision of services under this Agreement. We understand that your fees for the services described in this letter will be billed based on the number of hours incurred at your customary hourly rates and exclusive of out-of-pocket expenses which will be billed separately. Expenses that you incur in performing these services should be itemized separately and invoiced at cost. Bills should be submitted monthly as your work progresses and will be payable upon receipt.

VIII. **CONCLUSION**

We believe the foregoing correctly sets forth our understanding, but if you have any questions, please let me know. We very much appreciate your assistance in this matter and look forward to working with you on this important project.

Very truly yours,
Schwartz, Shaw and Griffith

By: _____
Paul W. Shaw

PWS:og

Feeley & Driscoll, P.C. Approval

_____

Date:

EXHIBIT XXIV.
Example of Marking Material System Preserving Privilege

SCHWARTZ, SHAW & GRIFFITH
PRIVILEGED DOCUMENT
ATTORNEY WORK PRODUCT
DO NOT COPY OR DISTRIBUTE

EXHIBIT XXV.
Examples of Joint Defense Agreements

Schwartz, Shaw and Griffith

Attorneys at law

Robert A. Griffith
Paul W. Shaw
Harvey A. Schwartz
Gregory J. Aceto
Jonathan B. Bruno
James F. O'Brien
William C. Taussig
Jerome B. Tichner
Robin J. Dimieri, Esq., P.C., Of Counsel

November 30, 1999

[Name]
[Address]

Re: Joint Litigation and Confidentiality Agreement[1]

Dear ____:

    This letter confirms our mutual understanding of our joint defense obligations. The joint defense arises from the representation of _____ by your firm, our firm, and _____ in connection with an investigation being conducted by the United States Attorney's Office in _____ and other federal agencies.

    We have mutually concluded, with the specific agreement of our respective clients, that the investigation and any proceedings that may result therefrom raise matters of common interest to our respective clients and that the sharing of information, factual materials, mental impressions, memoranda, interview reports, and communications with clients (hereinafter referred to as "defense materials"), will facilitate the rendition of professional legal services to our respective clients. These defense materials are privileged from disclosure to adverse or other parties as a result of the attorney-client privilege, the attorney work-product, and other applicable privileges.

    Such exchange of information and materials in connection with our joint defense efforts is not intended to waive any attorney-client or work-product privilege or other privilege otherwise available. We consider such disclosure of matters of common concern essential to the preparation of an effective defense by our clients and effective representation of them and that such exchanges and disclosures, therefore, are covered by the "joint defense doctrine" recognized in such cases as *In re Grand Jury Subpoenas*, 902 F.2d 244, 248-49 (4th Cir. 1990); *United States v. McPartlin*, 595 F.2d 1321, 1336-37 (7th Cir. 1979); *Hunydee v. United States*, 355 F.2d 183 (9th Cir. 1965); *Continental Oil Co. v. United States*, 330 F.2d 347 (9th Cir. 1964).

---

[1] This form is reprinted from the the AHLA *"Best Practices Handbook In Advising Clinets on Fraud & Abuse Issues,"* (1999).

30 Federal Street
Boston, Massachusetts 02110-2508

617 338 7277 Fax 617 338 1923
E mail: office@ssglaw.com
www.ssglaw.com

Schwartz, Shaw and Griffith

Attorneys at law

It is our mutual understanding that the sharing, or disclosure of defense materials among us and our respective clients will not diminish in any way the confidentiality of such materials and will not constitute a waiver of any available privilege. We have further agreed that neither we nor our clients will disclose defense materials received from each other to anyone except our respective clients, attorneys within our firms, or our employees or agents.

Defense materials (including all copies thereof) shall be returned upon request at any time to the attorney who famished them. Defense materials also shall be returned promptly to the attorney who furnished them in the event any attorney or his client concludes that the parties no longer have a common interest in the matter or if for any reason the joint defense effort or this agreement is terminated. At the conclusion of the investigation or any proceedings resulting therefrom, all copies of defense materials shall be returned to the attorney who furnished them. The obligations of the attorneys and their clients not to disclose defense materials, except in accordance with this agreement, shall not be affected by the return of such materials or termination of this agreement.

If any other person or entity requests or demands, by subpoena or otherwise, any defense materials obtained from another attorney or client, counsel will immediately notify each of the other attorneys. The person or entity seeking the defense materials will be informed that such materials are privileged and may not be disclosed without the consent of the party furnishing them unless ordered by the Court.

If this letter accurately summarizes our understandings, I would appreciate your signing, below and returning, the original to me.

Yours very truly,

_____
Robert A. Griffith

The foregoing is agreed to: _____

JOINT DEFENSE AND COMMON INTEREST AGREEMENT

The undersigned counsel ("Counsel") and their respective clients, ███████████████ have agreed as follows relating to all pending and future civil, administrative, legislative, and criminal investigations, proceedings or inquiries relating to the long-term care facility known as the ███████████████ (herein "the subject matter of this Agreement"). A civil action has been filed by ███████████████ to the subject matter of this Agreement (the "Civil Suit"). The parties specifically contemplate that this Agreement shall remain in force should any other government agency, self-regulatory organization, private entity or individual initiate any investigative activity or legal proceedings of whatever nature in connection with the subject matter of this Agreement.

1. Background

Each of the Clients, and if applicable, their individual employees, agents and members, may be a witness in the Civil Suit. The nature of this Civil Suit and the relationships among the Clients have led the parties to conclude that there are and will be legal and factual issues common to the Clients, thus warranting joint effort in preparation of a potential common defense. It is and has been the desire and purpose of the Clients that every lawful, ethical and proper step be taken to assure that they and their respective Counsel be able to share and exchange strategies, legal theories, confidences, information and documents which may be useful in each Counsel's representation of his Client(s). Accordingly, Clients and Counsel have determined that they share a common interest with respect to the subject matter of this Agreement and have undertaken to engage in such exchanges and sharing in furtherance of a joint defense pursuant to the provisions of this Joint Defense and Common Interest Agreement ("Agreement").

2. Maintenance of Privilege

In order to avoid any suggestion that any applicable privilege or work product doctrine has been waived, it is agreed that communications among Counsel and joint interviews of the Clients or other prospective witnesses, are confidential and are protected from disclosure to any third party under the attorney-client privilege, joint defense privilege and attorney work product doctrine. Counsel also believe that, from time to time, the mutual interests of their respective Clients will be best served by sharing legal research and analyses, trial strategies, documents, factual material, mental impressions, memoranda, interviews, reports and other information, including the confidences of their Clients (hereinafter referred to as "Defense Materials"). Some or all of the Defense Materials may be privileged and protected from disclosure to adverse and third parties as a result of the attorney-client privilege, the work product doctrine or other applicable privileges. By exchanging or disclosing Defense Materials under this Agreement,

Counsel and their Clients do not intend to waive or diminish in any way the confidentiality of such materials or any privilege attaching thereto.

Counsel specifically agree to preserve and to invoke in all further proceedings of whatever kind, to the fullest extent possible consistent with the terms of this Agreement, the work product doctrine and attorney-client privileges, the protections of the joint defense doctrine and all other applicable rights and privileges, including those recognized in such cases as United States v. Bay State Ambulance and Hospital Rental Service, 874 F.2d 20, 28-29 (1st Cir. 1989); United States v. McPartlin, 595 F.2d 1321, 1336-37 (7th Cir. 1979); Hunydee v. United States, 355 F.2d 183, 185 (9th Cir. 1965); and Continental Oil Company v. United States, 330 F.2d 347, 349-350 (9th Cir. 1964).

3. Consent and Other Rights

Counsel have further agreed that neither they nor their Clients will disclose Defense Materials received from each other, or the contents thereof, to anyone except their respective Clients, attorneys within their firms, their employees, agents or experts unless they have first obtained the consent of Counsel to the party from whom the materials were obtained. Counsel reserve the right to place further restrictions on the disclosure of specific items of confidential information under this Agreement. Counsel also recognize that any party to this Agreement may choose not to share with other parties information known to him or his Counsel. The failure of any Counsel or Client to disclose such information to other Counsel or Clients shall not in any way affect the binding effect of this Agreement or the application of its terms. Counsel also agree that neither they nor their Clients will disclose to any adverse party, including the Office of the Attorney General, the fact that the parties have entered into this Agreement without first obtaining consent of other Counsel.

4. Use of Defense Materials

Defense Materials that are shared, and the information contained therein, are to be used solely by Counsel, their Clients, employees, agents or experts, in the preparation of defenses to be raised in connection with the litigation referenced above and in connection with all pending or future administrative, civil, legislative or criminal proceedings arising from or relating to the subject matter of this Agreement. Neither the Defense Materials nor the information contained therein may be used for any other purpose. Counsel agree to designate specially and number consecutively the documentary Defense Materials that contain the confidences or statements of any of the Clients. Counsel receiving such specially-designated Defense Materials may make one duplicate copy of such materials for internal office use only, unless otherwise designated or agreed. Upon demand, Counsel receiving such specially-designated Defense Materials agree to return the original and copy to the disclosing party.

Counsel further agree that they and their Clients will use their best efforts to ensure that the confidentiality of Defense Materials is maintained at all times and that no disclosure is made that would result in a waiver or loss of any privilege or confidentiality right otherwise available. Specifically, in the event that any Counsel or Client receives a subpoena or request for voluntary production from any third party (including other parties to this Agreement), such Counsel shall immediately notify all Counsel who are parties to this Agreement of that fact and shall not voluntarily surrender any Defense Materials (except, if necessary those materials that were originated by the subpoenaed party) without permitting all affected Counsel an opportunity to protect their respective interests and assert any applicable privilege or the work product doctrine by motion in an appropriate court or through a similar mechanism. Counsel agree that this Agreement does not limit any Counsel's right to disclose documents or information that have been independently obtained by Counsel.

5. Changed Circumstances

Any party is free to withdraw from this Agreement, upon written notice to all other parties. Upon withdrawal from this Agreement, the withdrawing party agrees to return any Defense Materials (and copies thereof) obtained pursuant to this Agreement and all records that pertain to Defense Materials, to the party from which the Defense Materials were received, within ten days of withdrawal. Counsel agree that they and their Clients will continue to be bound by this Agreement notwithstanding any such withdrawal, with the exception that any communication made by a withdrawing party following withdrawal is not subject to this Agreement.

Counsel and their respective Clients agree that in the event that any party to this Agreement enters into any arrangement, formal or informal, with any adverse party, including the Office of the Attorney General, for cooperation, settlement, immunity, non-prosecution or a plea agreement, or decides to pursue a defense which is adverse to the position taken by any other party to this Agreement, then such party shall withdraw from this Agreement.

Counsel and their respective Clients further agree that in the event that any party to this Agreement chooses to withdraw from this Agreement for whatever reason, neither the fact that this Agreement exists, nor the communications and information sharing that take place pursuant to this Agreement shall create a conflict of interest or other basis so as to require the disqualification of any Counsel from the representation of their respective Clients. Moreover, Counsel and their respective Clients hereby expressly and knowingly waive any right to assert that any actual or perceived conflict of interest exists as a result of this Agreement. Each Counsel signing this Agreement acting on behalf of their Client, as well as any individual employee, agent or officer of a Client, and each Counsel party to this Agreement expressly and knowingly waives any right to seek the disqualification as Counsel of any other Counsel party to this Agreement based upon a counsel's receipt of any communication or Defense Materials pursuant to this Agreement.

6. Limitation of Duties and Conflicts

Each Client who is a party to this Agreement understands and acknowledges by their authorized signature hereto that they are represented only by their Counsel in this matter; and that while the Counsel representing the other Clients party to this Agreement have a duty to preserve the confidences disclosed to them pursuant to this Agreement, each Counsel will be acting only as the attorney for their respective Client and will owe a duty of loyalty only to their own Client. Each Client who is a party to this Agreement also knowingly and intelligently waives any actual or perceived conflict of interest that may arise from a Counsel who is a party to this Agreement, other than their own Counsel, examining them at any proceeding.

7. **Sole Purpose of the Agreement - No Effect on Liability**

The sole purpose of this Agreement is to facilitate the exchange of information between and among parties who share a common interest as stated above. Each Client who is a party to this Agreement understands and acknowledges that the declaration of a common interest among the parties, as evidence through this Agreement, does not in any way affect the liability, if any, that may be imposed upon each party to this Agreement as a result of the Civil Suit, the subject matter of this Agreement or any other matters in dispute between the parties.

8. **Injunctive Relief**

Counsel acknowledge on behalf of their Clients that disclosure of any communications in violation of this Agreement will cause the parties hereto to suffer irreparable harm for which there is no adequate remedy at law. Each party hereto acknowledges that immediate injunctive relief is an appropriate and necessary remedy for violation of this Agreement.

9. **Continuance of Agreement**

This Agreement shall continue in effect notwithstanding any conclusion or resolution as to any party hereto of the Civil Suit or any pending or future administrative, legislative, civil or criminal proceedings arising from or relating to it. Counsel agree that they and their Clients will continue to be bound by this Agreement following any such conclusions or resolution.

10. **Explanation**

By executing this Agreement, Counsel for each Client represents that he or she has advised his or her Client fully concerning the advantages and disadvantages of a joint defense agreement. It has been explained to each Client, and each Client understands, that in the event that the Client, or any agent, employee or member of the Client, should at some point become a witness at a trial relating to the subject matter of this Agreement, that the Counsel for other Clients party to this Agreement who are litigants in this case would have information that had been shared pursuant to this Agreement available to use to support cross-examination of the testifying witness. Such information may include statements of confidences the testifying witnesses shared with his or her Counsel.

In entering into this Agreement, each party knowingly and intelligently waives any objection that might otherwise be available to him or her to being cross-examined by Counsel for another Client party to this Agreement using information that has been shared pursuant to this Agreement. In waiving such objection, each Client specifically is aware of the fact that it will be the option of the Client's Counsel, acting upon the Client's authority, to contribute or withhold any particular information from the other parties to this Agreement.

11. <u>Modifications</u>

Any modifications to this Agreement must be in writing and signed by all parties.

12. <u>Application of Agreement to Previous Communications</u>

This Agreement also confirms that, to the extent that Counsel have already been in communication with one another and with other cients since the commencement of the investigation by the Office of the Attorney General and the Civil Suit concerning the subject matter of this Agreement, their communications and work product are subject to the joint defense privilege and now are subject to this written Agreement.

13. <u>Counterparts</u>

This Agreement may be signed in counterparts and each signed counterpart shall be deemed an original thereof.

14. <u>Additional Parties</u>

Additional Counsel and Clients may join this Agreement with the consent of the Clients and Counsel that have previously been, and who remain at that time, parties to this Agreement.

The undersigned have reviewed, and agree to the Agreement embodied herein, and each signs, under seal this ____ day of _____, 1999.

_____   _____

for   Boston, MA 02108

The undersigned have reviewed, and agree to the Agreement embodied herein, and each signs, under seal this ____ day of _____, 1999.

_____   _____

                                       Boston, MA 02210

EXHIBIT XXVI.
Example of Verified Complaint for Injunctive Relief and Supporting Affidavit

IN THE UNITED STATES DISTRICT COURT
FOR THE DISTRICT OF MARYLAND

UNITED STATES OF AMERICA :

    Plaintiff, :

v. : CIVIL NO. RTM-1c-2257

MARY HUEY WEI FANG CHANG, M.D. :
a/k/a   HUI FANG
      MARY FANG :
      MARY CHANG
10931 MARTINGALE COURT :
POTOMAC, MARYLAND
:
and
:
PETER CHANG
10931 MARTINGALE COURT :
POTOMAC, MARYLAND
:
    Defendants.
...oOo...

VERIFIED COMPLAINT FOR INJUNCTIVE RELIEF

Plaintiff, the United States of America, by its undersigned counsel, requests injunctive relief from this Honorable Court pursuant to 18 U.S.C. 1345, to enjoin a scheme to defraud health care insurers using the mails in violation of 18 U.S.C. 1341 and to preserve the assets derived from the scheme. In support of this verified Complaint, the United States alleges:

I. JURISDICTION AND VENUE

1. This action is brought by the United States of America for a temporary restraining order, preliminary and permanent injunction and other equitable relief pursuant to 18 U.S.C. §1345 to enjoin the Defendants from continuing to defraud health care insurers through the submission of fraudulent claims for medical services and pharmaceutical supplies. The United States

seeks such relief as is needed to redress the injury to the health care insurers resulting from the scheme and to prevent further injury.

2. This Court has jurisdiction under 18 U.S.C. § 1345 and 28 U.S.C. §1345. Venue is proper pursuant to 28 U.S.C. §1391(b).

II. **THE PARTIES**

3. Plaintiff is the United States of America. At all times material to this civil action, the United States seeks to protect the public from an ongoing or likely to reoccur health care fraud scheme that may extend to over 60 private health insurers. Additionally, the United States seeks to protect health insurers during the pendency of the criminal investigation into violations of 18 U.S.C. 1341, and possibly 18 U.S.C. 287, 371 and 1001, and 21 U.S.C. 331.

4. Defendant Mary Huey Wei Fang Chang, M.D. is an internist and is licensed to practice medicine in the State of Maryland under the name Mary Fang. Dr. Fang's business office is located at 121 Congressional Lane, Suite 310, Rockville, Maryland. She resides in the State of Maryland at 10931 Martingale Ct. Potomac, Maryland. In her dealings with various insurance companies Dr. Fang is known to use and submit claims for reimbursement under the names of Hui Fang, Mary Chang and Mary Fang. Additionally, Dr. Fang is known to use her in-laws address to receive insurance and reimbursement payments at 4515 Westbrook Lane, Kensington, Maryland.

5. Defendant Peter Y. Chang is the husband of Dr. Fang and resides at 10931 Martingale Ct. Potomac, Maryland. Mr. Chang is an active participant in Dr. Fang's medical billing practices and prepares at their home the claims for insurance reimbursement submitted to private and government health insurers.

THE FRAUDULENT SCHEMES

6. Defendants are engaged in the fraudulent submission of insurance reimbursement claims through the U.S. Mails for medical services not rendered and for the sale of free drug samples. Defendants' fraud scheme involves the submission of insurance claims under different and misleading names and addresses to achieve payments of money for which there is no legal entitlement. Defendants are depositing the proceeds of fraudulently obtained insurance reimbursements into numerous bank accounts at several different financial institution in the name of the Defendants and/or in the names of their four minor children.

7. The United States has probable cause to believe a violation of 1341 is ongoing or likely to occur in the future absent relief from the Court. Attached hereto as Exhibit A is the Affidavit of Special Agent Kelly Johnstone, Food and Drug Administration, Office of Criminal Investigation is support of the Complaint for Injunctive Relief. Dr. Fang continues to practice medicine, continues to have possession of controlled substances, continues to dispense controlled substances, and continues to submits claims to health care insurers for reimbursement. There is no compelling reason to assume that absent relief from the Court

these activities are now free of illegality or that the scheme to defraud will not reoccur during the government's investigation.

8. The United States, through the Food and Drug Administration, Drug Enforcement Administration, and Federal Bureau of Investigation and the State of Maryland, through the Montgomery County Police Special Investigations Division, are conducting a criminal investigation into violations of 18 U.S.C. 1341 as well as other criminal statutes. The investigation is not complete and will require additional efforts to determine the scope of the fraud on health care insurers.

9. On July 10, 1996 a state search warrant was executed on the business and residential addresses of Mary Fang as well as the residential premises of Peter Chang's parents. Attached hereto as Exhibit B is a copy of the warrant. Referenced in the warrant is an undercover operation by the Montgomery County Police Special Investigations Division, which has produced evidence of false insurance claims submitted to insurers under the names of Mary Fang and Hui Fang.

10. During the execution of the warrant, agents seized approximately nine boxes of records and observed other records on the premises. Additionally, during the execution of the search warrant, Dr. Fang voluntarily provided interviews to SA Johnstone and DEA IA Kathy Ingram. The investigation to date reveals the following:

A. Though Dr. Fang's medical practice is located at 121 Congressional Lane, Rockville, Maryland, she retains her patients medical and billing records at her home in Potomac, Maryland. Dr. Fang's husband, Peter Chang, prepares for submission all insurance claims on behalf of or associated with her medical practice. Dr. Fang instructs her husband for which services to bill.

B. Dr. Fang is licensed to practice medicine in the State of Maryland under the name Mary Fang. Dr. Fang and Peter Chang prepare and cause to be submitted claims for health insurance reimbursement under the names of Mary Fang, Mary Chang and Hui Fang. They direct that reimbursement payments in the name of Hui Fang be mailed to 4515 Westbrook Lane, the home of Mr. Chang's parents.

C. From the records reviewed to date, it is believed that Dr. Fang has submitted or caused to be submitted insurance claims to approximately sixty (60) health insurers under several different names. Reimbursements to Dr. Fang have been paid under the names of Dr. Fang, Dr. Hui Fang and Dr. Mary Chang.

D. Dr. Fang has submitted false insurance claims for services rendered under the various names. She has acknowledged billing health insurers for services not rendered and for repackaged free drug samples since 1992. Dr. Fang described that she uses different identifying numbers on reimbursement claims, such as a social security number for one name and a taxpayer identification number when using other names.

11. The proceeds received from health insurers are deposited into Dr. Fang's business account. Dr. Fang then withdraws or transfers the proceeds to joint account with her husband, Peter

Chang. Monies from both Business Account and the Chang Joint Account are deposited into various other financial accounts. In addition to the Business Account and Chang Joint Account, the investigation has determined the existence of approximately nine (9) additional accounts in the names of the Changs and their minor children. The United States asserts that the monies in these accounts are derived from Dr. Fang's medical practice with the possible exception of Mr. Chang's bi-weekly paycheck of $2,000 which, until November 1995, was deposited into the Chang Joint Account.

12. The United States asserts that the monies in these accounts derive from the Defendants' fraudulent billing schemes and are, therefore, subject to injunctive relief under 18 U.S.C. 1345.

13. The United States asserts that current investigative information reasonably forecasts that the magnitude of the fraud perpetrated by the Defendants is massive and may extend to sixty (60) insurers. Defendants have prepared and cause to have submitted claims under the name of Hui Fang, M.D. to approximately eleven (11) insurers. Two insurance companies have advised that they have processed reimbursement claims for Hui Fang, M.D. in the amount of $ 73,959.00 from January 1995 to April 1996. Additionally, an initial review of records from the Changs show insurance payments to Hui Fang in the amount of $40,000 from eight (8) different insurers. During the search of the premises, investigators observed claims information for numerous other insurers, including the Medicare intermediary (XACT, Camp Hill, PA) that services

Montgomery and Prince George's Counties, Maryland. From what the government can determine now, 11 insurers out of possibly 60 have suffered approximately $120,000 in damages in the last 18 months. Dr. Fang describes she has engaged in these billing practices since 1992. The potential financial victimization in this case could very likely extend into hundreds of thousand of dollars. Such a scenario, moreover, appears consistent with Dr. Fang's description of her income as a practicing internist as she has reported to the agents during her interview that her net income in 1995 was approximately $350,000 to $400,000.

14. For the purposes of executing this scheme, Defendants knowingly and willfully have used, or have caused to be used, the United States mails in violation of the federal mail fraud statute, 18 U.S.C. §1341. These violations are either ongoing or are reasonably likely to resume if no injunctive relief is granted. Dr. Fang continues to practice medicine and submit claims for insurance reimbursement presumably under the different and misleading names and addresses and these claims continue to be prepared for submission and mailing by Peter Chang. Therefore, through their fraudulent activity, Defendants are causing a continuing and substantial public injury.

15. Under 18 U.S.C. § 1345, this court may issue both preliminary and permanent injunctive relief in order to prevent **"a continuing and substantial injury to the United States or to any person or class of persons for whose protection the action is brought."** The United State seeks this relief to protect health

care insurers victimized by the Defendants fraudulent scheme and asserts that over 60 insurers may have received, are receiving or will be receiving, fraudulent claims in the multiple names of Mary Fang, Mary Chang, or Hui Chang.

VI. PRAYER FOR RELIEF

WHEREFORE, Plaintiff requests, pursuant to 18 U.S.C. §1345 and the Court's inherent equitable powers that this Honorable Court:

(a) issue a temporary restraining order and a preliminary injunction barring Defendants, their agents (including financial institutions and other entities having possession or control of defendants' assets), officers, employees and all persons in active concert or participating with them in their affairs:

(1) from using the mails or causing use of the mails to fraudulently obtain payments or reimbursements from health insurers;

(2) from accepting, disposing of or otherwise taking any action with respect to monies received from health insurers as a result of their fraudulent scheme;

(3) from failing to maintain all business, financial, and accounting records and from disposing of business, financial, patient and accounting records and from altering patient insurance records;

(4) from withdrawing or transferring any money or sums presently deposited, or held on their behalf by any financial institution, trust fund, brokerage agency or other financial

agency, public or private; except that the defendants may petition the Court, and the Court may order, that the defendants may conduct normal, day-to-day business activities and pay for the same on a monthly basis, in an amount not to exceed that determined by the Court; provided, however, Defendants provide a verified disclosure of all assets and liabilities;

(5) from transferring, selling, assigning, dissipating, concealing, encumbering, impairing, or otherwise disposing of, in any manner, assets in real or personal property, owned, gained or acquired by defendants.

Respectfully submitted,

Lynne A. Battaglia
United States Attorney

By: /s/ Kathleen McDermott
Kathleen McDermott
Assistant United States Attorney
604 United States Courthouse
101 West Lombard Street
Baltimore, Maryland 21201-2692
410/962-4822 ext. 464

EXHIBIT XXVII.
Example of Temporary Restraining Order

IN THE UNITED STATES DISTRICT COURT
FOR THE DISTRICT OF MARYLAND

UNITED STATES OF AMERICA :

    Plaintiff, :

v. : CIVIL NO. PJM 96-2354

MARY HUEY WEI FANG CHANG, M.D. :
a/k/a HUI FANG
    MARY FANG :
    MARY CHANG
10931 MARTINGALE COURT :
POTOMAC, MARYLAND
and :
PETER CHANG
10931 MARTINGALE COURT :
POTOMAC, MARYLAND
    :
    Defendants

...oOo...

TEMPORARY RESTRAINING ORDER

The Court has considered the United States' Application for Temporary Restraining Order, Verified Complaint For Injunctive Relief, and Memorandum of Law.

The Court finds that a Temporary Restraining Order should issue under 18 U.S.C. §1345 because the United States has shown probable cause to believe that Defendants are engaged in an ongoing scheme to defraud in violation of 18 U.S.C. §1341.

THEREFORE, at 11 o'clock a.m., on this 29th day of July, 1996, this Court issues a Temporary Restraining Order **PROHIBITING:**

(1) the Defendants from using the mails or causing use of the mails to fraudulently obtain payments from health care insurers;

(2) the Defendants from accepting, disposing of, or otherwise taking any action with respect to monies received from the health care insurers, the United States or financial institutions as a result of their fraudulent scheme;

(3) financial institutions and other entities having possession or control of Defendants' assets from disposing of or transferring such assets from the time of service on them of a copy hereof;

(4) the Defendants from failing to maintain business, financial, patient, and accounting records and from disposing of business, financial, patient and accounting records or from altering in any way the same described records;

(5) the Defendants from withdrawing or transferring any money or sums presently deposited, or held on their behalf by any financial institution, trust fund, brokerage agency or other financial agency, public or private, including those custodial accounts in the names of their minor children; except that the Defendants may petition the Court, and the Court may order, that the Defendants may conduct normal, day-to-day business activities and pay for the same on a monthly basis, in an amount not to exceed that determined by the Court, provided, however, that the Defendants produce to the Court and the government a verified disclosure of all assets and liabilities; and

(6) the Defendants from transferring, selling, assigning, dissipating, concealing, encumbering, impairing, or otherwise disposing of, in any manner, assets in real or personal property, owned, gained or acquired by Defendants.

This Temporary Restraining Order will expire at 11:00 a.m. on the 7th day of August, 1996 and a hearing on the United State's Motion For Preliminary Injunction is set for 10:00 a.m. August 6, 1996.

／s／ Peter J. Messitte
Peter J. Messitte
United States District Judge

UNITED STATES DISTRICT COURT
DISTRICT OF CONNECTICUT

FILED
Jun 22 8:41 AM '99

UNITED STATES OF AMERICA,
          Plaintiff

v.

          Defendant

Civil No. _____ - (PCD)

JUNE 21, 1999

TEMPORARY RESTRAINING ORDER

The Court has considered the United States' motion for Ex Parte Temporary Restraining Order, Verified Complaint for Injunctive Relief, Memorandum of Law, and supporting documents.

Pursuant to Federal Rule of Civil Procedure 65 and 18 U.S.C. § 1345, the Court finds that there is reasonable probability the defendant, _____, has committed Federal health care fraud offenses as described in 18 U.S.C. §§ 24 and 1345. The Court therefore finds that a temporary restraining order should enter under 18 U.S.C. § 1345(a)(2)(B).

THEREFORE, at 4:00 o'clock p.m., on this 21 St day of June, 1999, it is hereby

ORDERED:

1. The defendant, _____ his agents, representatives, or employees, or anyone acting under his direction or control, shall not commit any Federal health care fraud offense;

2. The defendant shall not fail to maintain business, financial, patient, personal and accounting records, shall not dispose of business, financial, patient, personal, and accounting records or alter in any way any such

records;

3. The defendant or his agents, assigns, representatives, employees, or any other person acting at defendant's direction or within his control, shall not withdraw, transfer, remove, dissipate, or dispose of the following property:

   (a) Bank Accounts
   Webster Bank
       CD   Acct. No.
       Savings Acct. No.

   Fleet Bank
       Checking Acct. No.

   New Haven Savings Bank
       CD No.

   Merrill Lynch
       Cash Management Acct. No.
       IRA   Acct. No.
       IRA   Acct. No.

   (b) Real Property
       , Connecticut
       , Connecticut

4. The financial institutions involved, namely,   Bank,   Bank,   Bank, and   shall not permit any withdrawal, transfer, or removal from the subject accounts in the foregoing paragraph;

5. Pursuant to § 1345(b), the defendant shall submit to civil discovery, including a deposition, before a hearing on the plaintiff's motion for preliminary injunction is held; and

It is hereby further **ORDERED**:

6. In lieu of the appointment of a temporary receiver under 18 U.S.C. 1345(a)(2)(B)(ii), plaintiff is granted expedited financial discovery, whereby the defendant shall produce within three days an accounting of all bank accounts, stock accounts, real property, and any chattel property valued over $10,000, identifying the location and value of each asset;

7. In the alternative to the relief granted in paragraphs 3, 4, and 6, the defendant may post a surety bond in the amount of $1,000,000 or place the same in an interest bearing account suitable to the United States with a federally insured bank or escrow agent; and

8. Service of this Order and related documents upon the defendant and the subject financial institutions may be made by Special Agents of the Office of the Inspector General of the Department of Health and Human Services, Federal Bureau of Investigation, or any other federal law enforcement officer.

This Temporary Restraining Order will expire at 4:00 p.m. on the 1st day of July 1999, and a hearing on the United States' Motion for Preliminary Injunction is set for 9:00 a.m., Friday, June 25th, 1999, in Courtroom One .

SO ORDERED.

Dated at New Haven, Connecticut, June 21, 1999.

_____
Peter C. Dorsey
United States District Court

UNITED STATES DISTRICT COURT
DISTRICT OF CONNECTICUT

UNITED STATES OF AMERICA,
        Plaintiff

v.   Civil No.   (PCD)

        Defendant   :   JUNE 21, 1999

ORDER TO SHOW CAUSE

Pursuant to the Court's Temporary Restraining Order, entered today, it is hereby ORDERED that the defendant,   shall appear and show good cause why a Preliminary Injunction, as prayed, should not enter, at a hearing to be held on Friday, June 25, 1999, at 9:00 a.m., United States Courthouse, 141 Church Street, New Haven, Connecticut, Courtroom One. It is further ORDERED that the plaintiff shall serve a copy of this Order and the papers upon which this order is issued on the defendant on or before Wednesday, June 23, 1999.

SO ORDERED.

Dated at New Haven, Connecticut, June 21, 1999.

                                              Peter C. Dorsey
                                             United States District Court

EXHIBIT XXVIII.
Example of Preliminary Injunction

UNITED STATES DISTRICT COURT
DISTRICT OF CONNECTICUT

UNITED STATES OF AMERICA,
           Plaintiff

v.

           Defendant

Civil No. 3:99cv1163 (PCD)

JULY 30, 1999

PRELIMINARY INJUNCTION

The Court having heard the parties and reviewed the memoranda on the United States' Motion for Preliminary Injunction, IT IS HEREBY ORDERED:

Pursuant to 18 U.S.C. § 1345, the Court finds that there is probable cause that the defendant,   , has committed Federal health care fraud offenses as described in 18 U.S.C. §§ 24 and 1345. The Court therefore finds that a preliminary injunction should enter under 18 U.S.C. § 1345(a)(2)(B).

THEREFORE, it is hereby **ORDERED**:

1. The defendant,   , his agents, representatives, or employees, or anyone acting under his direction or control, shall not commit any Federal health care fraud offense;

2. The defendant shall not fail to maintain business, financial, patient, personal and accounting records, shall not dispose of business, financial, patient, personal, and accounting records or alter in any way any such records;

3. The defendant or his agents, assigns, representatives, employees, or any other person acting at defendant's direction or within his control, shall n[ot] withdraw, transfer, remove, dissipate, or dispose of the following proper[ty]

   (a) <u>Bank Accounts</u>

   (b) <u>Real Property</u>

4. In addition to the accounts above, the parties agree that the plaintiff, and any one acting under his direction or control, shall not withdraw such funds from Merril Lynch IRA account no. ⸱⸱⸱ that cause the balance in the account to fall below $828,000. In other words, such fund[s] in account no. ⸱⸱⸱ in excess of $828,000 may be withdrawn, and are not frozen under this order.

5. The financial institutions involved, namely. ⸱⸱⸱ ⸱ shall not permit any withdrawal, transfer, or removal from the subject accounts in the foregoi[ng] paragraphs 3 and 4, except as set forth in paragraph 4;

2

It is hereby further **ORDERED**:

6. In the alternative to the relief granted in paragraphs 3, 4, and 5, the defendant may post a surety bond in the amount of $1,000,000 or place the same in an interest bearing account suitable to the United States with a federally insured bank or escrow agent; and

7. Service of this Order and related documents upon the defendant and the subject financial institutions may be made by Special Agents of the Office of the Inspector General of the Department of Health and Human Services, Federal Bureau of Investigation, or any other federal law enforcement officer.

The Preliminary Injunction will remain in effect until further order of the Court.

SO ORDERED.

Dated at New Haven, Connecticut, July 30, 1999.

_____
Peter C. Dorsey
United States District Judge

EXHIBIT XXIX.
Example of HCFA Notice of Overpayment Based on Random Sampling

August 27, 1999

RE: COMPREHENSIVE MEDICAL REVIEW

Dear Physicians:

National Heritage Insurance Company (NHIC) as the Medicare Carrier for the state of Maine, Massachusetts, New Hampshire and Vermont is required by the Health Care Financing Administration (HCFA) to periodically conduct routine postpayment reviews on physicians' services which are billed to Medicare. The primary objective of this postpayment process is to identify providers who, for various reasons, appear to warrant an in-depth review in order to: 1) verify that reimbursements are made only for those services which are considered to be medically necessary, 2) identify problems regarding any unusual practice patterns and 3) rule out over utilization or abuse of the Medicare Program.

A *Statistically Valid Random Sampling (SVRS) review* was conducted on your use of procedure code 99285 (Emergency department visit for the evaluation and management of a patient, which requires these three components within the constrains imposed by the urgency of the patient's clinical condition and mental status: a comprehensive history; a comprehensive examination; and medical decision making of high complexity). All services included in our 1998 postpayment review processed for payment from August 1, 1996 through July 31, 1998.

Records were requested and reviewed on 201 beneficiaries. Our consultant's determination with regard to procedure code 99285 is as follows:

1. Scope of Audit for CPT Procedure Code 99285 (Emergency department visit for the evaluation and management of a patient, which requires these three components within the constrains imposed by the urgency of the patient's clinical condition and mental status: a comprehensive history; a comprehensive examination; and medical decision making of high complexity).

   A. This audit covers services that were paid by Medicare from August 1, 1996 to July 31, 1998.

   B. The audit revealed the following problems in your billing and practice patterns:

   o documentation in most records did not support the level of care billed as defined by the CPT.

   o occasionally documentation was missing such as the medical records, a dictated note and/or a handwritten note by the ER physician.

SVRS Letter W

2. Issues/Determinations

A nurse reviewer consulted during the audit process using documentation guidelines and CPT definitions. Claims and submitted records of 393 services were reviewed. The nurse reviewer determinations are detailed in the following discussion of issues and determinations:

- 50 or 13% of 393 services had documentation which supported procedure code 99285
- 179 or 46% of 393 services had documentation which supported a lower level procedure code 99284
- 92 or 23% of 393 services had documentation which supported a lower level procedure code 99283
- 41 or 10% of 393 services had documentation which supported a lower level procedure code 99282
- 9 or 2% of 393 services had documentation which supported a lower level procedure code 99281
- 21 or 5% of 393 services had no medical record, ER MD note or record was incomplete
- 1 or <1% of 393 services duplicate service billed

Based on available information, we believe you knew or should have known that the services were not medically necessary and reasonable. You knew or should have known that the services were not reasonable and necessary because documentation submitted for review was not sufficient to support the level of care billed as described in the CPT manual. Medicare will only pay for services that are determined to be "reasonable and necessary" under section 1862(a)(1) of the Medicare law. If Medicare determines that a particular service, although it would be otherwise covered, is "not reasonable and necessary" under Medicare program standards, Medicare will deny payment for that service.

We have made the determination that you were not "without fault" in causing the overpayment. Therefore, we are not waiving your obligation to repay. We cannot find you without fault because, the documentation does not substantiate the service which was billed. Pertinent information was available from the law and regulations section 1862(a)(1) of Medicare law, and published in articles titled:

"Physician does not submit documentation to substantiate that he performed services billed to program where there is a question as to whether they were actually performed."
MCM Section 7103.1

"Waiver of Liability"	Medicare B Newsletters	Oct 1991	page 4
"Waiver of Liability"	Medicare B Newsletters	July 1992	page 7
"Waiver of Liability"	Medicare B Newsletters	Apr 1994	pages 31-33
"Waiver of Liability"	Medicare B HealthResource	Feb/Mar 1996	pages 90-93

"A Message From The Medical Director" (re: documentation)
    Medicare B Newsletters   March 1994   page 1
"Documentation Guidelines For Evaluation and Management Services"
    Medicare B Newsletters   Nov 1994   pages 10, 22-30
"Evaluation and Management Services - Questions and Answers Related to Documentation Guidelines"
    Medicare B Newsletters   July/August 1995
"Focused Medical Review"   Medicare B HealthResource   May 1996   page 15
"Documentation Quality"   Medicare B HealthResource   Oct/Nov 1996   page 8

For your edification:

"Evaluation and Management Services; Documentation Guidelines"
        Medicare B HealthResource   August 1997   pages 1-23

"Evaluation and Management Services - review of documentation"
        Medicare B HealthResource   Oct/Nov 1997   page 14

3. Calculation of Overpayment

Summary of Data for Time Period in Review: August 1, 1996 - July 31, 1998

Procedure Code Reviewed: 99285

Summary of Sample and Universe of Claims

	Totals
Beneficiaries in sample	201
Beneficiaries in universe	2564
Total $ Paid in sample	$47,256.21
Total $ paid in universe	$456,251.18

Actual Overpayment Calculated from Sample

	Totals
$ denied should be (S/B) 99284	$7,846.67
$ denied should be (S/B) 99283	$6,513.43
$ denied should be (S/B) 99282	$3,771.98
$ denied should be (S/B) 99281	$933.94
$ denied no note or medical record	$1,487.93
$ denied no physical exam	$973.82
$ denied duplicate service billed	$124.96
$ denied no service by ER MD	$124.96
Total $ overpaid (actual)	$21,777.69

Projected Overpayment Calculated

A.

Total $ overpaid in sample divided by Total $ paid in sample = Percent (%) of $ overpaid in sample

For example: $21,777.69 divided by $47,256.21 =   46%

B.

% of $ overpaid in sample X total $ paid in universe = Projected overpayment across universe

For example: 46% X $456,251.18 = $209,875.54

Projected Overpayment Calculated

	Totals
A.) % overpaid per sample	46%
B.) Projected overpayment across universe	$209,875.54

Therefore an overpayment of $209,875.54 has been calculated. The list of sampled beneficiaries, date of service, procedure codes and overpayment is contained in the attachment of this letter.

As a Carrier for the Medicare Program, we are responsible for recovering overpayments. Therefore, in accordance with this responsibility, we are requesting that you refund the amount of $209,875.54 to the Medicare Program. Please make your check or money order payable to National Heritage Insurance Company, and direct it to the following department along with a copy of this letter using the enclosed self-addressed return envelope.

> National Heritage Insurance Company
> Post Office Box 9103
> Hingham, MA 02044 - 9103

The entire amount of $209,875.54 is expected within thirty (30) days of the date of this letter. If we do not hear from you within thirty (30) days, interest will accrue and any payments due on claims in process or submitted will be used to offset the overpayment obligation. Please be advised that in accordance with Public Law 97-248, interest will be assessed at the current rate of 13..25% on the amount due unless full payment is made within thirty (30) days. Any payment received or any amount offset from other payments due you, will be applied first to the accrued interest and then to the principal amount.

If you are unable to repay the amount within that time period, we are authorized to consider repayment in installments up to one hundred eight (180) calendar days based on financial hardship, or an Extended Repayment Plan (ERP) may be applied for and, if approved may extend the time over which a potential overpayment must be paid.

If repayment of the amount due, in a lump sum or on an approved installment plan is not forthcoming, HCFA may, at their option, forward the case to the Department of Justice or the Internal Revenue Services for collection or to the Office of Inspector General for consideration of suspension action.

If you feel the overpayment, as determined by the Carrier, is not justified and you wish to dispute our findings, you may do so by requesting a Hearing. You may request an in-person. You may attend the Hearing in person or send someone to represent you. Your representative can be anyone you choose. Please note on your request who will attend the Hearing. ***Your request for a Hearing must be sent to my attention. I will forward it to Hearing, who will then contact you to set up arrangements.*** If you do not wish to have an in-person Hearing, you are entitled to a Hearing over the telephone or you may ask that a decision be made based on the facts in the file. A copy of the decision will be sent to you.

However, if you choose to request a Hearing, it does not postpone repayment of the overpayment. If the amount due is not paid within the time frame mentioned above, interest will be applied and offset will be initiated. If the Hearing decision is favorable, all moneys collected from you will be refunded.

Should this improper billing practice continue, it is our responsibility to advise you that under the provisions of the Social Security Act, Section 1128(a) and 1128(b), as amended by Section 2105 of the Omnibus Budget Reconciliation Act of 1982 (Pub. L. 97-35) and Section 137(b)(2) of the Tax Equity and Fiscal Responsibility Act of 1983 (Pub.L. 97-248) that civil monetary penalties will be assessed if false or certain other improper claims or requests for payment are made from the Medicare program. Violators may be fined up to $2,000 as penalty for each false and improper item or service claimed and additional assessment of up to twice the amounts falsely claimed. This statue also permits an individual upon whom the Department imposes a civil monetary penalty or assessment to be suspended from participation in the Medicare and Medicaid programs.

I would like to thank you for your anticipated cooperation in this matter. Should you have any questions, please contact me at (207) 294-4300 extension.

Sincerely,

Mary L. Gabriele, RN
Utilization Review Analyst
Medical Review for Program Safeguards

CC: Schwartz, Shaw and Griffith
Attn: Paul W. Shaw
Attorneys at Law
30 Federal Street
Boston, Massachusetts 02110-2508

EXHIBIT XXX.
Example of Appeal to a Carrier for Hearing

DR. JOHN JONES'
APPEAL REGARDING THE
TENNESSEE CARRIER'S
SEPTEMBER 1, 1998 AND FEBRUARY 1, 1999 AUDIT
DETERMINATIONS

Respectfully Submitted,

Robert A. Griffith
BBO # 211900
Jerome Tichner
BBO # 640838
Schwartz, Shaw & Griffith
30 Federal Street
Boston, Massachusetts 02110-2508
(617) 338-7277
October 28, 1999 (617) 338-1923 FAX

INTRODUCTION:		1
STATEMENT OF FACTS:		3
ANALYSIS		5

    A.   The Carrier's LMRP Restricts and Conflicts With U.S. Statutes, Federal Regulations and Medicare Guidelines and as such 142 of the Carrier's denials should be reversed 5

        1.   <u>Tennessee Law</u> 5

        2.   <u>Podiatric Services are covered by Medicare</u> 5

        3.   <u>HCFA Restricts the Carrier's Ability to Enact LMRPs</u> 7

        4.   <u>The Carrier's LMRP restricts national policy regarding the reimbursement of podiatrists and as such should be disregarded</u> 8

    B.   Even In the Face of this Inappropriate LMRP, the Carrier's own Rules Dictate That At Least 34 of the Carrier's Denials for Failure to Obtain an Attending Physician's Written Order Should be Overturned 10

        1.   <u>The Carrier Has Indicated That Debridement of Mycotic Nails Is a Specifically Covered Service</u> 12

        2.   <u>As Dr. Jones' Records Documented Mycosis, Pain Causing Difficulty with Ambulation and/or Infection These Debridement Procedures Were Covered Services</u> 13

    C.   The Notes Contained Within the Dr. Jones' Medical Records Fully State His Patients' Medical Conditions As Well As Any Relevant Medical History. 14

    D.   Ten of the Carrier's Denials Were Based Upon the Carrier's Faulty Conclusion that Evaluation and Management Services Were Not Properly Documented. 16

        1.   <u>As Dr. Jones has Clearly Performed E&M Services On the Patient's In Question, He Is Entitled to Reimbursement for His Services</u> 17

    E.   The Carrier's Denials Based Upon Assertions that Dr. Jones' Documentation Failed to Indicate Pain, or that Dr. Jones Performed the Claimed Procedure are Incorrect. 23

    F.   Any of the Carrier's Assertions that Dr. Jones' Treatments Represented Routine Care are Incorrect Due to the Symptomatic Nature of These Patient's Conditions 25

        1.   <u>The Three Services Denied</u> 25

        2.   <u>By definition, symptomatic care is non-routine</u> 25

        3.   <u>Review of Documentation Distributed by the Tennessee Carrier Supports the Claim That Symptomatic Care is Not Routine Care</u> 27

        4.   <u>Asymptomatic services are reimbursable in the presence of class findings</u> 28

    G.   The Carriers denials with regard to the treatment of Patient 20 on 02/01/97. 30

CONCLUSION 30

INTRODUCTION:

Pursuant to 42 C.F.R. 405.821, Dr. John Jones[1] ("Dr. Jones" or "The Petitioner") has claimed an appeal from the actions taken by Tennessee's Medicare Part B Carrier, Cigna Healthcare ("the Tennessee Carrier" or "the Carrier") in seeking a refund for certain payments made by the Carrier in 1997. In accordance with 42 C.F.R. 405.830, this document represents part of Dr. Jones' submission to the Hearing Officer assigned by the Carrier to review these determinations.

The Carrier has performed audits regarding payments made by the Carrier to Dr. Jones in 1997. An initial review was performed on a "non statistically valid sample" of 15 beneficiaries ("the Sub Sample") which resulted in a projected potential overpayment of $418, 902.65. (*See* Exhibit 1). Dr. Jones challenged this audit and requested that a statistically valid random sample ("SVRS") be reviewed. The Carrier's analysis of the SVRS resulted in an overpayment determination which was detailed in a March 1, 1999 letter. (*See* Exhibit 1). Within its March 1, 1999 letter, the Carrier asserted that Dr. Jones had received overpayments in a total amount equaling $418,638.63. This total represents a combination of $415,075.80 in overpayment regarding the SVRS and $3,562.83 in actual overpayment from the Sub Sample. In documents accompanying the Carrier's September 1, 1999 and February 1, 1999 letters a "Reason for Action" is disclosed for each assertion of overpayment. These "Reason for Action" disclosures provide the specific bases for the Carrier's overpayment determinations. Dr. Jones, herein discusses the appropriateness of each of these Reasons for Action and asserts that a majority if not all of the reasons upon which the Carrier's overpayment determinations are founded are inappropriate. The specific "Reasons for Action" were as follows:

- 61 of 75 code submissions from the SVRS and 81 of 94 code submissions from the Sub Sample were denied as a result of the following Reason for Action: "There is no documented order from the attending physician for this service. Therefore, this service is denied."

- 6 of the 75 code submissions reviewed in the SVRS and 4 of the 94 code submissions reviewed in the Sub Sample were denied as a result either of the following Reasons for Action: "There is no evaluation and management service documented on this date of service" or "[t]here is no documentation of any evaluation and management service being provided. Therefore the service is denied."

- 3 of the 75 code submissions from the SVRS were denied as a result of either of the following Reasons for Action: "[n]o documentation of pain/difficulty with ambulation. Documentation does not support service billed." or "[t]he documentation submitted does not show that this patient had any secondary infection or pain with ambulation. Therefore, this service is denied."

---

[1] Dr. Jones is a fictional individual whose name is utilized solely for the purpose of this example. All references to patients and particular dates of service are also fictitious.

- 2 of the 75 code submissions from the SVRS and 6 of the 94 code submissions from the Sub Sample were denied as a result of either of the following Reasons for Action: "There is no documentation supporting that a debridement of 6 or more nails was performed", "There is no documentation of a debridement of 6 or more mycotic nails on this date.", "There is no documentation supporting debridement of nails","There is no documentation to support payment for this service," or "There is no criteria documented to support payment of this service."

- 3 of the 75 code submissions from the SVRS were denied as a result of the following Reason for Action: "This service appears to be routine foot care. Documentation does not show that class findings were present. Therefore, this service is denied."

- 3 of the 94 code submissions from the Sub Sample were denied as a result of the following Reason for Action: "No Documentation Provided for this date of service."

STATEMENT OF FACTS:

Dr. Jones is an approved Medicare provider with a regional office located at 1 Main Street, Nashville, TN. Prior to Cigna's recent review, Dr. Jones had never been the subject of a pre- or post-payment review or any type of corrective or recovery action by the Medicare program.

During the course of his practice, Dr. Jones engages in the evaluation and treatment of symptomatic foot conditions. Unlike many podiatrists, Dr. Jones' practice focuses primarily on the treatment of patients suffering from severe conditions and symptoms. Virtually every one of Dr. Jones' patient's is suffering from severe mycosis of the nails coupled with other symptoms. Demonstrating the level of severity of the conditions of these patients, Attached as Exhibit 2 are photographs of the feet of a number of the patients referenced in this matter.

Often, Dr. Jones' patients reside in nursing homes. Dr. Jones' treatments generally involve the performance of one or more of a variety of procedures as dictated by the medical needs and conditions of each of his patients. The Nursing Homes where Dr. Jones provides services desperately need and rely upon his services, a number of nurses and physicians have written letters regarding the value and types of services provided by Dr. Jones have indicated the supervision/ordering of treatment. (See Exhibit 3). Specifically, Dr. Jones' treatments may or may not include, but are not limited to, nail debridement, lesion debridement, ulcer debridement and in some instances routine care. When appropriate, Dr. Jones submits bills to Medicare for his provision of these services.

On or around February 1, 1997 a Local Medical Review Policy ("LMRP") regarding "PRN" Orders" in nursing homes was made effective by the Carrier. A PRN order generally represents an order by a patient's attending physician stating that the patient is to receive an indicated type of medical care as needed. Specifically, the LMRP issued by the

Carrier stated:

> Medicare will not cover/pay for EM services, procedures or other services rendered in a nursing home in compliance with a PRN standing order...
>
> **Document Requirements:** There should be a specific order for services requested from another provider, this may be written by the attending physician or give[n] telephonically and signed later on.

Cigna, Medicare Bulletin GR96-6, November/December, 1996,
TN Insert Page 13 (Attached as Exhibit 4) (emphasis added).

This LMRP provided the basis for the Carrier's denial of 142 of Dr. Jones' claims.

ANALYSIS

A. The Carrier's LMRP Restricts and Conflicts With U.S. Statutes, Federal Regulations and Medicare Guidelines and as such 142 of the Carrier's denials should be reversed

1. <u>Tennessee Law</u>

Dr. Jones is a licensed podiatrist in Tennessee and as such is entitled to perform all of the services discussed under the laws and rules regarding podiatrists in that state. In Tennessee a Podiatrist is one who "examines, diagnoses or treats medically, mechanically or surgically, the ailments of the human foot...." <u>Tennessee Board of Registration in Podiatry</u>, *General Rules Governing the Practice of Podiatry*, Ch. 1155-2. Additionally, these rules define the scope of podiatric practice as follows: "any person in Tennessee who possesses a valid and current license in Podiatry issued by the Board has the right to use the title licensed podiatrist." *Id.* Ch. 1155-2-.02. All of the services performed by Dr. Jones, and at issue here, fall under these definitions and were performed while he held a valid license in Tennessee.

2. <u>Podiatric Services are covered by Medicare</u>

As a threshold issue, there is no question that in the absence of some clear exclusion, podiatric services of the type rendered by Dr. Jones are covered by the Medicare program. It is axiomatic that Medicare will pay for "medical and other health" services performed by a physician. In turn, Congress has defined the term "physician" as including "a doctor of podiatric medicine...with respect to functions which he is legally authorized to perform as such by the State in which he performs them." 42 U.S.C. 1395x(r).

Additionally, federal regulations recognize podiatric services as falling within the definition of physicians' services:

> **42 C.F.R. § 410.20 Physicians' Services**
>
> (a) *Included services.* Medicare Part B pays for physicians' services, including diagnosis, therapy, surgery, consultations and home, office, and institutional calls.
>
> (b) *By whom services must be furnished.* Medicare Part B pays for the services specified in paragraph (a) of this section if they are furnished by one of the following professionals who is legally authorized to practice by the State in which he or she performs the functions or actions, and who is acting within the scope of his or her license....
>
>   (1) A doctor of medicine or osteopathy...
>   (2) ....
>   (3) **A doctor of podiatric medicine**.
>
> (C) *Limitations on services.* The services specified in paragraph (a) of this section may be covered under Medicare Part B if they are furnished within the limitations specified in §§410.22 through 410.25

42 C.F.R. § § 410.20 (emphasis added)

Even the "limitations on services" discussed within this federal regulation act to incorporate podiatric services within the definition of physicians' services. 42 C.F.R. § 410.25 states:

> Medicare Part B pays for the services of a doctor of podiatric medicine, acting within the scope of his or her license, if the services would be covered as physicians' services when performed by a doctor of medicine or osteopathy.

42 C.F.R. § 410.25

Moreover, the Health Care Financing Agency ("HCFA"), following these statutes and regulations, includes podiatry within the definition of physicians and recognizes that the services performed by podiatrists are reimbursable.

> A doctor of podiatric medicine is included within the definition of 'physician,' but only with respect to those functions which he is legally authorized to perform in the state in which he performs them. This means that the professional services provided by a doctor of podiatric medicine within the scope of his applicable state license....are 'physician's services' payable under the Fee Schedule....

Podiatrists' Services, CCH-EXP, MED-GUIDE, ¶3110.67.

The primary effect of these statutes, federal regulations and Medicare guidelines is to ensure that the full panoply of podiatric medical services are reimbursable by the Medicare program unless otherwise excluded by law. The only enumerated services that have been excluded are those not reasonable and medically necessary, the provision of orthopedic shoes or other supportive devices for the feet, treatments for flat feet, prescriptions for supportive devices, treatments for subluxations and routine foot care in some circumstances. *See* 42 C.F.R. §411.15.

3. <u>HCFA Restricts the Carrier's Ability to Enact LMRPs</u>

Carriers are prevented from enacting policy that would in any way limit, restrict or conflict with existing national policy regarding reimbursement. The Medicare Carriers Manual ("Carriers Manual"), HCFA's instructions/guidelines to carriers, directly states that, "[A] LMRP must be clear, concise, **and not restrict or conflict with national policy**." Medicare Carriers Manual, §7501.2 (emphasis added).

Furthermore, the Carriers Manual further narrows the scenarios under which Carriers' enactment of LMRPs is appropriate by suggesting that LMRPs are to be enacted only when national policy does not exist regarding a particular issue. Specifically, the Carriers Manual states that, "**In the absence of national policy**, [a LMRP] is generally developed to specify criteria that describes whether the item/service is covered and under what clinical circumstances it is considered to be reasonable, necessary and appropriate." *Id.* (emphasis added). The clear purpose of these guidelines is to proscribe Carriers from overriding national policies regarding coverage established by Congress and HCFA.

In light of these HCFA instructions, a LMRP that is enacted when national policy exists is most likely inappropriate and a LMRP that in any way limits, restricts or conflicts with national policy is clearly improper and should be disregarded.

4. <u>The Carrier's LMRP restricts national policy regarding the reimbursement of podiatrists and as such should be disregarded</u>

As described in detail above, U.S. statutes, federal regulations and Medicare guidelines set forth the national policy that podiatrists are to be treated as physicians for reimbursement purposes. Restating from above, 42 C.F.R. § 410.20 further establishes the national policy that, subject to particular exclusions established by statute, regulation and HCFA, "Medicare Part B pays for physician's services including diagnosis, therapy, surgery, consultations and home, office, and <u>institutional calls</u>." 42 C.F.R § 410.20. Detailed review of the laws and regulations regarding physician reimbursement, reveals that there appear to be no specific requirements that any physician treating a patient at a nursing home obtain authorization form that patient's attending physician prior to providing services to that patient. A Government Accounting Office Report summarizes HCFA's rules regarding nursing homes and states that "under HCFA's provision's for reimbursement, providers can bill Medicare directly, without the nursing facility or attending physician affirming whether the items were necessary or provided as claimed." *GAO Report,* GAO/HEHS-96-18, Med Guide 1996-1 Med-Guide-TB ¶ 44,015, January 24, 1996.

It is clear, therefore that pursuant to national policy, physicians (podiatrists included) are entitled to receive reimbursement for services provided to patients in nursing homes without those patients' attending physicians' authorization so long as those services are otherwise covered services (i.e., not otherwise be excluded under federal laws, regulations or HCFA rules). In contrast, under the Carrier's LMRP, and regardless of whether or not a service is otherwise covered under Medicare, a physician may only be reimbursed if he or she has particular documentation exhibiting an authorization for the service by the patient's attending physician. This LMRP, therefore, severely limits national policy regarding the reimbursement of physicians. The sweeping manner in which this LMRP limits national policy is evidenced by the fact that **under this LMRP ANY otherwise reimbursable service may be disallowed by the Carrier** so long as specific authorization by the attending physician is not documented.

By requiring authorization and documentation otherwise not required by Medicare the Carrier has inappropriately limited national reimbursement policy. Once again, HCFA directs that:

> [A] LMRP must be clear, concise, **and not restrict or conflict with national policy**."

Medicare Carriers Manual, §7501.2 (emphasis added).

This policy should be disregarded as inappropriate and each of the 142 denials based upon failure to document an order from the attending physician should be reversed.[2]

B. **Even In the Face of this Inappropriate LMRP, the Carrier's own Rules Dictate That At Least 34 of the Carrier's Denials for Failure to Obtain an Attending Physician's Written Order Should be Overturned**

Even under this LMRP, the Carrier's denials with regard to 34 claims were incorrect under the Carrier's own policy statements. These specific claims are as follows:

#	Patient Name	Date of Service	Code Submitted
1	Patient 2*	06/01/97	11721
2	Patient 3*	07/22/97	11721
3	Patient 5*	07/20/97	11721
4	Patient 7*	06/01/97 10/01/97	11721 11721
5	Patient 8*	06/01/97	11721

---

[2] Hearing Officers' authority with regard to LMRPs is discussed in detail in HCFA-Pub. 60AB, (March 1, 1997).

#	Patient Name	Date of Service	Code Submitted
6	Patient 9*	06/01/97 08/01/97 10/01/97	11721 11721 11721
7	Patient 10*	06/01/97 07/01/97	11721 11721
8	Patient 11*	06/01/97 08/01/97	11721 11721
9	Patient 12*	02/01/97 06/01/97 08/01/97	11721 11721 11721
10	Patient 13*	06/01/97	11721
11	Patient 14*	02/01/97 04/01/97 07/01/97 09/01/97	11721 11721 11721 11721
12	Patient 15*	02/01/97 04/01/97 07/01/97	11721 11721 11721
13	Patient 16*	08/01/97 11/01/97	11721 11721
14	Patient 17*	02/01/97 05/01/97 07/01/97 09/01/97	11721 11721 11721 11721
15	Patient 1	09/01/97	11721
16	Patient 3	03/01/97	11721
17	Patient 8	04/01/97	11721
18	Patient 9	09/01/97	11721

* Indicates patients from the Sub Sample

In March, 1997 the Carrier publicly issued podiatry billing guidelines in a document entitled "Meeting Medicare." (See Exhibit 4). Within this document, the following was stated:

> Medicare, under certain circumstances, will allow coverage for the treatment by debridement of mycotic nails in the absence of a systemic condition. It is not necessary for a patient first to be diagnosed by an M.D. or D.O. for the presence of a systemic condition before receiving treatment of mycotic nails. Therefore, **providers will not need to report a referring/treating M.D. or D.O. on the claim for treatment of mycotic nails (CPT codes 11720, 11721).**

Cigna, Meeting Medicare, Podiatry, Pg. 4, March, 1997. See Exhibit 4.

Under the Carrier's own policy, therefore, any of Dr. Jones' claims for the debridement of mycotic nails did not require an authorization by an attending physician. As the Carrier has established this exception to its own LMRP, the only remaining issue with regard to these claims is whether they are otherwise appropriately reimbursable under the codes submitted by Dr. Jones. Dr. Jones asserts that each of these claims was appropriate.

    1.   <u>The Carrier Has Indicated That Debridement of Mycotic Nails Is a Specifically Covered Service</u>

The Carrier has clearly stated that debridement of mycotic nails is a covered service if performed upon patients exhibiting particular symptoms. *See* Cigna, Meeting Medicare, Podiatry, Pg. 4. (March, 1997) (Exhibit 4). Specifically, this publication established that where a patient has "markedly thickened toenail(s)" resulting in pain **and/or** secondary infection (paronychia-soft tissue infection) debridement shall be considered a covered service. *See* id. Although the Carrier stated within this publication that for coverage of debridement procedures both infection and pain are required to accompany markedly thickened nails, the Carrier contradicts itself and states that **either pain or infection** is a sufficient precursor for coverage when accompanying thickened nails. Specifically, the Carrier went so far as to provide an example of an appropriate claim for debridement which established that **either pain or infection** was sufficient. This example contained the following statement:

> This example represents a claim for Debridement of Mycotic Nails, in which the patient meets coverage criteria of a diagnosis of mycotic nails and severe pain that causes marked limitation of ambulation.

Cigna, Meeting Medicare, Podiatry, Pg. 10, March, 1997. (Exhibit 4)

Note that within this example, which is clearly intended for use as a guideline by podiatrists, the Carrier stated that coverage criteria was met without any indication of infection. As the Carrier specifically instructed providers that debridement of mycotic nails was a covered service where mycosis was diagnosed and where pain affecting ambulation was noted, this is the standard upon which Dr. Jones' claims for debridement must be judged.

    2.   <u>As Dr. Jones' Records Documented Mycosis, Pain Causing Difficulty with Ambulation and/or Infection These Debridement Procedures Were Covered Services</u>

Examination of the records regarding Dr. Jones' debridement claims reveals that **severe mycosis resulting in thickened nails and pain causing difficulty with ambulation was indicated for each claim submitted.** (*See* Exhibit 5). As such, Dr. Jones' debridement procedures were covered services and, as discussed above, under the Carrier's own rules Dr. Jones was not required to indicate or obtain authorization from any other physician. Regardless of whether the Carrier's inappropriate LMRP is applied here, under the carrier's own rules in the 34 cases where Dr.

Jones performed debridement on patients whose records clearly indicate severe mycosis causing pain/difficulty with ambulation and/or infection, the Carrier's denials should be overturned.

C. **The Notes Contained Within the Dr. Jones' Medical Records Fully State His Patients' Medical Conditions As Well As Any Relevant Medical History.**

A number of issues raised by the Carrier stem from the Carrier's review and interpretation of Dr. Jones' medical records. Specifically, these records reflect the details of the examinations and services performed by Dr. Jones, the relevant medical conditions of these patients and indications of negative medical findings (e.g., the lack of edema, etc.). In general, Dr. Jones' records consist of a standard paragraph detailing certain common findings (e.g., thickened painful nails) along with lists of potential symptoms, conditions and class findings with relevant findings circled. Additionally, virtually every record also contains handwritten notations from Dr. Jones providing further detail regarding his patient's conditions.

The primary reasoning for the use of this format is the fact that **every patient for whom a form was used was suffering from severe mycosis causing nail thickening and pain**. As stated above, Dr. Jones' practice is unusual in that the patients he treats are primarily suffering from severe conditions. Importantly, although these forms allow the efficient recording of symptoms commonly shared by Dr. Jones' patients (e.g., mycotic painful nails), the data contained within each of these records speaks to the individual treatment, symptoms and diagnoses of these patients. The data included within these records must be appropriately analyzed and taken into consideration when reviewing the appropriateness of Dr. Jones' billing.

The fact that the Dr. Jones' records are in "checklist" format do not reduce their value in supporting Dr. Jones' submitted claims. Checklists of this sort are not prohibited by HCFA regulations or guidelines and in fact are utilized by numerous hospitals and other providers in the documentation of patient treatment. Such checklist formats enable providers to maintain organized data designed to allow easy tracking of patient improvement, tracking of significant patient illness and compliance with Medicare billing requirements[3]. In general, where providers treat numerous patients suffering from common symptoms or conditions, the use of forms such as this allows providers to avoid wasting significant amounts of time writing out the symptoms common to each patient. This practice enables providers to focus their efforts more on patient treatment than on the repetetive aspects of documentation while still allowing the providers the ability to effectively track and indicate each patient's individual condition, history, etc.

---

[3] For example, many of Dr. Jones' records set forth the particular class findings in their respective categories. This enables Dr. Jones to easily determine whether class finding requirements have been satisfied.

D. **Ten of the Carrier's Denials Were Based Upon the Carrier's Faulty Conclusion that Evaluation and Management Services Were Not Properly Documented.**

The Tennessee Carrier denied 10 claims[4] on the grounds that "There [was] no evaluation and management service documented on [the] date of service[5]." The specific patients, the codes submitted and the dates of service regarding these claims are as follows:

#	Patient Name	Date of Service	Code Submitted
1	Patient 4	01/01/97	99301
2	Patient 5	11/01/96	99301
3	Patient 7	12/01/96	99302
4	Patient 8	12/01/96	99302
5	Patient 9	12/01/96	99303
6	Patient 13	09/01/97	99312
7	Patient 3*	12/01/96	99303
8	Patient 7*	01/1/97	99312
9	Patient 9*	12/01/96	99302
10	Patient 15*	12/01/96	99313

* Patients from "Non Statistically Valid" Sub Sample

Contrary to the Carrier's assertion, the medical records for these patients clearly establish that Dr. Jones performed the Evaluation & Management ("E&M") services claimed. *See* Exhibit 5. The records for these services demonstrate that Dr. Jones ascertained that each patient was suffering from mycosis causing thickened painful nails. Additionally, each of these records contains Dr. Jones' recordings of the presence of other relevant symptoms and relevant patient history. For example, these records contain indications regarding which of the patients' feet, if any, exhibited subungual debris, whether the patients exhibited difficulty in walking, whether the patient suffered from peripheral vascular disease ("PVD") or whether the patient had Hammertoe Digit Syndrome ("HDS"). Dr. Jones' notation of these conditions acts as clear evidence that he performed E&M services upon these patients.

---

[4] Note that four of these claims were denied from the "non statistically valid" sample and are included in the Carrier's claim of overpayment as actual overpayments. Six claims were reviewed and denied as part of the "statistically valid sample" and are included in the Carrier's extrapolation calculations.

[5] Note that the grounds for denial of these six claims from the "statistically valid sample" reads as follows, "There is no evaluation and management service documented on this date of service. Also, use of the modifier is incorrect as there is no separately identifiable E/M service documented. Therefore, this service is denied."

1. <u>As Dr. Jones has Clearly Performed E&M Services On the Patient's In Question, He Is Entitled to Reimbursement for His Services</u>

The codes Dr. Jones submitted for his E&M services were appropriate and as such, he is entitled to reimbursement. It is clear that as with any other providers, podiatrists should be entitled to some compensation for the time and effort required to evaluate and manage their patients' conditions. The E&M codes in question are defined as follows:

99301	**Establishment and management** of a new or established patient involving an annual nursing facility assessment which requires these three key components: • **a detailed interval history;** • **an comprehensive examination;** • **medical decision making that is straightforward or of low complexity.**
99302	**Establishment and management** of a new or established patient involving an annual nursing facility assessment which requires these three key components: • **a detailed interval history;** • **a comprehensive examination;** • **medical decision making of moderate to high complexity;**
99303	**Establishment and management** of a new or established patient involving an annual nursing facility assessment which requires these three key components: • **a comprehensive history;** • **a comprehensive examination;** • **medical decision making of moderate to high complexity;**
99312	**Subsequent nursing facility care**, per day, for the evaluation and management of a new or established patient, which requires at least two of these three components: • **an expanded problem focused interval history;** • **an expanded problem focused examination;** • **medical decision making of moderate complexity.**
99313	**Subsequent nursing facility care**, per day, for the evaluation and management of a new or established patient, which requires at least two of these three components: • **a detailed interval history;** • **a detailed examination;** • **medical decision making of moderate to high complexity.**

American Medical Association, CPT'97, Pg. 29-32

Dr. Jones argues that as codes 99301-99303 are generally used for the initial evaluation of patients in nursing facilities and as he performs this function to the extent that it is appropriate within his profession, he should be entitled for reimbursement under these codes.

Podiatrists are generally restricted from engaging in full physical examinations of their patients as full examinations are generally outside of the scope of podiatry. Accordingly, podiatrists generally engage in more moderate examinations generally focused on patients' lower extremities. Currently, however, the definitions of the codes in question allow for the use of codes 99301-99303 only where comprehensive examinations are performed.[6] As podiatrists may not generally engage in full body examinations the issue arises as to what CPT code represents the appropriate vehicle for podiatrists to be fairly compensated for their initial evaluations of patients in nursing facilities. Note that the introduction and definitions of codes 99301-99303 do not excluded their use in podiatry. The only other codes that may be appropriate in these circumstances are codes 99311-99313 which, are designated for "subsequent nursing facility care" but indicate treatment of "new" patients. *See* AMA, CPT'97, Pg. 30-32. Specifically, the introduction for Subsequent Nursing Facility Care states that codes 99311-99313 "are used to report the services provided to residents of nursing facilities who do not require a comprehensive assessment, and/or who have not had a major, permanent change of status. Id. at 30.

As it is clear that Dr. Jones provided E&M services to these patients, and as it is clear that podiatrists should be entitled to some compensation for the time spent on evaluating and managing their patient's care, Dr. Jones requests that his claims for E&M services be allowed. If, however, it is determined that Dr. Jones shall not be compensated for reimbursement under codes 99301-99303 it is appropriate and fair that he at least be reimbursed under codes 99311-99313.

An analysis of each of the ten claims in question follows:

Patient 4, DOS: 1/01/97, Code: 99301:

The record for Patient 4 exhibits that Dr. Jones identified that the patient presented with painful, thickened,

---

[6] A comprehensive examination is defined as " a general multi-system examination or a complete examination of a single organ system. The following organ systems are recognized:
- Eyes
- Ears, nose, and throat
- Cardiovascular
- Respiratory
- Gastrointestinal
- Genitourinary
- Musculoskeletal
- Skin
- Neurologic
- Psychiatric
- Hematologic/lymphatic/immunologic"

American Medical Association, CPT'97, Pg. 7-8

mycotic nails, that Dr. Jones tested both the dorsalis pedis and posterior tibial pulses of the patient, that subungual debris was noted on both feet and that the patient exhibited onychocryptosis of the right hallux nail. This record exhibits that Dr. Jones examined this patients feet carefully and recorded relevant findings. This record clearly establishes, contrary to the Carrier's grounds for denial, that Dr. Jones performed significant E&M services on this date.

Dr. Jones argues that the condition of this patient, the history taken and Dr. Jones' thorough evaluation of this patient's feet entitles him to reimbursement under CPT code 99301. In the alternative, Dr. Jones should otherwise be reimbursed under CPT code 99312 which has a **clinical example** stating "Scheduled follow up visit with an afebrile [i.e.,having normal temperature] demented resident who has a mild cough, requiring no change in the medical plan of care." See AMA, CPT'97, Pg. 31. This clinical example offered by the CPT'97 represents a condition considerably less severe than treatment of a nursing home resident experiencing pain and limited ambulation. Consequently, Dr. Jones' services should be reimbursed at no less than a 99312 level.

Patient 5, DOS: 11/01/96, Code: 99301:

The record for this patient exhibits that Dr. Jones identified a painful area on the patient's 5th digit, left foot (lateral), that there was serous drainage and pain but that no infection or purulent drainage was present. Additionally, Dr. Jones noted that the patient suffered from mycotic nails. Although discussions regarding patient history were held with nursing facility staff and competent patients, no medical history relevant to the podiatric treatment of this patient was obtained. This record establishes, contrary to the Carrier's ground's for denial, that Dr. Jones performed significant E&M services on this date.

Dr. Jones' evaluation and treatment of this patient entitles him to reimbursement under CPT code 99301. In the alternative, Dr. Jones should be reimbursed under CPT code 99312 which has a **clinical example** stating "Scheduled follow up visit with an afebrile [i.e.,having normal temperature] demented resident who has a mild cough, requiring no change in the medical plan of care." See AMA, CPT'97, Pg. 31. This clinical example offered by the CPT'97 represents a condition considerably less severe than treatment of a nursing home resident experiencing mycosis, pain and serous drainage. Consequently, Dr. Jones' services should be reimbursed at no less than a 99312 level.

Patient 7, DOS: 12/01/96, Code: 99302:

The record for this patient exhibits that Dr. Jones identified that the patient presented with painful, thickened, mycotic nails, that Dr. Jones tested both the dorsalis pedis and posterior tibial pulses of the patient, that subungual debris was noted on both feet and that the patient had hammertoes. This record exhibits that Dr. Jones examined this patients feet carefully and recorded relevant findings. Although discussions regarding patient history were held with nursing facility staff and competent patients, no medical history relevant to the podiatric treatment of this patient was obtained. This record clearly establishes, contrary to the Carrier's grounds for denial, that Dr. Jones performed significant E&M services on this date.

Dr. Jones' evaluation and treatment of this patient entitles him to reimbursement under CPT code 99301 (original code submitted: 99302). In the alternative, Dr. Jones should be reimbursed under CPT code 99312 which has a **clinical example** stating "Scheduled follow up visit with an afebrile [i.e., having normal temperature] demented resident who has a mild cough, requiring no change in the medical plan of care." See AMA, CPT'97, Pg. 31. This clinical example offered by the CPT'97 represents a condition considerably less severe than treatment of a nursing home resident with mycosis, pain and hammertoes. Consequently, Dr. Jones' services should be reimbursed at no less than a 99312 level.

(SUMMARIES FOR THE SEVEN OTHER PATIENTS HAVE BEEN OMITTED)

E. **The Carrier's Denials Based Upon Assertions that Dr. Jones' Documentation Failed to Indicate Pain, or that Dr. Jones Performed the Claimed Procedure are Incorrect.**

The Carrier denied 11 claims for nail debridement upon the grounds that either Dr. Jones' records failed to demonstrate that the patient exhibited pain or that Dr. Jones' records failed to demonstrate that Dr. Jones performed the debridement services claimed. These assertions by the Carrier are simply incorrect. Review of the documentation for these claimed services clearly reveals that Dr. Jones' records indicate both the presence of pain/difficulty with ambulation for each of these patients and that debridement was performed. Additionally, Dr. Jones' use of these debridement codes was appropriate under the Carrier's rules regarding mycotic nail debridement. The specific patients, dates of services and eleven claims submitted for these seven patients are as follows:

#	Patient Name	Date of Service	Code(s) Submitted
1	Patient 5	01/1/97	11721
2	Patien 14	12/1/96	11700 11701
3	Patient 17	06/1/97	11721
4	Patient 19	09/1/97	11721
5	Patient 3*	12/01/96	11700 11701
6	Patient 7*	12/01/96	11700 11701

#	Patient Name	Date of Service	Code(s) Submitted
7	Patient 15*	12/01/96	11700 11701

* Indicates patients from Sub Sample

Initially, each of the records for these submitted claims contains the information that the Carrier declares is undocumented. As Dr. Jones practice solely entails the treatment of individuals suffering from severe pedal ailments which <u>invariably include mycotic conditions</u>, Dr. Jones utilized standard forms to assist him with his documentation. Restating from above, Dr. Jones forms generally include standard statements to the effect that the patient presented with mycotic nails causing pain/difficulty with ambulation. As each and every patient treated suffers from these symptoms, this statement whether circled, hand written or typed as part of the form applies to each of the patient's treated by Dr. Jones and at issue here. The Carrier's assertion that no pain/difficulty with ambulation was noted within these record's is incorrect.

Additionally, within each of these patients' records Dr. Jones has circled the appropriate foot upon which debridement was performed. Therefore, contrary to the Carrier's declaration that no notation of debridement existed, Dr. Jones has specifically indicated that debridement occurred and upon which foot it was performed. As each of these records clearly contains indications of pain/difficulty with ambulation and debridement procedures the Carrier's denial of these claims should be reversed.

Not only were these claims appropriately documented but the documentation supported coverage of the debridement codes submitted. As each of these patients presented with mycotic nails and pain causing limited ambulation the Carrier's rules regarding coverage of mycotic nail debridement establish that these treatments are covered services. *See above*, Part B discussion of mycotic nail debridement.

F. **Any of the Carrier's Assertions that Dr. Jones' Treatments Represented Routine Care are Incorrect Due to the Symptomatic Nature of These Patient's Conditions**

The Carrier denied 3 of Dr. Jones claims on the basis that the services rendered appeared to be routine foot care. Not only are the Carrier's assertions about these 3 particular claims incorrect and any attempt to characterize any of the services at issue here as routine foot care is incorrect due to the symptomatic nature of each of Dr. Jones patients.

1. <u>The Three Services Denied</u>

Each of the three services denied on "routine care" grounds were performed upon Patient 17 on either 6/01/97 or 9/01/97. The codes submitted were for the avulsion of nail plates (Codes 11730 and 11731). Specifically, Patient 17 presented on both of these occasions exhibitng mycotic nails, onychcryptosis (specifically "severe" on 6/24/97), pain upon palpation and shoe wear, subungual debris bilaterally and an ingrown nail on 6/24/97. These conditions represent significant sympomatic conditions and establish that Dr. Jones' services fell outside of the scope of routine care.

2. By definition, symptomatic care is non-routine

Medicare defines routine foot care as:

> The cutting or removal of corns, or callouses, the trimming of nails routine hygienic care (preventative maintenance care ordinarily within the realm of self care), and any service performed in the **absence of localized illness, injury or symptoms involving the feet.**

42 C.F.R §411.15(l)(i) (Emphasis supplied)

This definition is substantially similar to the position statement drafted by the Government/Federal Health Policy Committee of the American Podiatric Medical Association (AMPMA) and distributed in March of 1994:

> Routine foot care is the cutting or removal of **asymptomatic** corns and callouses, the trimming of nails , and other hygiene care in the realm of self care, such as cleaning, soaking and applications of skin creams.

Reported in APMA News, Volume 15, Number 5, May 1994. (Emphasis supplied).

Both of the above definitions of routine foot care serve to emphasize that while routine services a patient could reasonably expect to perform on his or her own will not be covered by Medicare, **symptomatic medical care is not considered routine.** As a result, payment may not be denied for the removal of corns and calluses, the trimming of nails, the debridement of nails and other services generally denominated routine care **in the presence of pain and/or other conditions affecting ambulation.**[7] Stated another way, the presence of pain and/or other conditions affecting ambulation necessarily takes the services outside the scope of routine care.

3. Review of Documentation Distributed by the Tennessee Carrier Supports the Claim That Symptomatic Care is Not Routine Care

The Tennessee Carrier issued policy statements during 1997 discussing the scope and billing of routine care.

---

[7]This interpretation is further buttressed by the fact that Medicare, through federal regulations, has stated that routine footcare does not include the cutting or removal of corns or callouses, the trimming of nails or other hygienic care which is performed as: (1) incident to, at the same time as, or as a necessary integral part of a primary covered procedure performed on the foot; or (2) as initial diagnositc services (regardless of the resulting diagnosis) in connection with a specific symptom or complaint that might arise from a condition whose treatment would be covered. 42 C.F.R. 411.6(l)(2)(iii).

[2]Close review of these publicly issued statements reveals that the Carrier's definition of routine foot care closely parallels Medicare's definition.

Within the Carrier's "Meeting Medicare, Podiatry" publication the Carrier defines routine foot care as including:

> C. Routine Foot Care (M0101)
> 1.
> 2. Routine foot care includes:
>   (a) the cutting or removal of corns or callouses;
>   (b) the trimming of nails, including mycotic nails;
>   (c) other hygenic and preventative self-care...
>   (d) any service performed in the absence of localized illness, injury or symptoms involving the feet.

Cigna, Meeting Medicare, Podiatry, Pg. 10, March, 1997.

As with Medicare's definition, the Carrier's definition of routine care emphasizes that **symptomatic medical care is not considered routine**. As a result, under the Carrier's definition, payment may not be denied for the removal of corns and calluses, the trimming of nails, and other services generally denominated routine care **in the presence of localized illness, injury, or symptoms involving the foot**.

The Carrier's definition further indicates that routine foot care involves treatment utilized for purposes of "hygenic and preventative self-care." This definition acts to exclude from its scope treatments utilized in the presence of localized illness, injury, or symptoms involving the foot from its scope. Consequently, Dr. Jones' treatment of this patient's nails falls outside the scope of routine care because the avulsion of painful mycotic nail plates represents treatment of current symptomatic conditions and was not for the purposes of preventative or hygenic care.

Although Dr. Jones does not dispute that treatments such as the trimming, cutting and debridement of nails may be considered routine, he asserts that the determinative factor of whether such services are within the scope of routine care is whether these services were performed in response to the presence of localized illness, injury or symptoms involving the foot. For, if such injury, illness or symptoms are present then Medicare's definition of routine care, the American Podiatric Medical Association's definition of routine care and significantly the Carrier's definition of routine care removes these types of treatments from the scope of routine care.

Any assertion by the Carrier that Dr. Jones' treatment of any of the patients at issue in the Carrier's audit is routine is incorrect because each of these patients presented with mycotic nails, pain and a variety of other problems that were fully documented with the record.

4. Asymptomatic services are reimbursable in the presence of class findings

In certain circumstances, even routine foot care is covered by Medicare. Medicare reimburses for the provision of routine foot care when the patient receiving care is compromised or at risk due to a systemic condition that has resulted in severe circulatory embarrassment or areas of densensitization in the legs and feet. These systemic conditions are known as "class findings." In essence, Medicare has recognized that in the presence of class findings such as peripheral vascular disease, diabetes mellitus, chronic thrombophlebitis, and peripheral neuropathies associated with malnutrition and vitamin deficiency, carcinoma, drugs and toxins, payment is proper because the performance of these otherwise routine services would become hazardous to the patient if not performed by a professional. Class findings represent special classifications for which payment will be made for routine services irrespective of whether or not the patient presents localized illness, injury or symptoms of the foot. Significantly, class findings are **not** the equivalent of "symptomatic" conditions.

As a result, in the context of the Medicare regulatory scheme, the Carrier must initially undertake a two-part inquiry when analyzing reimbursement claims. First, the medical reviewer must determine whether there is adequate documentation to demonstrate whether the patient presented with localized illness, injury or symptoms involving the feet. If the patient presents any such conditions or symptoms then the provider should be reimbursed for otherwise routine services such as the cutting of corns and calloues and the debridement of nails. If the patient presents without localized illness, injury or symptoms involving the feet, then the Carrier must take the additional step of determining whether class findings are present. If class findings are present, reimbursement is proper. If class findings are not present, the services are deemed routine foot care and payment is properly denied.

The Carrier's clearly adopts this approach in its publications and as such any claim denied on the basis of routine care must be evaluated for the potential of a class finding exclusion. *See* Cigna, Meeting Medicare, Podiatry, Pg. 2-4.

G. The Carriers denials with regard to the treatment of Patient 20 on 02/01/97.

The Carrier denied three claims submitted regarding the treatment of Patient 20 on the basis that records for the date of service, 02/01/97, were not provided to the Carrier. Dr. Jones conducted a second search of his records regarding the treatment of this patient on 02/01/96. The record for this date of service was located and is attached as Exhibit 6.

CONCLUSION

Scrutinization of Dr. Jones' records regarding these patients establishes that a majority, if not all, of the bases for the Carrier's denials are inappropriate. The Carrier's denials are primarily based upon the application of an overreaching local medical review policy, upon the disregard of documentation kept in a format utilized by numerous doctors, hospitals and other medical providers, and upon incorrect application of standards established by H.C.F.A and by the Carrier itself. A majority of these claims were appropriately submitted and as such should be approved.

EXHIBIT XXXI.
Example of Notice Describing Options for Consent Settlement Procedure

NHIC   **MEDICARE**

National Heritage Insurance Company

43 Landry Street • Biddeford, ME 04005

July 16, 1998

Dear Dr.

Under Section 1842 (a)(1)(C) of the Social Security Act, carriers under contract to the Health Care Financing Administration are authorized to "make......... audits of the records of providers of services as may be necessary to assure that proper payments are made under this part". We are responsible for conducting audits of physicians and suppliers to ensure that Medicare Part B claims have been billed and paid appropriately.

On October 14, 1997, your office and several nursing homes received our request for medical records. The purpose of this letter and attachments is to describe the steps involved in the audit process, to highlight problems in your billing and practice patterns identified as a result of our audit, and to outline the three (3) options available to you.

Our normal full-scale audit process entails the extensive review of records for a large number of randomly selected beneficiaries. However, in the interest of economy and expediency for both you and the Medicare program, as a first step, we elected to perform a limited audit. We reviewed claims and medical records for services rendered to 20 beneficiaries over a 12 month time period, from September 14, 1995 to September 5, 1996. While the 20 beneficiaries were randomly selected for our sample from a larger universe of beneficiaries for whom you provided services, it is not considered to be a statistically valid random sample (SVRS). A SVRS normally involves a much larger sample.

You were chosen for an audit because statistical data indicated a significant utilization of the following procedure code(s): 99312 - Subsequent nursing facility care, per day, for the evaluation and management of a new or established patient, which require at least two of these three key components: and expanded problem focused interval history; an expanded problem focused examination; medical decision making of moderate complexity.

We selected the 20 beneficiaries by telling the computer the over utilized procedure codes. The computer was then instructed to include in the universe only those beneficiaries for whom you rendered and billed at least one of these procedure codes that was paid by Medicare during the review period. From this universe of beneficiaries, the computer randomly selected the beneficiaries to be included in the sample. All claims for the procedure codes at issue which were rendered to the sampled beneficiaries and paid within the time period were audited. The list of sampled beneficiaries, dates of service and procedure codes is contained in the attachment to this letter.

The 20 beneficiaries included in our audit resulted in 105 claims being paid by Medicare between January 1, 1996 and December 31, 1996. These claims and their corresponding medical records were audited, resulting in a potential overpayment of $35,586.89 including an actual overpayment of $2,237.94 for 20 beneficiaries. Item 3 under "Audit Results" explains how we calculated the potential overpayment. Please review the attached documents containing the audit results and options along with an explanation of the Extended Repayment Plan.

Based on the results of this audit we are requiring that you submit documentation with claims for procedure codes 99311, 99312, 99213 and 99232 billed to Medicare after August 14, 1998. This is to ensure that you are complying with the policies for the Evaluation and Management documentation guidelines. Copies of these policies are included in this mailing.

We must have your response to this letter within thirty (30) days of the date of this letter, by August 14, 1998. If we do not have any response from you within thirty (30) days, Option 3 will be chosen for you by default (see attached discussion of audit results). Be advised that by signing this letter your legal options may be affected. You may wish to have legal counsel review this letter before signing it. If you have any questions, please contact me at (207) 294-4300, extension 3034.

Sincerely,

Ruth Morin
Utilization Review Analyst
Medical Review for Program Safeguards

5 Enclosures

RM/Consent312.doc

Audit Results - 99312

Provider Name: | Date: 7/16/98

Provider Address:
|

Provider Number:

1. Scope of Audit

    A. This audit covers services that were paid by Medicare from January 1, 1996 to December 31, 1996.

    B. The audit revealed the following problems in your billing and practice patterns:

    o The documentation reviewed indicated that a brief history and exam with either a straightforward or moderate decision making was involved. See attached worksheets for each beneficiary reviewed.

    o No records were received for six patients, therefore these services are not payable.

2. Issues/Determinations

    A Nurse reviewer consulted during the audit process. Claims and submitted records of 106 services were reviewed. The nurse reviewer's determinations are detailed in the following discussion of issues and determinations:

    o 10 or 9% of the 106 services reviewed had documentation which supported procedure code 99312
    o 59 or 56% of the 106 services reviewed had documentation which supported a lower level procedure code 99311
    o 25 or 24% of the 106 services reviewed had no record submitted after request to nursing homes
    o 12 or 11% of the 106 services reviewed had no note in the medical record

Based on available information, we believe you knew or should have known that the services were not medically necessary and reasonable. You knew or should have known that the services were not reasonable and necessary because documentation submitted for review was not sufficient to support the level of care billed as described in the CPT manual. Medicare will only pay for services that are determined to be "reasonable and necessary" under section 1862(a)(1) of the Medicare law. If Medicare determines that a particular service, although it would be otherwise covered, is "not reasonable and necessary" under Medicare program standards, Medicare will deny payment for that service.

99312/Asaker_wb

Audit Results - 99312

We have made the determination that you were not "without fault" in causing the overpayment. Therefore, we are not waiving your obligation to repay. We cannot find you without fault because, the documentation does not substantiate the service which was billed. Pertinent information was available from the law and regulations section 1862(a)(1) of Medicare law, and published in articles titled "Waiver of Liability", In Medicare B Newsletters October 1991 and July 1992 and MCM Section 7103.1, "physician does not submit documentation to substantiate that he performed services billed to program where there is a question as to whether they were actually performed." Also enclosed is the "Documentation Guidelines for Evaluation and Management Services" published in November 1994 Medicare B Newsletter. For your edification I have also enclosed a copy of the August 1997 Special Edition Medicare B Newsletter regarding "Documentation Guidelines for Evaluation and Management Services."

3. Calculations:

A copy of our calculation worksheet is enclosed for your information. To calculate the <u>potential projected overpayment</u> amount for each denied procedure code, we used the following formulas:

Full Summary Data for Year in Review - All 5 Strata:

Total beneficiaries in universe	400
Total 99312 paid in universe:	$61,592.61

Summary of Samples in Each Stratum

	Stratum 1	Stratum 2	Stratum 3	Stratum 4	Stratum 5	Totals all Strata
Beneficiaries in sample	4	4	4	4	4	20
Beneficiaries in universe strata	180	72	87	52	9	400
Total $ Paid in sample	$283.93	$719.46	$890.27	$1,092.54	$1,295.40	$4,281.60
Total $ paid in universe strata	$12,784.76	$12,348.55	$19,513.19	$14,031.14	$2,914.97	$61,592.61

Actual Overpayment Calculated

	Stratum 1	Stratum 2	Stratum 3	Stratum 4	Stratum 5	Totals all Strata
$ denied should be (S/B) 99311	$37.75	$100.24	$188.59	$226.18	$188.27	$741.03
$ denied no note for this date in record	$0.00	$0.00	$80.72	$80.72	$323.35	$484.79
$ denied no record received	$162.38	$363.89	$202.27	$243.10	$40.48	$1,012.12
Total $ overpaid (actual)	$200.13	$464.13	$471.58	$550.00	$552.10	**$2,237.94**

AVG $ Overpaid:

A.

Total $ overpaid in stratum / Total $ paid in stratum sample =
Percent (%) of $ overpaid (per stratum)

For example: $200.13 / $283.93 =   70%

B.

Percent (%) of $ overpaid X Total $ in stratum universe =
Projected overpayment

For example: 70% X $12,784.76 = $8,949.33

C.

The sum of each projected overpayments for each universe stratum = Projected overpayment for universe

For example: $8,949.33 + $8,026.56 + $10,341.99 + $7,015.57 + $1,253.44 = $35,586.89

Projected Overpayment Calculated Across Universe

	Stratum 1	Stratum 2	Stratum 3	Stratum 4	Stratum 5	Totals all Strata
A.) % of $ overpaid (per stratum)	70%	65%	53%	50%	43%	C.
B.) Projected overpayment	$8,949.33	$8,026.56	$10,341.99	$7,015.57	$1,253.44	*$35,586.89*

The actual overpayment amount is $2,237.94. The projected procedure code potential overpayments, including the actual overpayment amount is $35,586.89.

4. Options

You must now select one (1) of the three (3) options explained below. Our normal audit process entails the routine use of Option Three. However, we are now making two (2) additional options available to you as a Consent Settlement.

Should you fail to notify us of your selected option, Option Three (election to Proceed to a Statistically Valid Random Sample) will automatically be selected for you by default. You should be aware that when a statistically valid random sample is selected for audit, records for all of the services at issue must be available for review.

Your response to the options listed below must be received within thirty (30) days from the date of this letter, August 14, 1998.

Regardless of the option selected, beneficiaries may not be billed for any of the overpayment amount.

Option One - Acceptance of Potential Projected Overpayment

You agree to refund the entire potential overpayment amount (which includes the actual overpayment for the sample beneficiaries) of $35,586.89 and do not wish to submit additional medical documentation. The potential overpayment amount may be paid by check written to National Heritage Insurance Company. Any balance not paid within thirty (30) days of the date you select this option will be subject to offset, whereby future Medicare payments made to you will be withheld and applied to the potential overpayment. An Extended Repayment Plan (ERP) may be applied for and, if approved, may extend the time over which a potential overpayment must be paid. Please refer to Attachment 5 for an explanation of the ERP. As explained in Item 5 below, interest will be assessed on any balance outstanding thirty (30) days from the date of this letter, which is August 14, 1998.

By selecting this option, you agree that there was a problem in your billing as identified by the carrier, you intend to correct this in future billings, and you understand the sampling methodology used and the methodology to project the potential overpayment. Because you agree that there was a problem and agree to make changes in your practice to address this problem, you waive your right to appeal the sampled individual overpayments, the potential overpayment resulting from the projection and the sampling procedures. The appeal rights you are waiving include a hearing before a Hearing Officer, an Administrative Law Judge, or in the Courts. You also waive any rights you have under Section 1870 and/or 1879 of the Social Security Act. (Please see Items 6 and 7 in this attachment for a discussion of these rights.)

Election of Option One means that, in the absence of fraud, we will not audit your claims for any procedure codes projected in our audit during the audit time frame again. In the event of fraud and/or if you fail to correct the identified problems, we reserve the right to audit prior years' claims and claims for any procedure codes for the time period considered in this audit.

Option Two - Acceptance of Capped Potential Projected Overpayment

You agree to repay the potential projected overpayment, including the actual overpayment on the sample beneficiaries, after providing additional medical documentation relevant to the 20 beneficiaries involved in our sample which was in existence at the time the services were rendered. This information would then be reviewed and would result in one (1) of three (3) decisions.

1) All services in contention could be determined to be appropriate and allowed as originally determined when the claims were processed, and the question of any potential overpayment would be eliminated; or

2) A portion of the services in question could be determined to be appropriate and allowed as originally processed, and the amount of the potential overpayment would decrease accordingly; or

3) The audit results could remain the same and the potential projected overpayment would then remain at $35,586.89.

You may request a meeting to explain the additional documentation or to provide other information relevant to the redetermination.

If you select Option Two, you agree to refund the revised potential overpayment amount, if any, which will not exceed the dollar amount calculated in Item 3 of this attachment and printed above. **The revised potential overpayment amount will not exceed this capped amount.**

The form and manner of repayment will be the same as that listed under Option One.

By selecting this option, you agree that there was a problem in your billing as identified by the carrier, you intend to correct this in future billings, and you understand how we reached the potential overpayment, i.e., you understand the sampling methodology used and the methodology to project the potential overpayment. Because you agree that there was a problem and agree to make changes in your practice to resolve this problem, you waive your right to appeal the sampled individual overpayments, the potential overpayment resulting from the projection and the sampling procedures. The appeal rights you are waiving include a hearing before a Hearing Officer, Administrative Law Judge, or in the Courts. You also waive any rights you have under Section 1870 and/or 1879 of the Social Security Act. (Please see Items 6 and 7 in this attachment for a discussion of these rights). Election of Option Two means that, in the absence of fraud, we will not audit your claims for any procedure codes projected in our audit during the audit time frame again. In the event of fraud and/or if you fail to correct the identified problems, we reserve the right to audit prior years' claims and claims for any procedure codes for the time period considered in this audit.

Option Three - Election to Proceed to a Statistically Valid Random Sample

If you do not choose either Option One or Two, we will proceed with Option Three. If we do not hear from you within thirty (30) days from the date of this letter, August 14, 1998, this option will be chosen for you by default. This is the second step in the audit process if you have been offered a consent settlement on a potential overpayment but do not accept the offer. This step utilizes a Statistically Valid Random Sample (SVRS) for the same universe or time period. Your right to appeal to a Hearing Officer, an Administrative Law Judge or to the Court remains if you should choose this option. Also, any rights available to you under Section 1870 and/or 1879 of the Social Security Act remain.

You should be aware that this option, either by your selection or by default, means that you will be required to submit medical documentation for _all_ of the services at issue in the SVRS (just as you would have had to do if we had not first offered you the opportunity for a consent settlement on a potential overpayment). You should also be aware that this option, whether selected by you or by default, withdraws the option of a consent settlement, as described in Options One and Two.

If you elect (or accept by default) Option 3, it is important that you understand the following information concerning our actions and your responsibilities with regard to the actual overpayments found for the claims involved in the limited audit:

- The potential projected overpayment referred to in this correspondence is based on a sample of 20 beneficiaries. We audited claims and medical documentation of the 20 beneficiaries in the sample to arrive at an actual overpayment for these claims. The actual overpayment amount was then projected to the universe of procedure codes to develop the potential projected overpayment. (See Item 3 above for the actual overpayment amount and the potential projected overpayment amount.)

- Options One and Two involved repayment of the potential projected overpayment, which includes the actual overpayment amount. Choosing Option Three does not eliminate your obligation to repay the actual overpayment. Recoupment of the actual overpayment identified for the claims in the limited audit will be pursued individually, but their recovery will be credited against any projected overpayment for the universe to which the claims belong. Your obligation to repay the overpayment for these claims will begin on the date of the official notification of overpayment. You will be notified of your appeal rights on these claims at this same time.

5. **Assessment of Interest**

We wish to make you aware, should you elect Option One, that interest will be assessed on any balance outstanding thirty (30) days from the date of your signed selection, or, if you choose Option Two, thirty (30) days from the date of the letter notifying you of a final potential overpayment, if any. Should you choose Option 3, interest will be assessed on any balance outstanding thirty (30) days from the date of the letter notifying you of a final overpayment determination. We must assess interest as provided in 42 CFR SS405.376. Interest will accrue on the unpaid balance for each thirty (30) day period (or portion thereof) that repayment is delayed. The current interest rate is 14.00%.

6. **Limitation of Liability**

Section 1879 of the Social Security Act (42 UCS SS 1395pp, 42 Code of Federal Regulations (CFR) SS411.406) permits Medicare payment to be made to providers on assigned claims for certain services otherwise not covered because they were not reasonable or necessary for the diagnosis or treatment of illness or injury or to improve the functioning of a malformed body member, or were custodial services if neither the beneficiary nor the physician knew, or could reasonably be expected to know, that the services were not medically necessary or were for custodial care. Services affected are those disallowed as not reasonable or necessary for the diagnosis or treatment of illness or injury, or to improve the functioning of a malformed body member and those disallowed as custodial services.

7. **Waiver of Obligation to Repay under Section 1870 of the Social Security Act**

Section 1870 of the Social Security Act (42 USC SS 1395gg, 42 CFR SS405.704(b) (14)) permits you to request waiver of an overpayment on the grounds that you were "without fault" with respect to causing the overpayment. This determination is made after Section 1879 (see Item 6 above) is considered.

If it is determined that you or the beneficiary knew or should have known that the service was not medically necessary and reasonable or constituted custodial care as described under the provisions of 1879, we address 1870 and determine whether you were "without fault" with respect to causing the overpayment.

8. **General**

We wish to ensure that you are aware of regulations and provisions of the law relating to continuation of the problems discussed herein. They include exclusion from the Medicare Program in accordance with SS 1128(b) of the Social Security Act (42 USC SS 1320 a-7), civil monetary penalties or other actions in accordance with SS 1128A of the Social Security Act (42 USC SS 1320a-7a), and/or, if appropriate, withholding payment under 42 CFR SS 405.370.

Your decision regarding this matter must be in writing and received by this office by August 14, 1998. If your decision is not received by the above-mentioned date, Option 3, Election to Proceed to a statistically Valid Random Sample, will be selected for you by default.

We have enclosed two copies each of the three option forms for your convenience. Select one of the options, complete and sign both forms corresponding to that option, and send them to my personal attention at the address shown below.

The physician must personally sign the forms. A signature stamp, or the signature of a staff member or attorney is not acceptable. After receipt of the two identical option forms with authorized signatures, we will in turn sign both forms and return one to you.

Ruth Morin
Utilization Review Analyst
Medical Review for Program Safeguards

43 Landry Street
Biddeford, ME 04005

(207) 294-4300, Extension 3034

Option One - Acceptance of Potential Projected Overpayment   Enclosure 2

I,

- have read the results of the audit findings in the letter dated July 16, 1998.

- understand the issues the carrier presented and the calculation of the projected potential overpayment and agree to settle the issue of a potential projected overpayment by refunding $35,586.89 to Medicare. This amount was derived by reviewing a sample of my claims and determining that a potential overpayment did exist within the universe of my claims.

- understand that if the settlement amount is not paid in full within thirty (30) days from the date I sign this agreement, the unpaid balance is subject to offset. I may apply for an Extended Repayment Plan and if approved, may make payments over an approved period of time.

- understand that interest on the amount accrues from the date I sign this consent agreement, but that this interest will be waived if repayment is made within thirty (30) days from the date I sign this consent agreement.

- understand that claims paid to me from January 1, 1996 to December 31, 1996 will not be audited in the future. I further understand that in the event of fraud and/or if I fail to correct the identified problems, the carrier reserves the right to audit prior years' claims and claims for any procedure codes for the time period considered in this audit.

I, _____, agree by settling this:

- That my right to appeal, which includes a Medicare part B Hearing Officer Hearing, Administrative Law Judge Hearing, or any Court appeals regarding this matter is waived I also understand any rights available to me under Section 1870 and/or 1879 of the Social Security Act are waived.

Overpayment instructions will be provided upon Medicare's receipt of the signed option agreement. Please do not enclose a check with the option form.

Physician signature: _____

Date signed: _____

Printed or typed name: _____

Title of signatory: _____

Carrier Representative signature: _____

Date signed: _____

Printed or typed name: _____

Title of signatory: _____

Please submit **both copies** of the selected option form, with original signatures, in the enclosed envelope. Upon completion, a file copy will be returned to you.

Option Two - Acceptance of Capped Potential Projected Overpayment   Enclosure 3

I,

- have read the results of the audit findings in the letter dated July 16, 1998.

- understand the issues the carrier presented and the calculation of the projected potential overpayment and agree to settle the issue of a potential projected overpayment by refunding a redetermined amount of up to $35,586.89 to Medicare. This amount was derived by reviewing a sample of my claims and determining that a potential overpayment did exist within the universe of my claims.

- have enclosed additional documentation which you will review for the purpose of redetermining the potential overpayment. I understand that I may request a meeting to explain the additional documentation or to provide other information relevant to the redetermination. I understand the redetermined potential overpayment, if any, will not exceed the amount shown above.

- understand that if the redetermined settlement amount is not refunded to Medicare within thirty (30) days from the date of the redetermined potential overpayment notice, the unpaid balance is subject to offset. I may apply for an Extended Repayment Plan and, if approved, may make payments over an approved period of time.

- understand that interest on the amount accrues from the date of the final potential overpayment determination, but that this interest will be waived if repayment is made within thirty (30) days from the date of the final potential overpayment determination.

- understand that claims paid to me from January 1, 1996 to December 31, 1996 will not be audited in the future. I further understand that in the event of fraud and/or if I fail to correct the identified problems, the carrier reserves the right to audit prior years' claims and claims for any procedure codes for the time period considered in this audit.

I, _____, agree by settling this:

- That my right to appeal, which includes a Medicare part B Hearing Officer Hearing, Administrative Law Judge Hearing or any Court appeals regarding this matter is waived I also understand any rights available to me under Section 1870 and/or 1879 of the Social Security Act are waived.

I, _____, do/do not (circle one) wish to request a meeting at this time to discuss the additional documentation I have submitted.

Physician signature: _____

Date signed: _____

Printed or typed name: _____

Title of signatory: _____

Carrier Representative signature: _____

Date signed: _____

Printed or typed name: _____

Title of signatory: _____

Please submit <u>both copies</u> of the selected option form, with original signatures, in the enclosed envelope. Upon completion, a file copy will be returned to you.

Option Three - Election to Proceed to a Statistically Valid Random Sample   Enclosure 4

I,

- have read the results of the audit findings in the letter dated July 16, 1998.

- elect to proceed to your full-scale audit process, involving a Statistically Valid Random Sample (SVRS) for the same universe of procedure codes and time period as the limited audit, as explained in the letter. I understand the full-scale audit process is the normal audit process, and that the limited audit was offered to me only in the interest of economy and expediency. Upon selection of Option Three, I understand that the offer of a consent settlement as stated in options One and Two is withdrawn.

- understand that I and/or my office staff will be required to submit medical documentation for all services at issue in the SVRS, upon request by the carrier.

- understand that all applicable appeals rights, including any right to a Hearing Officer Hearing, an Administrative Law Judge Hearing, or Court review are available to me. I also retain any rights available under Section 1870 and/or 1879 of the Social Security Act, as appropriate.

- understand that claims paid from the above-referenced limited audit will not be selected for inclusion in the SVRS; the SVRS will be a new and independent audit.

- understand that the overpayment identified for claims in the limited audit will be pursued on an individual basis, and that this overpayment will be subtracted from any overpayment resulting from the SVRS; that I will be provided with appeal rights regarding the overpayment amount on the claims in the limited audit at a later date; and that any interest on the overpayment amount on the claims in the limited audit will be calculated from the date of this later notice with appeal rights.

Physician signature: _____

Date signed: _____

Printed or typed name: _____

Title of signatory: _____

Carrier Representative signature: _____

Date signed: _____

Printed or typed name: _____

Title of signatory: _____

Please submit **both copies** of the selected option form, with original signatures, in the enclosed envelope. Upon completion, a file copy will be returned to you.

Enclosure 5

EXTENDED REPAYMENT PLAN (ERP)

As indicated, it has been determined by an audit that there is a potential overpayment amount due to Medicare. It is expected that you will remit the entire amount in one payment within thirty (30) days of the date you sign Consent Agreement Option One (Acceptance of Potential Projected Overpayment) or, if you select Consent Agreement Option Two (Acceptance of Potential Projected Overpayment), the date of the final potential overpayment determination, or, if you select Option Three (Election to Proceed to a Statistically Valid Random Sample), the date of the final overpayment determination. However, if you are unable to repay the amount within that time we are authorized to consider repayment in installments based on validated financial hardship. Installments can range from 2-6 months based on the amount of overpayment. You should be aware that if the repayment is not made within thirty (30) days, interest will be due. For Option One, interest accrues from the date you sign Consent Agreement Option One or, if you select Consent Agreement Option Two, interest accrues from the date of the final potential overpayment determination, or if you elect Option Three, interest accrues from the date of the final overpayment determination (see 42 C.F.R. 405.376). Interest will be waived if repayment is made within thirty (30) days of the applicable date cited above for the option chosen. The current rate of interest is 14.00%. If you wish to claim financial hardship you should contact me to obtain the Financial Statement of Debtor form (HCFA-379). This form must be completed and returned with your request for approval of an installment schedule. If compliance with the above is not acceptable to you, it is suggested that you seek a private or commercial loan to satisfy the obligation.

If repayment of the amount due, in a lump sum or on an approved installment plan, is not forthcoming, the Health Care Financing Administration may, at its option, forward the case to the Department of Justice or the Internal Revenue Service for enforced collection.

RM/Consent312.DOC

EXHIBIT XXXII.
Example of Chart of Investigation of Physician Practices

PATIENT MARY DOE.

#	Date of Treatment	Drugs Prescribed by Dr. John Doe (key to abbreviations on last page)	Total Daily Dosage Prescribed by Dr. John Doe	PDR Dosage & Admin. Range [A]	Dosing Guideline's Accepted Dosage (mg/day) [B]	Amount Supplied: (# of Days worth of Drugs)	Days Before Next Treatment
1	10/2/91	No Drugs Prescribed					26
2	10/28/91	Doxepin 25mg II hs #10	50mg	75-300mg	75-300mg	5	4
3	11/1/91	Doxepin 50mg II h.s. #10	100mg	75-300mg	75-300mg	5	18
4	11/19/91	Doxepin 50mg II h.s. #14 Buspar 5mg I t.i.d #21	100mg 15mg	75-300mg 15-60mg	75-300mg 15-60mg	7 7	10 10
5	11/29/91	Doxepin 50mg II h.s. #14 Buspar 10mg I t.i.d #21	100mg 30mg	75-300mg 15-60mg	75-300mg 15-60mg	7 7	4 4
	12/2/91	**Personality Evaluation by Dr. John Smith, Phd.**					
6	12/3/91	Prozac 20mg I a.m. #7 Doxepin 50mg II h.s. #14	20mg 100mg	20-80mg 75-300mg	10-80mg 75-300mg	7 7	7 7

1. Dr. John Doe treated Patient Mary Doe 13 times from 10/2/91 to 4/9/92. This represents a period of approximately 6 months.

2. On 9/13/90 Mary Doe taken to City Memorial Hospital by ambulance, found lying on ground at 4th and Jones Street complaining of abdominal pains.

3. On 2/9/91 Mary Doe claimed he ingested a large quantity of alcohol and was having difficulty breathing. City fire department responds and transports to St. Susan's hospital. The government identifies this as an OD.

4. Dr. John Doe wrote a total of 22 prescriptions during this period, none of which were for benzodiazepines.

5. The only drugs prescribed to Patient Mary Doe during this period were Buspar, Doxepin and Prozac.

6. Dr. John Doe treated Patient Mary Doe twice in October of 1991 (Treatments 1 & 2), three times in November of 1991 (Treatments 3,4 &5), twice in December of 1991 (Treatments 6 & 7), once in January of 1992 (Treatment 8), four times in February of 1992 (Treatments 9, 10, 11 &12) and once in April 1992 (treatment 13). Dr. John Doe did not prescribe any medication to Patient Mary Doe during Treatment #1. During Treatments 2 & 3 Dr. John Doe prescribed Doxepin to Patient Mary Doe. During Treatments 4 & 5 Dr. John Doe prescribed a combination of Doxipin and Buspar to Patient Mary Doe. During Treatments 6-13 Dr. John Doe prescribed consistent amount of Prozac (20mg I a.m. #7) and Doxepin (50mg II h.s. #14) to Patient Mary Doe, the only variation of which occurred during Treatments 12 & 13 whereupon Dr. John Doe increased Patient Mary Doe's Prozac prescription to 20mg I b.i.d.

7. Every drug prescribed to Patient Mary Doe during this period was prescribed in amounts that were either well within or below lower half of the acceptable PDR dosage and administration range.

8. Every drug prescribed to Patient Mary Doe during this period was prescribed in amounts well within or below the Dosing Guideline's range published in Primary Psychiatry in 1995.

EXHIBIT XXXIII.
Example of Position Statement Letter to U.S. Attorney's Office with Memorandum of Law

Schwartz, Shaw and Griffith

Attorneys at law

Robert A. Griffith
Paul W. Shaw
Harvey A. Schwartz

Gregory J. Aceto
Jonathan B. Bruno
James F. O'Brien
William C. Taussig
Jerome B. Tichner

Robin J. Dimieri, Esq., P.C.,
Of Counsel

October 10, 1997

Michael K. Loucks, Assistant United States Attorney
Susan G. Winkler, Assistant United States Attorney
United States Attorney's Office
1003 John W. McCormack Post Office &Courthouse.
Congress Street
Boston, MA 02109

Re: **John Doe, former General Manager,
Damon Clinical Laboratories, Inc., Any City, Any State**

Dear Mr. Loucks and Ms. Winkler:

We are writing about your decision to include John Doe in the group of former Damon officers and employees targeted for indictment.[1] Mr. Doe adopts the joint submission made by Wilkie Farr & Gallagher regarding Damon's alleged improper addition of laboratory tests, as well as the arguments made by attorney John Wall on behalf of William Smith. Those two submissions provide compelling reasons why the prosecution of Mr. Doe and the others should not proceed and would be fundamentally unfair given the regulatory framework that existed during 1988-1989.

The purpose of this submission is to focus on our client, John Doe, who was neither an officer, shareholder, regional manager, nor in a position to affect or determine policy at Damon. He was simply the manager of one of Damon's regional laboratories. During our conversations with you about this matter, the government has advised that John Doe is included within those targeted for criminal prosecution based solely on the fact that, at the direction of the corporate office, he drafted some document addressing the addition of ferritin tests to the Lab Scan panel in the fall of 1988.

---

[1] This letter is submitted pursuant to Fed.R.Evid. 410(4) and Fed.R.Crim.P. 11(e)(6).

30 Federal Street
Boston, Massachusetts 02110-2508

617 338 7277 Fax 617 338 1923
E mail: office@ssglaw.com
www.ssglaw.com

Michael K. Loucks, Assistant United States Attorney
Susan G. Winkler, Assistant United States Attorney
October 10, 1997
Page 2

Ferritin Was Added To The Lab Scan Panel
At The Direction Of The Corporate Office

The government has had the opportunity to meet and question Mr. Doe about his position with Damon and involvement in the addition of tests during his tenure with the company. It should be abundantly clear that he did not initiate the addition of the ferritin test to the Lab Scan panel during 1988 but was directed to do so by his regional manager after the test had been added by other regional offices and in particular the Dallas regional office. Indeed, the Government conceded this point in the October 1996 criminal information it filed against Damon, in which it charged that Mr. Doe was instructed to add ferritin to the Lab Scan profile.

United States District Court
District of Massachusetts

United States of America	)	Criminal No. 96-10256-REK
	)	Violation:
v.	)	18 U.S.C. §371
	)	Conspiracy to Defraud
Damon Clinical	)	The United States
Laboratories, Inc.	)	
Defendant	)	
	)	

INFORMATION

The United States Attorney Charges that:
...

Bundling Ferritin and Iron Tests

...
20b.   In or about early 1988, executive officers of Damon instructed employees of Any City, Any State laboratory to add the ferritin test to Lab Scan profile in order to generate increased revenue from the Medicare program.

---

[1] *United States v. Damon Clinical Laboratories,* No. 96-10256-REK, ¶20b.

Schwartz, Shaw and Griffith

Attorneys at law

Michael K. Loucks, Assistant United States Attorney
Susan G. Winkler, Assistant United States Attorney
October 10, 1997

It is beyond our comprehension why Mr. Doe is targeted for prosecution when other mid-level managers who similarly acted at the direction of their superiors will not be indicted, especially when you agree that in the entire history of the "labscam" probe by the various United States Attorneys' Offices, no employee has ever been charged with a criminal offense arising from this investigation, from the National Health Laboratories case to the present. It would be both unprecedented and unfair to charge an employee in the position of Mr. Doe, who was only following the directives of the company, with a federal criminal offense that will result in his being incarcerated for a significant period under the federal sentencing guidelines in the event of a conviction.[2]

Not only would a prosecution be unprecedented and unfair, but there is simply no basis for it. The facts the government now alleges relative to Mr. Doe are essentially contrary to the facts alleged by the government and filed in the criminal information against Damon. Neither is the government's most recent version of the facts supported by Damon's internal business records. The thrust of the information filed against Damon is that it billed for medically unnecessary tests for the objective of maximizing company revenues to offset Medicare fee reductions scheduled for April 1, 1988. The government alleged that in furtherance of this objective, five regional laboratories thereafter added the serum ferritin test to the Lab Scan:

---

[2] Mr. Doe faces certain imprisonment if convicted of any prosecution for conspiracy to defraud Medicare. You have stated that the amount of loss to Medicare from billings for ferritin from the Phoenix office was in the area of $5 million. This would put the Base Offense Level at 20 under the U.S.S.G § 2F1.1(b)(1)(O), resulting in a range of imprisonment of 33-41 months.

Schwartz, Shaw and Griffith

Attorneys at law

Michael K. Loucks, Assistant United States Attorney
Susan G. Winkler, Assistant United States Attorney
October 10, 1997
Page 4

#	Date	Act Alleged and Citation in Criminal Information
1	Early 1988	Executive officers instruct regional laboratories to bundle test with Lab Scan panel. Information. ¶20a.[3]
2	Early 1988	Executive officers instruct Any City laboratory to add ferritin to Lab Scan. ¶20b.
3	April 1, 1988	Dallas, TX, regional laboratory adds serum ferritin to the Lab Scan. ¶20h.
4	May 1, 1988	Berwyn, IL, regional laboratory adds serum ferritin to the Lab Scan. ¶20i.
5	May 15, 1988	Newbury Park, CA, regional laboratory adds serum ferritin to the Lab Scan. ¶20l.
6	May, 1988	San Francisco, CA regional laboratory adds serum ferritin to the Lab Scan. ¶20m.
7	Oct. 1, 1988	Any City, Any State regional laboratory adds serum ferritin to the Lab Scan. ¶20k.

As the foregoing table illustrates, by the government's own admission the Any City regional laboratory was the last of at least five regional laboratories to add ferritin to the Lab Scan panel (nine to ten months after "the executive directors . . . instructed . . . the regional laboratory in Any City, AZ to add the ferritin to the Lab Scan"). As the government well knows from the proffer sessions of other uncharged Damon executives, Damon Clinical Laboratories operated under a "highly centralized management structure." The structure was such that central management had software systems in place designed to 1) standardize the billing system in each regional laboratory, 2) ensure that no test was billed which was not performed, and 3) be in compliance with all payment regulations and

---

[3] All paragraph references in this table are to the information filed in *United States v. Damon Clinical Laboratories*, No. 96-10256-REK.

requirements. This system was company-wide and managed from Boston, not from Any City. Furthermore, Damon had a comptroller at headquarters whose duties included exercising judgment as to whether or not laboratory panels had to be billed as offered to the physicians or billed in any manner not conflicting with Medicare laws, regulations and carrier bulletins.

We wish to stress that just as Damon corporate executives instructed Any City to add the ferritin test to the Lab Scan, corporate approval and authorization would have been required to remove it. Therefore, while John Doe as the general manager of the Any City regional laboratory may have been required to gather the financial information from his regional accounting staff regarding the addition of ferritin, he was powerless to act on this information. We raise these factual assertions because they only serve to further highlight our contention that just as John Doe had nothing to do with implementing the addition of ferritins on a national basis, on the regional basis he merely gathered the information from many sources which was sought by corporate headquarters and transferred it to his superiors. It is our understanding that based upon this information and the information from the other regional laboratories that already had added ferritin to the Lab Scan, Damon made its decision to offer this particular panel in Any State.

Furthermore, even though John Doe was the general manager of the Any City laboratory, he nonetheless had to seek authorization to purchase the equipment to perform the ferritin test, despite the fact that four other regional laboratories had already implemented the Lab Scan with ferritin following corporate authorization. Simply stated the addition of ferritin to the Lab Scan was something Mr. Doe was expected to implement in Arizona absent a compelling reason otherwise. Where the government has already represented to the court that it was Damon's executive officers who instructed the Any City regional laboratory employees to add the ferritin test, John Doe certainly should not be charged in a scheme to defraud Medicare.

We also wish to draw your attention to the fact that Mr. Doe never directly profited from the addition of ferritin or any other tests. His bonus structure was based upon the overall operation of the Any City laboratory, and in fact he does not believe he ever received a bonus of more than several thousand dollars in any year. Indeed, at no time

Schwartz, Shaw and Griffith

Attorneys at law

Michael K. Loucks, Assistant United States Attorney
Susan G. Winkler, Assistant United States Attorney
October 10, 1997
Page 6

during his tenure as "General Manager" of the Any City office did he make more than $72,000 per year.

The Documents Relied Upon By The Government
Do Not Support Its Theory Of Prosecution.

The government has represented its case is supported by two specific documents which are allegedly indicative of criminal intent. These two documents, one from 1988 - the other from 1990, have been culled from thousands of documents provided by the Damon Clinical Laboratories. We submit that neither is the "smoking gun" the government asserts it to be.

1. Capital Expenditure Request (9-14-88)

The first document the government relies upon is the capital expenditure request for new equipment to perform the ferritin tests. This document is dated October 14, 1988. [DAM 0005895-96]. A capital expenditure request had to be completed by every regional office whenever new equipment purchases were proposed. The capital expenditure report completed by John Doe and submitted to his supervisor, Bill Smith, followed a standard informational format. The government has taken this memorandum completely out of context by focusing on the term "Revenue Enhancement" contained on the second page of the document. The government asserts that based on the information provided under this heading, John Doe knew or should have known the reason for adding the test to the panel was solely to increase revenues from Medicare.

We dispute this conclusion, because the government has completely ignored the remaining section of the document. For example in the cover sheet of Mr. Doe's memo to Mr. Thurston, Mr. Doe clearly articulates that the objective of adding ferritin and TSH was "[t]o strengthen our competitive posture in the marketplace." Mr. Doe reviewed the major variances between Damon's panel and those of its competitors, including MetPath and National Health. It was those competitive concerns which the corporate officers had instructed each regional laboratory to address and Mr. Doe complied with those

Michael K. Loucks, Assistant United States Attorney
Susan G. Winkler, Assistant United States Attorney
October 10, 1997
Page 7

instructions. Mr. Doe states, "[a]s can be gleaned from the above, we must position ourselves to respond to market needs."

You also allege this document demonstrates John Doe knew or should have known ferritin was a medically unnecessary test. This is based on the fact that prior to the addition of ferritin to the Lab Scan, the Any City office only billed approximately 150 tests to Medicare each month but that after it was added, the number rose to 2,500 per month. The government argues Mr. Doe either was or should have been put on notice by the increase that the ferritin test was medically unnecessary. We disagree the government's conclusion because such an increase would be expected when any test, and not just ferritin, was added to a panel. Indeed, the government's argument is deflated by the fact that Medicare itself never objected or denied any of these claims as being medically unnecessary, even when it was being billed for thousands of such tests in conjunction with the billing for a standard panel of tests that Medicare had never previously encountered in bills submitted by Damon.

It is our contention that the government's position ignores a significant amount of the evidence. The memorandum itself recites Mr. Doe's belief that adding ferritins offered a "more medically sound and beneficial" test than the common iron test, thereby giving Damon a "marketing edge over our competition." Indeed, the "Benefit" section of the memorandum states in full:

> In addition to offering more medically sound and beneficial procedures, this will give us a marketing edge over our competition. This will renew interest in existing profiles and force greater contact with existing clients, as well as potential for new ones. The final result of the changes will be realizing increased new revenues from our new features and benefits.

[DAM 0005895]. This supports Mr. Doe's statement during the proffer session that ferritin was added to enable Damon to compete economically with other labs and that he believed they were medically sound and beneficial.

While you may disagree with his belief, it is quite evident that Mr. Doe did not arrive at this understanding based upon his own knowledge. This understanding, however

Schwartz, Shaw and Griffith

Attorneys at law

Michael K. Loucks, Assistant United States Attorney
Susan G. Winkler, Assistant United States Attorney
October 10, 1997
Page 8

controversial the government may claim it to be, arose directly out of information provided to him as the general manager of the Any City laboratory. During his interview, Mr. Doe told the government that it was the lab director and medical director of the Any City laboratory who provided him with the information about the benefits of the ferritin test over other iron profiles. In fact, several other general managers were provided with similar information from their medical directors, as evidenced in their separate capital expenditure requests. Indeed, we know of no document circulated to any general manager claiming the ferritin test was not medically beneficial and there can be no disagreement that it is a beneficial test.[4] As indicated in the letter from attorney John Wall, the government has in its possession documents and articles supporting the position that ferritin had significant medical value as a coronary risk indicator. [See DAM 0030927-0030943].

The following comment by the OIG in 1996 confirms that Medicare was well aware that its regulations did not provide sufficient guidance on the issue of custom panels:

> . . . custom panels - packages developed by the laboratory that do not correspond with defined organ and disease panels - are still generally being billed as individual tests to Medicare. Current Medicare guidelines do not address the problem of custom panels as a marketing mechanism of the laboratory industry nor the problem of the industry billing the contents of custom panels individually. Also, HCFA's policies have not emphasized the medical necessity element in the processing of claims for clinical laboratory services.

"Follow-up Report to 'Changes are Needed in the Way Medicare Pays for Clinical Laboratory Tests," (Office of the Inspector General, January 1996), at I. That same report

---

[4] We have used the term "beneficial" rather than the term "necessary" because as Mr. Doe told the government, he was lead to believe ferritin was a beneficial test and he was never made aware of any significant difference between the term "beneficial" and "necessary". At this juncture, we would also like to draw your attention to the fact that the term "medically necessary" is not defined in the statute.

Schwartz, Shaw and Griffith

Attorneys at law

Michael K. Loucks, Assistant United States Attorney
Susan G. Winkler, Assistant United States Attorney
October 10, 1997
Page 9

noted that physicians ordered such added tests "because the patient could potentially benefit from the additional screening tests." Id. p.10.

2. <u>Great Lake Medical Group (1-9-90)</u>

You also assert that the January 8, 1990 letter from the attorney for the Great Lake Medical Group placed John Doe on notice that there was a potential problem with the Medicare billing. [DAM 000574-000574]. Once again, the government is reading far too much into this document. As Mr. Doe informed you during his proffer, prior to the letter being written, Great Lake had requested the requisition form be changed as a result of the 'sponsoring organizations' not wanting the ferritin test bundled with the basic panel. This was not a major issue for Mr. Doe, as Damon would have made a similar change for any physician who requested it. The mere fact the Great Lake 'insurers' did not want the ferritin or other specialized tests bundled with the standard profile would not cause a person in John Doe's position to believe that the bundling was improper.

Furthermore, although John Doe was the addressee of the letter, there should be no dispute that all negotiations with Great Lake were handled by the corporate office because of the size and complexity of the account. In fact, you have evidence demonstrating that Damon's corporate counsel, John Goodman, took credit for handling the Great Lake negotiations. [DAM 0049359-360]. Mr. Doe functioned solely in an operational capacity in servicing the Great Lake account, such as staffing and equipment decisions. As he explained during his proffer, upon receipt of the letter, he immediately passed it on to his superior for response, as he had already made the requested change to the requisition form, as indicated in the letter itself. As he explained, changing the requisition forms was simply accommodating a large account. It did not raise any "red flags" that bundling of the test was inappropriate or improper.

There is no evidence of criminal intent.

Michael K. Loucks, Assistant United States Attorney
Susan G. Winkler, Assistant United States Attorney
October 10, 1997
Page 10

There is simply no evidence of criminal intent on the part of John Doe. The conduct at issue was pervasive throughout the clinical laboratory industry and was viewed as being routine and acceptable. There was absolutely no reason for John Doe to be on notice that his conduct or that of Damon was improper, let alone illegal. While you opine that Mr. Doe is liable under the doctrine of "wilful blindness", it is respectfully submitted that the facts of this case cannot and do not warrant such a conclusion. See generally *United States v. Gabrielle*, 63 F.3d 61, 66 (1st Cir. 1995). We make this statement based upon several grounds. The first is that there were no facts which reasonably could have alerted Mr. Doe to the fact that Damon, as the government claims, was billing for unnecessary tests. As we discussed in detail above, Mr. Doe was informed by the Any City regional laboratories medical director that the test was medically beneficial . . . "it would be a good test to add." Any impression he was under regarding the benefits of the test were confirmed by the fact that four other regional laboratories had already added ferritin to the Lab Scan. Although the government continues to refer to the discrepancy between the number of ferritin tests performed before and after it was added to the Lab Scan, we question the strength of this argument for the reasons set forth above.

Conclusion

As representatives of the United States government, you have had the opportunity to meet John Doe. We are confident that you were left with the impression that he is a sincere, honest man who would not knowingly engage in criminal activity. Whatever your theories of criminal responsibility in the context of corporate employees may be, there can be no doubt that Mr. Doe never believed his conduct in relation to ferritin was wrong, much less criminal. Indeed, until the highly publicized indictment in the NHL case in December 1992, everyone in the laboratory industry believed bundling of tests was both appropriate and legal. In summation of our general contention regarding whether or not Mr. Doe was "wilfully blind," we stress that there were no "red flags" in 1988 that would lead a reasonable person in Mr. Doe's position as general manager of the Any City office to believe that the addition of ferritin to the Lab Scan, initiated and approved by corporate headquarters and previously implemented by four other regional laboratories, was inappropriate.

Michael K. Loucks, Assistant United States Attorney
Susan G. Winkler, Assistant United States Attorney
October 10, 1997
Page 11

Mr. Doe left Damon on October 1, 1992. Damon had gone through an unfriendly take-over and his last three years with them had not been enjoyable. Anticipating his leaving the business, on June 1, 1992, he and his wife started their own business, CorporateWear. This is a registered specialty advertising company that provides customized products and wearables for companies. To date, the Does have a very successful small business with five full-time employees.

We would conclude by citing to the Department of Justice's *Principles of Federal Prosecution*, as it is a compelling statement for why a prosecution should not be instituted:

> a determination to prosecute represents a policy judgment that the fundamental interests of society require the application of the criminal laws to a particular set of circumstances -- recognizing both that serious violations of federal law must be prosecuted, and that prosecution entails profound consequences for the accused and the family of the accused whether or not a conviction ultimately results." § 9-27.001.

We submit that the interests of justice would not be served by bringing a prosecution for conduct that occurred almost ten years in the past. For all the foregoing reasons and those advanced by affiliated counsel, we respectfully request that Mr. Doe not be indicted.

Very truly yours,

Robert A. Griffith

Paul W. Shaw

RAG\dmp

cc: Donald Stern, United States Attorney
Mark Pearlstein, First Assistant United States Attorney
James Farmer, Criminal Division Chief

EXHIBIT XXXIV.
Example of Declaratory Judgment Action

COMMONWEALTH OF MASSACHUSETTS

SUFFOLK, SS

SUPERIOR COURT DEPARTMENT
OF THE TRIAL COURT
CIVIL ACTION NO.

SOUTHEAST MEDICAL SERVICES GROUP,)
  a medical group practice partnership,)
  by its Members and Agent,)
    Plaintiffs)
)
    v.) **COMPLAINT**
)
L. SCOTT HARSHBARGER, Attorney General,)
  Defendant)

INTRODUCTION

1. This is an action for a declaratory judgment brought against the Massachusetts Attorney General by the members and agent of a Massachusetts medical group practice partnership known as Southeast Medical Services Group ("SMSG"). Through its members and agent, SMSG seeks a declaration that it is a valid group practice and permitted to pay "gatekeeper" fees, as more fully described below. A controversy exists with the Attorney General since his Medicaid Fraud Control Unit currently disputes the validity of SMSG's payment of "gatekeeper" fees and is preparing to bring suit against SMSG to recover sums paid.

PARTIES

2. Plaintiff Southeast Medical Services Group ("SMSG") is a general partnership formed under Massachusetts law with a principal place of business of 67 G.A.R. Highway, Somerset, Massachusetts.

3. Plaintiff Gregory Squillante ("Squillante") is an individual who resides in Somerset, Massachusetts and at all relevant times, has served as an agent of SMSG.

4. The remaining plaintiffs are all physicians and osteopaths and/or professional corporations comprised of physicians and osteopaths licensed to practice medicine in the Commonwealth of Massachusetts and all are members of the SMSG group practice. These plaintiffs are as follows (and are collectively referred to as "SMSG members"): Rajaratnam T. Abraham, M.D.; Rajaratnam T. Abraham, M.D., P.C.; Moustafa Ali, M.D.; Americo B. Almeida, M.D.; Somerset Medical Associates, Inc.; Greg Angell, M.D.; John Costa, M.D.; Robert Courey, M.D.; Murray Dimant, M.D.; Fares Gennaoui, M.D.; Debra Kimball, M.D.; Christopher Lebo, D.O.; Somerset Swansea Medical Center, Inc.; David Maddock, M.D.; Manuela Mendes, M.D.; Majed Mouded, M.D.; Majed Mouded, M.D., P.C.; Bassem Nasser, M.D.; Michael Nissensohn, M.D.; John Pedrotty, M.D.; John Pedrotty, M.D., P.C.; Richard Perkins, M.D.; Richard Perkins, M.D., P.C.; Frederick Schnure, M.D.; Gastroenterology Associates of Fall River and New Bedford, P.C.; Carmela Sofia, M.D.; Jesus Sosa, M.D.; Jose Sousa, M.D.; James Stubbert, M.D.; Donald Sutherland, D.O.; Elie Tawa, M.D.; Henry Vicini, M.D.; Fall River Family Practice Associates; and Stephen Zuehlke, M.D.

5. The defendant Attorney General is the chief law officer of the Commonwealth. By reason of Mass. G.L. c. 118E, § 44, the Attorney General is empowered to bring civil actions to enforce the state Medicaid statutes.

JURISDICTION

6. This court has jurisdiction over this matter pursuant to Mass. G.L. c. 231A, §§ 1-4 and its inherent equity powers.

STATEMENT OF FACTS

7. As stated above, the SMSG members are all physicians and osteopaths licensed to practice medicine in the Commonwealth of Massachusetts. All are actively engaged in the practice of medicine in the Fall River area of southeastern Massachusetts and all are or were partners in the Southeast Medical Service Group general partnership formed in July 1992 pursuant to a general partnership agreement. SMSG is a multi-specialty medical group practice modeled on the "group practice without walls" concept and composed of primary care and specialist physicians.

8. Physician members of a multi-specialty group practice are permitted to reimburse primary care physicians for services rendered in connection with patients who are referred to specialist members of the group practice. This is commonly called a "gatekeeper fee" system.

9. Between 1992 and 1994, SMSG established a gatekeeper fee system and paid such fees to various primary care physicians within the group practice.

10. The SMSG members all joined SMSG in reliance on the advice of counsel that the business organization was a valid partnership.

11. The SMSG members also believed in good faith that SMSG was validly organized as a medical group practice that operated in compliance with all applicable laws and regulations.

12. At all times the SMSG members believed the gatekeeper fee system complied with all applicable laws and regulations.

PRESENT CONTROVERSY WITH THE
DEPARTMENT OF THE ATTORNEY GENERAL

13. The Attorney General, through his Medicaid Fraud Control Unit, has taken the position that the SMSG partnership was not a legitimate group practice, but instead was a sham business organization created for the purpose of making referrals and receiving "kickbacks" that are prohibited by Mass. G.L. c. 118E, §41.

14. The Attorney General has further alleged that the SMSG members created SMSG knowing that it was not a legally constituted group practice.

15. The Attorney General has notified a number of third parties that the activities of SMSG are criminal and violative of both state and federal law.

16. The Attorney General has also threatened to bring a civil monetary penalty action against the SMSG members and its agents to recover civil fines and penalties for the alleged violations of state law in connection with the gatekeeper fee system.

17. The conduct of the Attorney General has called into question the continued viability of SMSG as a group practice, and SMSG is unclear as to whether or not it may continue to hold itself out as a group practice and otherwise pay gatekeeper fees.

18. An actual, justiciable controversy now exists between the parties concerning SMSG's right to continue operating as a group practice and to continue with the "gatekeeper fee" structure.

19. Unless this controversy is resolved shortly, the plaintiffs will continue to be threatened by the Attorney General and will sustain further losses to both their businesses

and reputations.

20. SMSG and the Attorney General can not settle the existing controversy without the aid of this Court's judgment as to whether or not SMSG constituted a group practice under existing law and regulation and whether payment of gatekeeper fees is permitted under Mass. G. L. c. 118E, §41.

WHEREFORE, the plaintiffs request this Court to:

a. Enter a declaratory judgment that the Southeast Medical Services Group is a legitimately constituted "group practice" under existing law and regulation.

b. Enter a declaratory judgment that SMSG's gatekeeper fee system did not violate the provisions of Mass. G.L. c. 118E, §41.

c. And grant such further relief as the Court may deem equitable and just in the circumstances.

Respectfully submitted,
Americo B. Almeida, M.D.
Somerset Medical Associates, Inc.
Majed Mouded, M.D.
Majed Mouded, M.D., P.C.
Frederick Schnure, M.D.
Gastroenterology Associates of
 Fall River and New Bedford, P.C.
Gregory Squillante

Respectfully submitted,
Moustafa Ali, M.D.
Greg Angell, M.D.
Jose Sousa, M.D.

BY: _____
ROBERT A. GRIFFITH
(B.B.O. No. 211900)
PAUL W. SHAW
(B.B.O. No. 455500)
Schwartz, Shaw & Griffith
Boston, MA 02114
(617) 227-2414

BY: _____
WILLIAM M. MANDELL, ESQ.
Pierce & Mandell
One Beacon Street
Boston, MA 02108
(617) 720-2444

Respectfully submitted,
   Robert Courey, M.D.
   Murray Dimant, M.D.
   Fares Gennaoui, M.D.
   Debra Kimball, M.D.
   David Maddock, M.D.
   Bassem Nasser, M.D.
   Michael Nissensohn, M.D.
   Carmela Sofia, M.D.
   Jesus Sosa, M.D.
   Donald Sutherland, D.O.
   Stephen Zuehlke, M.D.

BY: _____
   THOMAS J. BUTTERS, ESQ.
   Cullen & Butters
   One Beacon Street
   Boston, MA 02108
   (617) 367-2600

Respectfully submitted,
   Rajaratnam T. Abraham, M.D.
   Rajaratnam T. Abraham, M.D., P.C.
   John Costa, M.D.
   Christopher Lebo, D.O.
   Somerset Swansea Medical Ctr., Inc.
   Manuela Mendes, M.D.
   John Pedrotty, M.D.
   John Pedrotty, M.D., P.C.
   Richard Perkins, M.D.
   Richard Perkins, M.D., P.C.
   James Stubbert, M.D.
   Elie Tawa, M.D.
   Henry Vicini, M.D.
   Fall River Family Practice Associates

BY: _____
   WILLIAM A. BROWN, ESQ.
   50 Milk Street
   Boston, MA 02109
   (617) 482-1001

EXHIBIT XXXV.
Examples of Voluntary Disclosure Involving Employee Dishonesty

**BROWN
RUDNICK
FREED &
GESMER**

PAUL W. SHAW
ATTORNEY AT LAW

Direct Dial: (617) 856-8363
E-Mail: pshaw@brfg.com

http://www.brownrudnick.com

April 10, 2000

VIA MESSENGER

Bruce Bullen, Commissioner
Division of Medical Assistance
600 Washington Street -5th Floor
Boston, MA 02111

Re: <u>Notice of Potential Overpayments to the XYZ Hospital and Rehabilitation Center</u>

Dear Commissioner Bullen:

This office serves as counsel to the XYZ Hospital and Rehabilitation Center, Boston, MA. By way of this letter, we would like to advise the Division of the receipt of potential overpayments by XYZ Hospital ("ZYX") during 1998. As you may be aware, this past summer, the Board of Directors of XYZ replaced the President and Chief Financial Officer. Under the stewardship of the Board of Directors and the new administration, a review of the operations and billing practices of ZYX was initiated. In connection with this review of the claims submission process, it is believed that a number of claims were incorrectly and inappropriately coded for resubmission to the Division of Medical Assistance during the period of January - April 1998. After discovering that certain claim forms had been changed for resubmission to the Division, ZYX retained this law firm, which in turn retained an independent auditing firm to conduct a more detailed examination with the goal of determining the number of claims that had been changed.

The circumstances giving rise to this disclosure are as follows:

1. By January 1998, UNISYS on behalf of Medicaid had denied a number of claims submitted the preceding year for in-patient services because the principal diagnosis on the UB-92 claim form was for a "mental disorder." It appears that many of these claims that had a principal diagnosis of a mental disorder were denied by UNISYS, as ZYX was not a networked provider for psychiatric care with MBHP, the Division's contractor for mental health and substance abuse services.

A Partnership of
Professional Corporations

ONE FINANCIAL CENTER
BOSTON, MASSACHUSETTS 02111
617-856-8200
FAX: 617-856-8201

Hartford / Providence

Bruce Bullen, Commissioner
Division of Medical Assistance
April 10, 2000
Page 2

2.   In the Spring of 1998, senior fiscal personnel had a list of claims that had been denied by Medicaid based on Denial Code "539," which indicated it was denied because ZYX was not a MBHP provider. For each denied claim, employees within the billing department were instructed to make a copy of the system generated UB-92 claim form, to "white out" the principal diagnoses that had an ICD-9 diagnosis between #290-319 for "mental disorder," and to replace it with a non-mental disorder diagnosis appearing on the UB-92. According to the former billing manager, he was instructed to do so by his superior, who has since been terminated by ZYX. In conversations with staff, the former supervisor opined that the changes involved patients who came into the hospital with medical problems and therefor the diagnosis should be medical.

3.   Although the principal diagnosis code on the subject UB-92 forms was changed from a mental disorder code to a medical code, the "swapped" medical code was a valid diagnosis for each patient that had been coded by the Medical Records Department. In fact, it is submitted that while the procedure followed by the billing department to change the principal diagnosis code was inappropriate, certain of the resubmitted claims may have had an appropriate diagnosis code for the billing period involved.

As a result of the investigation by outside counsel, the Board of Directors and current administration have taken the following corrective actions. First, all senior staff involved have been terminated. One junior level billing supervisor who was directed by her superior to make the changes to the UB-92s has been reprimanded. In addition, independent of this concern, the new administration has been implementing a corporate compliance program with corresponding educational seminars. These efforts have been accelerated to address any outstanding concerns as soon as possible.

We would like to arrange a meeting with you to discuss this matter in greater detail.

Very truly yours,

Paul W. Shaw
Robert A. Griffith

PWS/og
cc: Board of Directors
       XYZ Hospital and Rehabilitation Center

BROWN RUDNICK FREED & GESMER

PAUL W. SHAW
ATTORNEY AT LAW

Direct Dial: (617) 856-8363
E-Mail: pshaw@brfg.com

http://www.brownrudnick.com

April 10, 2000

Paul D. Duplinsky, Manager
Program Integrity Unit
Associated Hospital Service of Maine
2 Gannett Drive
South Portland, Maine 04106-6911

Re: Notice of falsification of home care visits by a former employee of the XYZ Home Health Agency of Greater Boston, MA

Dear Mr. Duplinsky:

This office is counsel to the XYZ Home Health Agency of Greater Boston. It has been discovered that a registered nurse employed by XYZ falsified records of home care visits she allegedly provided. The employee, Sally Nurse, RN, was terminated on January 13, 1999.

Ms. Nurse was employed by XYZ Home Health from January 6, 1997 through January 13, 1999. She was hired as a psychiatric nurse on an hourly basis to provide home visits to patients in the Essex County area.[1] After a 30 day orientation period, Ms. Nurse was assigned a patient caseload on February 6, 1997. During her tenure with XYZ Home Health, Ms. Nurse averaged about 20 patient visits each week.

For every patient visit, each nurse is required to complete a patient encounter form detailing her findings, interventions and plan of care. XYZ Home Health requires that the patient/client sign the encounter form. These encounter forms are turned in daily or every other day to each nurse's supervisor, who reviews the document for completeness. During Ms. Nurse's tenure, her supervisor met with her on a regular basis. In July 1998, a new supervisor was assigned to the group of clinical nurses that included Ms. Nurse. This supervisor met weekly or bi-weekly with Ms. Nurse to discuss each of Ms. Nurse's patients and their continuing

---

[1] At the time she was hired, XYZ Home Health received letters of reference from her prior employers attesting to her clinical abilities. The Agency did a criminal record offender check as well as insured that she was currently licensed and in good standing with the Massachusetts and New Hampshire nursing boards.

A Partnership of
Professional Corporations

ONE FINANCIAL CENTER
BOSTON, MASSACHUSETTS 02111
617-856-8200
FAX: 617-856-8201

Hartford / Providence

Paul D. Duplinsky, Manager
Program Integrity Unit
Associated Hospital Service of Maine
April 10, 2000
Page 2

needs. Many of the patients assigned to Ms. Nurse had been with XYZ Home Health for an extended period and the supervisor herself had cared for a number of these patients. At no time during any of her regular meetings with Ms. Nurse did the supervisor have any indication that the visits were not being performed as claimed. All of the encounter forms were signed, and the supervisor had no reason to question the signatures. At no time prior to her termination did XYZ Home Health receive any calls or complaints from any patient or family member about Ms. Nurse not servicing the patient. Indeed, the agency received several letters from patients singling her out as being a good clinician and caregiver.

Ms. Nurse was terminated on January 13, 1999 after it was discovered that she had falsely reported three home visits for a patient who in fact was hospitalized at the time of the purported visits. After Ms. Nurse was terminated, her caseload was re-assigned to other nurses. Each nurse was asked to inquire of the patient whether Ms. Nurse had been to the patient's home and the frequency of her visits. While the patients serviced by Ms. Nurse are not the most reliable historians, it became apparent to the nursing staff from their questioning that Ms. Nurse did not provide the number of encounters that she had submitted paperwork for. For many, it was that she only saw the patient once a week or once a month when she claimed to have visited them several times a week.

In other cases, the situation was more egregious. For example, one patient was admitted on February 23, 1998 to be seen two or three times a week. Ms. Nurse submitted encounter forms for multiple visits each week from that date through the time of her termination. However, the patient reports she had not seen Ms. Nurse since July 1998. With another patient, although Ms. Nurse claimed she had visited the patient on a regular basis for a number of months, when the patient's family was contacted it was found that she was being serviced by another home health agency because Ms. Nurse had never returned after the initial visit some months before. For each of these visits, Ms. Nurse submitted a patient encounter form that contained a purported signature of the patient.

It is difficult at this stage of the review to accurately determine the number of falsified visits that were submitted by Ms. Nurse. Home Health has notified the nursing boards in both Massachusetts and New Hampshire about Ms. Nurse's conduct and requested that appropriate action be taken against her nursing license. We are continuing to review Ms. Nurse's caseload in an attempt to estimate which of the claimed visits did not occur. During her employment with XYZ Home Health, Ms. Nurse was diagnosed with a serious medical condition in May 1998 that caused her to be on medical leave for eight weeks (May 28, 1997 - August 4, 1997). While the

Paul D. Duplinsky, Manager
Program Integrity Unit
Associated Hospital Service of Maine
April 10, 2000
Page 3

administration of XYZ Home Health can not be certain, it does not appear that any problems with falsifying the encounters occurred prior to that date. The administration of XYZ Home Health would welcome any suggestions from Associated Hospital Service about how to identify the visits that were not performed.

We look forward to speaking to you at your earliest convenience about the situation.

Very truly yours,

Paul W. Shaw
Robert A. Griffith

PWS/og

cc: President/CEO
XYZ Home Health Agency
Ronald Ritchie, Program Integrity
Associated Hospital Service of Maine

EXHIBIT XXXVI.
Example of Plea Agreement

U.S. Department of Justice

United States Attorney
District of Massachusetts

Main Reception: (617) 748-3100

United States Courthouse, Suite 9200
1 Courthouse Way
Boston, Massachusetts 02210

January 13, 2000

BY HAND

ATTORNEY NAMES REDACTED

Dear Gentlemen:

This letter sets forth the Agreement between the United States Department of Justice and the United States Attorney for the District of Massachusetts (collectively the "United States"), and your client, ▓▓▓▓ INC., ("▓▓▓▓"), a Delaware corporation, (collectively referred to as "the Parties") as follows:

1. <u>Guilty Plea</u>

On or before January 19, 2000, or such other date as the Court may set, ▓▓▓▓ shall waive indictment and plead guilty to Count Two of the Information attached hereto as Exhibit A, which charges ▓▓▓▓ with a conspiracy to defraud the United States and one of its agencies, the Health Care Financing Administration, through the submission of false, fictitious and fraudulent claims to the Medicare Program, in violation of 18 U.S.C. Section 286.

2. Sentencing Guidelines

The United States and ▓▓▓▓▓ agree that the following provisions of the United States Sentencing Guidelines ("U.S.S.G.") apply to sentencing of ▓▓▓▓▓ with respect to Count Two of the Information:

    (a) pursuant to U.S.S.G. § 8C2.4(a), the loss to the United States from this offense for criminal sentencing purposes is $22,900,000;

    (b) pursuant to U.S.S.G. § 8C2.5, the culpability score is 7, calculated as follows:

        (1) base score of 5 pursuant to § 8C2.5(a);

        (2) add 4 points pursuant to § 8C2.5(b)(2)(A)(i) and (ii);

        (3) deduct 2 points pursuant to § 8C2.5(g)(2).

    (c) pursuant to § 8C2.6, the applicable range for a multiplier is 1.4 to 2.8, and the appropriate multiplier to be applied as to ▓▓▓▓▓ is 1.6.

    (d) the Parties agree that there is no basis for a departure under the Sentencing Guidelines, either upward or downward.

3. Agreed Disposition

The United States and ▓▓▓▓▓ agree pursuant to Fed. R. Crim. P. 11(e)(1)(C) that the following sentence is the appropriate disposition of Count Two of the Information:

    (a) a criminal fine in the amount of thirty six million six hundred forty thousand dollars, ($36,640,000) to be paid as follows:

        (1) an amount of eighteen million one hundred five thousand dollars ($18,105,000) shall be paid within 15 days of sentencing;

        (2) an amount of nine million two hundred sixty seven thousand dollars ($9,267,000) shall be paid on or before April 16, 2001; and

        (3) an amount of nine million two hundred sixty seven thousand dollars ($9,267,000) shall be paid on or before July 16, 2001.

(b) a mandatory special assessment of $400 pursuant to 18 U.S.C. § 3013, which shall be paid to the Clerk of Court on or before the date of sentencing.

███████ acknowledges that it is obligated, pursuant to 18 U.S.C. § 3612(f), to pay interest on that portion of the fine which is not paid on or before the fifteenth day after the Court enters judgment in this matter.

In light of the pending civil action, <u>United States ex rel. Jay A. Buford, et al. v. ███████ Inc., et al.</u>, Civil Action No. 95-10742-NG (D. Mass.), and the settlement agreement between ███████ and others and the United States relating to the civil action which is being signed contemporaneous with this Plea Agreement (the "civil Settlement Agreement"), the parties agree the complication and prolongation of the sentencing process that would result from an attempt to fashion a proper restitution order outweighs the need to provide restitution to the victims in this case, where, as here, the loss suffered by each of the federal health care programs will be recompensed from amounts paid as part of the civil Settlement Agreement. <u>See</u>, 18 U.S.C. § 3663(a)(1)(B)(ii). Therefore, the United States agrees that it will not seek a separate restitution order as to ███████ as part of the resolution of Count Two of the Information.

4. <u>No Further Prosecution of Defendant</u>

The United States agrees that, other than the charge in Count Two of the attached Information, it shall not further prosecute ███████ for conduct which (a) falls within the scope of the conspiracy which is charged in Count Two of the Information; (b) was within the scope of the grand jury investigation conducted by the U.S. Attorney; or (c) was known to the U.S. Attorney prior to the date of execution of this letter.

The U.S. Attorney expressly reserves the right to prosecute any individual, including but not limited to present and former officers, directors, employees and agents of ███████ in connection with the conduct encompassed by this Plea Agreement or within the scope of the grand jury investigation.

5. <u>Probation Department Not Bound By Agreement</u>

The Parties acknowledge that the disposition agreed upon by the Parties and their calculations under the Sentencing Guidelines are not binding upon the United States Probation Office.

6. <u>Fed. R. Crim. P. 11(e)(1)(C) Agreement</u>

███████'s plea shall be tendered pursuant to Fed. R. Crim. P. 11(e)(1)(C). ███████ cannot withdraw its plea of guilty unless the sentencing judge rejects this Plea Agreement. If the sentencing judge rejects the guilty plea, this Plea Agreement shall be null and void at the option of either the United States or ███████, except as set forth in Paragraph 8 below. If ███████'s guilty plea is withdrawn on ███████'s motion for any reason, this Plea Agreement shall be null and void at the option of the U.S. Attorney, except as set forth in Paragraph 8 below.

7. Civil and Administrative Liability

By entering into this Plea Agreement, the United States does not compromise any civil or administrative liability, including but not limited to any False Claims Act or tax liability, which ███████ may have incurred or may incur as a result of its conduct and its plea of guilty to Count Two of the Information.

8. Waiver of Defenses

In the event that ███████'s guilty plea is not accepted by the Court for whatever reason, or is later withdrawn for whatever reason, ███████ hereby waives, and agrees not to interpose, any defense to any charges brought against it which it might otherwise have under any statute of limitations or the Speedy Trial Act, except any such defense that ███████ may already have for conduct occurring before March 1, 1994, if charges are filed within 90 days of the date on which such guilty plea is rejected or withdrawn.

9. Breach of Agreement

If the United States Attorney determines that ███████ has failed to comply with any provision of this Plea Agreement, or has committed any crime between the date of this letter and the date of sentencing in this matter, the United States may, at its sole option, be released from its commitments under this Plea Agreement in their entirety by notifying ███████ through counsel or otherwise, in writing. The United States may also pursue all remedies available under the law, irrespective of whether it elects to be released from its commitments under this Plea Agreement. ███████ recognizes that no such breach by ███████ of any obligation under this Plea Agreement shall give rise to grounds for withdrawal of its guilty plea. ███████ understands that, should it breach any provision of this Plea Agreement, the United States will have the right to use against ███████ before any grand jury, at any trial or hearing, or for sentencing purposes, any statements which may be made by ███████ and any information, materials, documents or objects which may be provided by it to the government subsequent to this Plea Agreement, without any limitation.

10. Corporate Authorization

███████ shall provide to the United States and the Court a certified copy of a resolution of the Board of Directors of ███████ affirming that the Board of Directors has authority to enter into the Plea Agreement and has (1) reviewed the Information in this case and the proposed Plea Agreement; (2) consulted with legal counsel of ███████'s choice in connection with the matter; (3) voted to enter into the proposed Plea Agreement; (4) voted to authorize ██████ to plead guilty to Count Two of the attached Information; and (5) voted to authorize the corporate officer identified below to execute the Plea Agreement and all other documents necessary to carry out the provisions of the Plea Agreement. ██████ agrees that counsel identified below will appear on behalf of ██████ and enter the guilty plea and will also appear for the imposition of sentence.

11. <u>Who Is Bound By Agreement</u>

This Plea Agreement binds ██████ and the United States Department of Justice, including each of its United States Attorney's Offices, and can not and does not bind the Tax Division of the U.S. Department of Justice, the Internal Revenue Service of the U.S. Department of Treasury, or any other federal, state or local prosecutive authority.

12. <u>Complete Agreement</u>

With regard to the disposition of Count Two of the attached Information, this Plea Agreement is the complete and only agreement between the Parties. No promises, representations, agreements or conditions have been entered into other than those set forth in this letter in connection with Count Two. This Plea Agreement supersedes prior understandings, if any, of the parties, whether written or oral in connection with the disposition of Count Two. This Plea Agreement can be modified or supplemented only in a written memorandum signed by the Parties or on the record in court.

If this letter accurately reflects the Agreement entered into between the United States and your client ██████, please sign the Acknowledgment of Plea Agreement below, provide evidence of the requisite authorization to enter into this Plea Agreement, and return the original of this letter to Assistant U.S. Attorneys Susan G. Winkler and Susan Hanson-Philbrick.

Very truly yours,

By: _____
MARK W. PEARLSTEIN
Acting United States Attorney
District of Massachusetts

By: _____
JOHN C. KEENEY
Deputy Assistant Attorney General
Criminal Division
Department of Justice

CORPORATE ACKNOWLEDGMENT OF PLEA AGREEMENT

The Directors of ████████ have read this Plea Agreement and the attached criminal Information, in their entirety, and have discussed this matter with legal counsel of the corporation's choosing, including undersigned counsel. As set forth in the attached resolution, the Board of Directors has authorized me, as an officer of the corporation, to enter into this Plea Agreement on behalf of the corporation. I hereby acknowledge, on behalf of ████████ that this letter fully sets forth ████████'s agreement with the U.S. Attorney relating to the disposition of Count Two of the attached Information, and that no additional promises or representations have been made to the corporation by any official of the United States in connection with the disposition of that charge. ████████ Inc. is entering into this Agreement freely, voluntarily and knowingly because it is guilty of the offense set forth in Count Two of the Information and it believes this Plea Agreement is in its best interest.

EXHIBIT XXXVII.
Example of Civil Settlement Agreement

SETTLEMENT AGREEMENT AND RELEASE

PARTIES

This Settlement Agreement and Release ("Agreement") is entered between the United States of America, acting through the United States Attorney's Office for the District of Massachusetts ("USAO") and on behalf of the Office of Inspector General ("OIG-HHS") of the Department of Health and Human Services ("HHS")(collectively, the "United States"); and the Commonwealth of Massachusetts ("Massachusetts"), acting through the Medicaid Fraud Control Unit of the Attorney General's Office ("MFCU")(collectively with the United States, the "Government"); and ███████████ Foundation, Inc. ("███████ Foundation"). Collectively, all of the above will be referred to as "the Parties."

PREAMBLE

A. WHEREAS, this Agreement addresses the United States' and Massachusetts' civil claims against ███████ Foundation based upon the conduct described in Preamble Paragraphs E and F below;

B. WHEREAS, at all relevant times, ███████ Foundation submitted or caused to be submitted claims for payment to the Medicare Program ("Medicare), Title XVIII of the Social Security Act, 42 U.S.C. §§ 1395-1395ddd (1997), and to the Medicaid Program ("Medicaid"), 42 U.S.C. §§ 1396-1396v (1997);

C. WHEREAS, in or about February, 1996, the ███████ Foundation disclosed to OIG-HHS certain Medicare and Medicaid billing problems that occurred during the period May 1, 1989 through June 30, 1995, and was accepted into the OIG-HHS's Voluntary Disclosure Program shortly thereafter;

D. WHEREAS, as part of its voluntary disclosure, ▮▮▮ Foundation provided to the Government various audit analyses, summaries of witnesses interviews, and documents related to the Medicare and Medicaid billing problems identified by ▮▮▮ Foundation;

E. WHEREAS, based upon its investigation of the disclosures made ▮▮▮ Foundation, the Government contends that ▮▮▮ Foundation violated federal and state statutes and/or common law doctrine by submitting claims for payment to Medicare and Medicaid during the period May 1, 1989 through December 31, 1991, for services that included bills for (1) decalcification procedures (Current Procedural Terminology ("CPT") Code 88311) and (2) special stains (CPT Codes 88312 and 88313) which were not documented in the pathology reports;

F. WHEREAS, based upon its investigation of the disclosures made by ▮▮▮ Foundation, the Government contends that ▮▮▮ Foundation violated federal and state statutes and/or common law doctrine by submitting claims for payment to Medicare and Medicaid during the period January 1, 1992 through June 30, 1995, for (1) services including bills for decalcification procedures (Current Procedural Terminology ("CPT") Code 88311) which were not documented in the ▮▮▮ reports; (2) services including bills for special stains (CPT Codes 88312 and 88313) which were not documented in the ▮▮▮ reports; (3) services that were inappropriately billed a second time when an addendum was added to a surgical ▮▮▮ report; (4) services for examining multiple specimens of varying complexity using the higher reimbursing CPT code for each specimen rather than the appropriate CPT code for the less complex specimen (CPT Codes 88300, 88302,

88304, 88305, 88307 and 88309); (5) services for gross only examinations of certain specimens during surgical consultations (CPT Code 88329) that were inaccurately billed as if more complex microscopic analyses with frozen sections were performed (CPT Code 88331); (6) services for examining hysterectomy specimens that were billed separately for the component parts of the specimen (uterus, tubes and ovaries) where only a single specimen is allowed to be billed (CPT Codes 88305, 88307, and 88309); (7) services for examining multiple specimens of the same type when only one specimen is allowed to be billed (CPT Codes 88300 through 88309); and (8) services for cell marker studies performed on a flow cytometer that were improperly billed as a manual service (CPT 88346) rather than as performed on the automated machine (CPT 88180).

G. WHEREAS, the ▇▇▇▇ Foundation contends that it did not knowingly submit any inaccurate billings to Medicare, and that any erroneous billings that were submitted resulted from faulty computer prompts, inaccuracies in the computer dictionary, and processes that unintentionally reflected only the physician's initial diagnosis rather that his or her final diagnosis.

H. WHEREAS, the Parties mutually desire to reach a full and final compromise of all civil claims that the Government has or may have against ▇▇▇▇ Foundation as set forth in Paragraph 2 and 3, below, and further wish to avoid the delay, expense, inconvenience and uncertainty of protracted litigation of these claims;

TERMS AND CONDITIONS

NOW, THEREFORE, in reliance on the representations contained herein and in consideration of the mutual promises, covenants, and obligations in this Agreement, and for good and valuable consideration, receipt of which is hereby acknowledged, the Parties hereby agree as follows:

1. ███████ Foundation agrees to pay to the Government the sum of four hundred seventy six thousand one hundred sixty seven dollars ($476,167)(the "Settlement Amount") and this sum shall constitute a debt immediately due and owing to the Government on the execution of this Agreement. Of that settlement amount, four hundred twenty nine thousand six hundred forty seven dollars ($429,647) shall be electronically transferred to the United States pursuant to instructions provided by the USAO no later than the seventh business day following the date on which this Agreement is fully executed by the Parties. The remaining portion of the settlement amount, forty six thousand five hundred twenty dollars ($46,520) shall be electronically transferred to Massachusetts pursuant to instructions provided by the MFCU no later than the seventh business day following the date on which this Agreement is fully executed by the Parties.

2. Subject only to the exceptions specified in Paragraph 5 below, in consideration of the obligations of ███████ Foundation as set forth in this agreement, and conditioned upon ███████ Foundation's payment in full of the Settlement Amount, the United States, on behalf of itself, its officers, agents, agencies and departments, agrees to release the ███████ Foundation and its subsidiaries, successors, and assigns, and its present or former directors, officers, or employees from any civil or administrative monetary claims

(including recoupment claims) that the United States has or may have under the False Claims Act, 31 U.S.C. §§ 3729-3733; the Program Fraud Civil Remedies Act, 31 U.S.C. §§ 3801-3812; the Civil Monetary Penalties Law, 42 U.S.C. § 1320a-7a; or the common law theories of payment by mistake, unjust enrichment, breach of contract and fraud for the conduct described in Paragraphs E and F of the Preamble for the period May 1, 1989 through June 30, 1995 (the "Covered Conduct");

3. Subject only to the exceptions specified in Paragraph 5 below, in consideration of the obligations of ███████ Foundation as set forth in this agreement, and conditioned upon ███████ Foundation's payment in full of the Settlement Amount, the Commonwealth of Massachusetts, on behalf of itself, its officers, agents, agencies and departments, agrees to release the ███████ Foundation and its subsidiaries, successors, and assigns, and its present or former directors, officers, or employees from any civil or administrative claims (including recoupment claims) that Massachusetts has or may have under G.L. c. 118E, §§ 38, 44, and 46-46A, 130 C.M.R. § 450.258, or the common law theories of payment by mistake, unjust enrichment, breach of contract and fraud the Covered Conduct.

4. Subject only to the exceptions specified in Paragraph 5 below, in consideration of the obligations of ███████ Foundation as set forth in this agreement, and conditioned upon ███████ Foundation's payment in full of the Settlement Amount, the OIG-HHS agrees to release and refrain from instituting, directing or maintaining any administrative claim or any action seeking exclusion from the Medicare, Medicaid, or other Federal health care programs (as defined in 42 U.S.C. §1320a-7b(f)) against ███████ Foundation under 42 U.S.C. § 1320a-7a (Civil Monetary Penalties Law), 31 U.S.C. §§ 3801-3812 (Program Fraud Civil

Remedies Act), or 42 U.S.C. § 1320a-7(b)(permissive exclusion) for the Covered Conduct, except as reserved in this Paragraph. The OIG-HHS expressly reserves all rights to comply with any statutory obligations to exclude ■■■ Foundation from the Medicare, Medicaid or other Federal health care programs under 42 U.S.C. § 1320a-7(a) (mandatory exclusion) based on the Covered Conduct. Nothing in this Paragraph precludes the OIG-HHS from taking action against entities or persons, or for conduct or practices, for which civil claims have been reserved in Paragraph 5, below.

5. Notwithstanding any other provision in this Agreement, the Government specifically does not release ■■■ Foundation, or any other entity or individual under this Agreement, from any and all of the following: (a) any criminal liability; (b) except as explicitly stated in this Agreement, any administrative liability, including mandatory exclusion from Federal health care programs; (c) any potential criminal, civil or administrative claims arising under Title 26 U.S. Code (Internal Revenue Code), Massachusetts or local tax obligations, or under securities laws; (d) any potential liability to the Government (or any agencies thereof) for any conduct or any Medicare or Medicaid billings other than the Covered Conduct; (e) any obligations created by this Agreement; (f) any express or implied warranty claims or other claims for defective or deficient services, including quality of goods or services.

6. ■■■ Foundation has this day executed a Corporate Integrity Agreement with OIG-HHS, attached as Exhibit A, which is incorporated herein by reference.

7. ■■■ Foundation agrees that it will waive and will not assert any defense, which may be based in whole or in part on the Double Jeopardy or Excessive Fines Clauses of the Constitution and agrees that the amounts paid under this Agreement are not

punitive in nature or effect for purposes of any criminal prosecution or administrative action. Nothing in this Paragraph or any other provision of this Agreement constitutes an agreement by the Government concerning the characterization of the Settlement Amount for purposes of the Internal Revenue Laws, Title 26 of the United States Code or Chapters 62 and 63 of the Massachusetts General Laws.

8. ▓▓▓▓▓▓▓▓ Foundation agrees that all costs (as defined in the Federal Acquisition Regulations ("FAR") § 31.302-47 and in Titles XVIII and XIX of the Social Security Act, 42 U.S.C. §§ 1395-1395ddd (1997) and 1396-1396v (1997), and the regulations promulgated thereunder) incurred by or on behalf of ▓▓▓▓▓▓▓▓ Foundation in connection with (a) the matters covered by this Agreement; (b) the Government's investigation of matters covered by this Agreement; (c) ▓▓▓▓▓▓▓▓ Foundation's investigation, audits, defense, and corrective actions taken in response to the government's investigation in connection with matters covered by this Agreement, including without limitation attorneys fees; (d) the negotiation of this Settlement Agreement; and (e) the payments made to the Government pursuant to the provisions of this Settlement Agreement, are unallowable costs on Government contracts and under the Medicare Program, Medicaid Program, TRICARE Program, Veterans Affairs Program ("VA") and Federal Employee Health Benefits Program ("FEHBP") (hereafter, "unallowable costs"). These unallowable costs will be separately estimated and accounted for by ▓▓▓▓▓▓▓▓ Foundation and this entity will not charge such unallowable costs directly or indirectly to any contracts with the United States or Massachusetts, or any other state Medicaid program, or seek payment for such unallowable costs through any cost report, cost statement,

information statement or payment request submitted by Brigham Pathology Foundation to the Medicare, Medicaid, TRICARE, VA or FEHBP programs.

███████ Foundation further agrees that within 60 days of the effective date of this Agreement it will identify to applicable Medicare fiscal intermediaries, carriers and/or contractors and Medicaid fiscal agents, any unallowable costs (as defined in this paragraph) included in payments previously sought from the United States, or the Massachusetts Medicaid Program, including, but not limited to, payments sought in any cost reports, cost statements, information reports, or payment requests already submitted by ███████ Foundation and will request, and agree, that such cost reports, cost statements, information reports or payment requests, even if already settled, be adjusted to account for the effect of the inclusion of the unallowable costs. ███████ Foundation agrees that the Government will be entitled to recoup from ███████ Foundation any overpayment as a result of the inclusion of such unallowable costs on previously-submitted cost reports, information reports, cost statements or requests for payment. Any payments due after the adjustments have been made shall be paid to the United States pursuant to the direction of the Department of Justice, and/or the affected agencies. The Government reserves its rights to disagree with any calculations submitted by ███████ Foundation on the effect of inclusion of unallowable costs (as defined in this paragraph) of ███████ Foundation cost reports, cost statements or information reports. Nothing in this Agreement shall constitute a waiver of the rights of the Government to examine or reexamine the unallowable costs described in this Paragraph.

9. This Agreement is intended to be for the benefit of the Parties only, and by this instrument the Parties do not release any claims against any other person or entity in connection with the Covered Conduct or otherwise.

10. This Agreement shall be binding upon the Parties, their successors, assigns and heirs.

11. The United States, Massachusetts, OIG-HHS, and the ▮▮▮▮ Foundation agree that each of them will bear their own legal fees, audit costs, and all other costs incurred in connection with this matter, including but not limited to the preparation and performance of this Agreement.

12. ▮▮▮▮ Foundation represents that this Agreement is freely and voluntarily entered into without any degree of duress or compulsion whatsoever.

13. This Agreement is governed by the laws of the United States. The Parties agree that the exclusive jurisdiction and venue for any dispute arising between and among the Parties under this Agreement will be the United States District Court for the District of Massachusetts.

14. The undersigned individual signing this Agreement on behalf of ▮▮▮▮ Foundation represents and warrants that he/she is authorized by ▮▮▮▮ Foundation to execute this Agreement on behalf of that entity. The undersigned United States and Massachusetts signatories represent that they are signing this Agreement in their official capacity and that they are authorized to execute this Agreement.

15. The parties agree that this Agreement does not constitute an admission by any person or entity with respect to any issue of law or fact.

16. This Agreement shall become final and binding only upon signing by each respective party hereto.

17. This Agreement may not be changed, altered or modified, except in writing signed by all parties; with the sole exception of the Corporate Integrity Agreement which may be changed, altered, or modified in writing signed by OIG-HHS and ▓▓▓▓ Foundation.

18. This Agreement may be executed in counterparts, each of which shall constitute an original and all of which shall constitute one and the same Agreement.

19. This Agreement is effective on the date signed by the last signatory.

UNITED STATES OF AMERICA

By: *Susan Winkler*   Dated: 7/9/99
SUSAN G. WINKLER
Assistant United States Attorney
District of Massachusetts

By: _____   Dated: _____
LEWIS MORRIS
Assistant Inspector General
Office of Counsel to the Inspector General
Office of Inspector General
U.S. Department of Health and Human Services

16. This Agreement shall become final and binding only upon signing by each respective party hereto.

17. This Agreement may not be changed, altered or modified, except in writing signed by all parties; with the sole exception of the Corporate Integrity Agreement which may be changed, altered, or modified in writing signed by OIG-HHS and ▓▓▓▓▓▓▓ Foundation.

18. This Agreement may be executed in counterparts, each of which shall constitute an original and all of which shall constitute one and the same Agreement.

19. This Agreement is effective on the date signed by the last signatory.

UNITED STATES OF AMERICA

By: _____ Dated: _____
SUSAN G. WINKLER
Assistant United States Attorney
District of Massachusetts

By: _____ Dated: 6/9/99
LEWIS MORRIS
Assistant Inspector General
Office of Counsel to the Inspector General
Office of Inspector General
U.S. Department of Health and Human Services

COMMONWEALTH OF MASSACHUSETTS

By: _____ Dated: June 4, 1999
PETER CLARK
Assistant Attorney General
Medicaid Fraud Control Unit
Office of the Attorney General
Commonwealth of Massachusetts

██████████████████ FOUNDATION, INC.

By: _____ Dated: _____

By: _____ Dated: _____
Counsel to ███████ Foundation

COMMONWEALTH OF MASSACHUSETTS

By: _____   Dated: _____
    PETER CLARK
    Assistant Attorney General
    Medicaid Fraud Control Unit
    Office of the Attorney General
    Commonwealth of Massachusetts

███████████████ FOUNDATION, INC.

By: _____   Dated: June 30, 1999

By: _____   Dated: July 6, 1999
    Counsel to ███████ Foundation

EXHIBIT XXXVIII.
Example of Corporate Integrity Agreement

CORPORATE INTEGRITY AGREEMENT
Between The
Office of Inspector General
Of The
Department of Health and Human Services
And
▓▓▓▓▓▓▓▓▓▓▓▓▓▓▓▓ Foundation, Inc.

This Corporate Integrity Agreement is entered into between ▓▓▓▓▓▓▓▓▓▓▓▓▓▓▓▓ Foundation, Inc. ("▓▓▓▓▓▓▓▓ Foundation"); and the Office of Inspector General ("OIG") of the Department of Health and Human Services ("HHS"). Pursuant to this Agreement, ▓▓▓▓▓▓▓▓▓▓▓▓ Foundation agrees to undertake the compliance provisions outlined below.

I. PREAMBLE

▓▓▓▓▓▓▓▓▓▓ Foundation agrees to implement this Corporate Integrity Agreement (the "Agreement") so as to ensure, to the extent reasonably possible, that ▓▓▓▓▓▓▓▓▓▓ Foundation and each of its Board of Directors, officers, employees and contractors maintain the business integrity required of a participant in Medicare, Medicaid and other federal health care programs, as defined in 42 U.S.C. 1320a-7b(f), and that ▓▓▓▓▓▓▓▓▓▓▓▓ Foundation is in compliance with all laws and regulations applicable to such programs and with the terms of this Agreement. The period of future integrity obligations assumed by ▓▓▓▓▓▓▓▓▓▓▓▓ Foundation under this Agreement shall be three (3) years from the date of execution of this Agreement. The date of execution of this Agreement is the date the final signature is obtained.

II. CORPORATE COMPLIANCE PROGRAM

▓▓▓▓▓▓▓▓▓▓▓▓ Foundation agrees to continue to implement and maintain its voluntary "Corporate Compliance Program" which has been adopted by ▓▓▓▓▓▓▓▓▓▓ Foundation's Board of Directors. This document is attached to this Agreement, and incorporated by reference, as Attachment A. To the extent that any of the obligations required by this Agreement replicate provisions contained in the attached Corporate Compliance Program, those provisions are deemed acceptable for the purpose of ▓▓▓▓▓▓▓▓▓▓ Foundation meeting its obligations under this Agreement.

III. CORPORATE INTEGRITY PROGRAM

Within one hundred twenty (120) days of the date of execution of this Agreement, ▇▇▇▇▇▇▇ Foundation agrees to implement a Corporate Integrity Program (the "Program"), which shall include the provisions listed herein.

A. Corporate Compliance Committee and Corporate Compliance Officer

Within ninety (90) days of the date of execution of this Agreement, the Board of Directors of ▇▇▇▇▇▇▇ Foundation shall: (i) direct the creation of a Corporate Compliance Committee (the "Compliance Committee"); (ii) charge the Compliance Committee with the responsibility to establish and implement the Program; and (iii) appoint an individual to serve as the Compliance Officer ("CO").

The members of the Compliance Committee shall be appointed by the President of ▇▇▇▇▇▇▇ Foundation, and shall include the Compliance Officer, the ▇▇▇▇▇▇▇ Foundation's Administrator, and any others that ▇▇▇▇▇▇▇ Foundation deems appropriate.

The Compliance Officer shall chair the Compliance Committee and shall be responsible for the day-to-day activities engaged in by ▇▇▇▇▇▇▇ Foundation to further the operations of the Program.

The Compliance Officer shall submit annual reports to OIG's Office of Counsel to the Inspector General ("OIG") of the United States Department of Health and Human Services ("HHS"), in accordance with the terms of this Agreement.

B. Audit Requirement

Beginning on the effective date of this Agreement and continuing for the duration of the term of this Agreement, ▇▇▇▇▇▇▇ Foundation shall conduct ongoing audits in accordance with the following protocol:

1. Each week, a printout of all professional fee charges generated by the Foundation will be delivered to ▇▇▇▇▇▇▇ Administration before any final bills are generated. Each week, an administrator will review selected cases from the weekly printout for any potential charge code errors. The administrator shall select cases for review based upon the criteria described below. The risk areas shall be selected according to greatest risk, with a. being the greatest risk and f. presenting the least risk. In accordance with this Agreement,

███████ Foundation will review all cases in categories a. and b. ███████ Foundation will select random samples, with a minimum of ten cases per category, or the number of cases in the category, whichever is less, for categories c. through f. Cases selected for review under this section may include cases selected for administrative review as described in section III. B. 2.

   a. error codes stemming from the data transmission from the ███████ Hospital computer system to the ███████ Foundation computer system;

   b. Cases that have more than three (3) dissimilar specimen types;

   c. Cases that incorporate the highest level fee codes, whether singly or in conjunction with other specimens;

   d. Cases that have multiple charge codes for other services, such as frozen sections, special stains, decalcification of specimens, immunohistochemistry, etc.;

   e. Cases selected at random of different specimen types, especially those where there are unique rules as to the selection of proper codes (e.g., hysterectomy cases and the bundling of specimens); and

   f. Cases that have lower level charge codes, either in multiple units or singly.

2. Each week, a Foundation administrator also will review all cases flagged for administrative review by senior staff at the time of final case sign-out.

3. If there is any uncertainty about the correctness of the coding of a particular case, a physician reviewer in the Foundation will review the coding of a case and report back his/her opinion to the administrator, who will modify the charge coding, if necessary. An expert consultant also will be used on those occasions where more general clarification is needed on coding situations across a number of case types.

4. If any incorrect charges are identified during a particular case review, a list of those charges will be prepared and faxed to the

billing agent for the Foundation to correct the charges on that case before a bill is sent out.

5. At least bi-annually, the administrator or compliance officer (or designee) will review a sample of the faxed corrections to ensure that all billing documents were corrected prior to submission of the claim.

6. Follow-up communication as appropriate will be made to the physician or technical staff on coding errors discovered at time of case review, providing explanations of the error and suggesting steps to prevent future problems. This is part of the Foundation's on-going training in proper coding for staff as part of Foundation's Compliance Plan.

7. The Foundation will maintain detailed logs of all cases reviewed and the results of that review.

8. The central charge coding reviewer will, on an ongoing basis, validate the fee codes assigned to high risk cases, such as those with multiple frozen sections and/or multiple charge level V or VI parts. Charge errors, if any, will be corrected immediately by the reviewer. The reviewer will also report to the Compliance Officer regarding any trends or consistent errors that have been detected, and the Compliance Officer and administrator will initiate immediate corrective action as indicated.

9. A formal randomized sample of one hundred (100) Medicare/Medicaid patient records completed but not yet billed as of the concurrent audit date will be selected from all those available during the first week of each April and October. The complete pathology report, the interim patient account record, the ███████ consult requisition, and any other backup (e.g., ███████ intra-operative consult record, order for special stains, etc.) will be gathered together for each sampled patient record. All 100 patient records will initially be validated by the central charge coding reviewer, who will then turn over the complete record set and his findings with respect to each to an outside auditor. The outside auditor will independently verify the accuracy of the fee codes and the ICD-9-CM diagnosis codes assigned to each case, and he/she will immediately report any exception(s) to the Compliance Officer for corrective action as indicated. All of these actions will be

undertaken and completed prior to release of any of the 100 patient records for formal claim preparation and filing.

10. Immediately after the release of the preceding 100 patient records for claim preparation, hard copy reproduction of each such claim will be forwarded to the outside auditor. He/she will verify the efficacy of all claims, consisting of key data fields such as name of referring physician; disclosure of the identification number of the performing pathologist; correct ICD-9-CM and CPT billing codes and correct units of service per CPT billing code as determined by the previous audit step; correct CPT code modifier use; correct CPT number; and proper disclosure of Graduate Medical Education resident involvement in the case, as applicable. The outside auditor will promptly report the results of his/her review to the Compliance Officer, who in turn will initiate any corrective action as may be indicated.

11. The concurrent audit for each October will also include a post-payment review step. In particular, the outside auditor will conduct a detailed analysis of each patient account subject to the random sample steps set forth above. The analysis will assure proper filing on behalf of any secondary insurance and/or patient billing pertaining to deductible and/or coinsurance amounts. It will also verify that the Medicare Part B carrier paid the correct amount for the claim and that it properly and accurately adjudicated each account. The outside auditor will promptly report the results of his/her review to the Compliance Officer, who in turn will initiate any corrective action as may be indicated. Also, the Compliance Officer will modify the training and education program as appropriate in response to these audits.

C. **Overpayments and Material Deficiencies**

If, as a result of these audits, ▆▆▆▆▆ Foundation identifies any billing, coding or other policies, procedures and/or practices that result in an overpayment, ▆▆▆▆▆ Foundation shall notify the payor (e.g., Medicare fiscal intermediary or carrier) within 30 days of discovering the deficiency or overpayment and take remedial steps within 60 days of discovery (or such additional time as may be agreed to by the payor) to correct the problem, including preventing the deficiency from recurring. The notice to the payor shall include:

1. a statement that the refund, if appropriate, is being made pursuant to this CIA;

2. a description of the complete circumstances surrounding the overpayment;

3. the methodology by which the overpayment was determined;

4. the amount of the overpayment;

5. any claim-specific information used to determine the overpayment (e.g., beneficiary health insurance number, claim number, service date, and payment date); and

6. the provider identification number under which the repayment is being made.

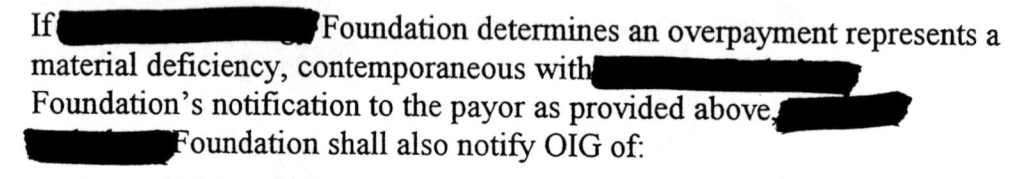

If ▒▒▒ Foundation determines an overpayment represents a material deficiency, contemporaneous with ▒▒▒ Foundation's notification to the payor as provided above, ▒▒▒ Foundation shall also notify OIG of:

1. a complete description of the material deficiency;

2. amount of overpayment due to the material deficiency;

3. ▒▒▒ Foundation's action(s) to correct and prevent such material deficiency from recurring;

4. the payor's name, address, and contact person where the overpayment was sent;

5. the date of the check and identification number (or electronic transaction number) on which the overpayment was repaid.

For purposes of this CIA, an "overpayment" shall mean the amount of money the provider has received in excess of the amount due and payable under the Federal health care programs' statutes, regulations or written program directives, and/or carrier and intermediary instructions.

For purposes of this CIA, a "material deficiency" shall mean anything that involves: (i) a substantial overpayment or improper payment relating to the Medicare and/or Medicaid programs; (ii) conduct or policies that clearly violate the Medicare and/or Medicaid statute, regulations or directives issued by HCFA and/or its agents; or (iii) serious quality of care implications for federal health care beneficiaries or recipients. A material deficiency may be the result of an isolated event or a series of occurrences.

D. **Corporate Integrity Policy**

Within one hundred twenty (120) days of the date of execution of this Agreement, ▮▮▮▮▮ Foundation shall develop and implement written policies regarding its commitment to accurate billings consistent with published Medicare and Medicaid statutes, regulations, program requirements and other written directives from HCFA or its agents.

These policies shall be adopted by ▮▮▮▮▮ Foundation's Board of Directors and distributed to all employees and independent contractors involved in submitting or preparing bills or claims on behalf of ▮▮▮▮▮ Foundation to the Medicare, Medicaid or other federal health care programs. ▮▮▮▮▮ Foundation shall post in a prominent place accessible to each employee a notice detailing its commitment to comply with all applicable Medicare, Medicaid and other federal health care programs' statutes, regulations, written directives and program requirements in the conduct of its business. A copy of the policies and notices will be available, upon request, for review by OIG or its duly authorized representative.

E. **Information and Education**

Within one hundred twenty (120) days of the date of execution of this Agreement, ▮▮▮▮▮ Foundation shall develop and institute an information and education program designed to ensure that each officer, Board of Directors member and employee who is involved directly or indirectly in the preparation or submission of claims for reimbursement to the Medicare, Medicaid and other federal health care programs is aware of all applicable statutes, regulations and written HCFA directives. The information and education program should also convey the standards of business conduct that each individual is expected to follow and the consequences both to the individual and ▮▮▮▮▮ Foundation that will ensue from any violation of these requirements.

The information and education program shall provide for no less than three (3) hours of formal training on an annual basis in: (i) the Corporate Integrity Program; (ii) the submission of accurate bills for services rendered to Medicare, Medicaid and other federal health care program patients; (iii) the personal obligation of each individual involved in the billing process to ensure that such billings are accurate; (iv) applicable reimbursement rules and laws; and (v) the legal sanctions for improper billings and examples of improper billing practices. Information concerning the format, dates, and a copy of the materials provided will be available, upon request, for review by OIG. Individuals whose contact with the billing process is both indirect and tangential, such as secretarial staff, are not required to have three (3) hours of training, but must have at least one and one-half hours of training (as described in this paragraph) per year.

The above-described training requirements shall be included in the formal orientation for new officers, Board of Directors members and staff (residents and any other hospital employees) who perform services on behalf of ▇▇▇▇▇▇▇ Foundation.

F. **Confidential Disclosure Program**

Within ninety (90) days of the date of execution of this Agreement, ▇▇▇▇▇▇▇ Foundation shall establish a confidential disclosure program enabling members, employees, contractors and physicians with staff privileges to disclose any practices or billing procedures alleged by such person to be inappropriate, to an identified individual not in that person's direct chain of command. ▇▇▇▇▇▇▇ Foundation shall, as part of this disclosure program, require the internal review of any disclosure that is sufficiently specific so that it: (i) permits a determination of the appropriateness of the practice alleged to be involved; and (ii) reasonably permits corrective action to be taken and ensure that proper follow-up is conducted. In an effort to address every disclosure, ▇▇▇▇▇▇▇ Foundation shall make a good faith preliminary inquiry for every disclosure instance to ensure that it has obtained all of the necessary information that is reasonably required to determine whether an internal review, in accordance with the language above, should be conducted. ▇▇▇▇▇▇▇ Foundation agrees that it will not take any retaliatory or adverse actions against any member, employee, contractor or physician with staff privileges who makes a confidential disclosure and that, to the extent possible, it will protect the anonymity of the person making the disclosure. This section does not preclude ▇▇▇▇▇▇▇ Foundation from taking disciplinary action (up to and including termination) against a member, employee, contractor or physician with staff privileges for actions or conduct unrelated to the making of the confidential disclosure.

▇▇▇▇▇▇▇ Foundation shall include in its Annual Report to OIG a summary of communications received from the Confidential Disclosure

Program and the findings of any investigations performed as a result of these disclosures. ███████████ Foundation shall make the results of the investigations available to OIG upon its request. At OIG's option, OIG may also review the documentation on ███████████ Foundation's premises. In turn, ███████████ Foundation agrees to maintain such reports in a manner agreeable to OIG so that they will be readily available to OIG for a minimum of one (1) year longer than the duration of this Agreement.

G. Ineligible Persons

For purposes of this CIA, an "Ineligible Person" shall be any individual or entity who: (i) is currently excluded, suspended, debarred or otherwise ineligible to participate in the Federal health care programs; or (ii) has been convicted of a criminal offense related to the provision of health care items or services and has not been reinstated in the Federal health care programs after a period of exclusion, suspension, debarment, or ineligibility.

███████████ Foundation shall not hire or engage as contractors any Ineligible Person. To prevent hiring or contracting with any Ineligible Person, ███████████ Foundation shall screen all prospective members, employees, and contractors prior to engaging their services and screen physicians prior to granting staff privileges by (i) requiring applicants to disclose whether they are Ineligible Persons, and (ii) reviewing the General Services Administration's List of Parties Excluded from Federal Programs (available through the Internet at http://www.arnet.gov/epls) and the HHS/OIG List of Excluded Individuals/Entities (available through the Internet at http://dhhs.gov/progorg/oig) (these lists and reports will hereinafter be referred to as the "Exclusion Lists").

Within ninety (90) days of the effective date of this CIA, ███████████ Foundation will review its list of current members, employees, contractors and physicians with staff privileges against the Exclusion Lists. Thereafter, ███████████ Foundation will review the list once semi-annually. If ███████████ Foundation has notice that a member, employee, contractor, or physician with staff privileges has become an Ineligible Person, ███████████ Foundation will remove such person from responsibility for, or involvement with, ███████████ Foundation's business operations related to the Federal health care programs and shall remove such person from any position for which the person's salary or the items or services rendered, ordered, or prescribed by the person are paid in whole or part, directly or indirectly, by Federal health care programs or otherwise with Federal funds at least until such time as the person is reinstated into participation in the Federal health care programs.

If ▇▇▇▇ Foundation has notice that a member, employee, contractor or physician with staff privileges is charged with a criminal offense related to any Federal health care program, or is suspended or proposed for exclusion during his or her employment or contract with ▇▇▇▇ Foundation, within 10 days of receiving such notice ▇▇▇▇ Foundation will remove such individual from responsibility for, or involvement with ▇▇▇▇ Foundation's business operations related to the Federal health care programs until the resolution of such criminal action, suspension, or proposed exclusion.

▇▇▇▇ Foundation shall not knowingly allow, or cause to be allowed, any person convicted in any local, state or federal court of any felony involving health care matters to hold the position of officer or member of the Board of Directors of ▇▇▇▇ Foundation, or any of its subsidiaries either through an employment agreement or an independent contract.

Should ▇▇▇▇ Foundation discover that it has employed an individual, allowed a physician to become a member, granted staff privileges to a physician or entered into a consultant agreement in contravention of this provision, ▇▇▇▇ Foundation will have thirty (30) days to take the necessary steps to cure the problem, in accordance with this section,

H.   Reporting on Investigations

Within fourteen (14) days of becoming aware of the existence of any investigation or legal proceeding conducted or brought by a governmental entity involving an allegation that ▇▇▇▇ Foundation has committed a crime or has engaged in fraudulent activities, ▇▇▇▇ Foundation shall notify OIG of such investigation or legal proceeding. The notification shall include a description of the allegation, the identity of the investigating or prosecuting agency, and the status of such investigation or legal proceeding. Within fourteen (14) days of the resolution of the investigation or legal proceeding, ▇▇▇▇ Foundation shall notify OIG, identifying the findings or results of the investigation or legal proceeding.

IV. OIG INSPECTION, AUDIT AND REVIEW RIGHTS

In addition to any other right OIG may have by statute, regulation, contract or pursuant to this Agreement, OIG or its duly authorized representative(s) may examine ████████ Foundation's books, records, and other company documents and supporting materials for the purpose of verifying and evaluating: (i) ████████ Foundation's compliance with the terms of this Agreement; and (ii) ████████ Foundation's compliance with the requirements of the Medicare, Medicaid and other federal health care programs. The documentation described above shall be made available by ████████ Foundation at all reasonable times for inspection, audit or reproduction. Furthermore, for purposes of this provision, OIG or its authorized representative(s) may interview any of ████████ Foundation's employees, members or physicians with staff privileges who consent to be interviewed at the Department of ████ of ████████ Hospital during normal business hours or at such other place and time as may be mutually agreed upon between the individual and OIG. ████████ Foundation agrees to cooperate with OIG in contacting and arranging interviews with such individuals upon OIG's request. Individuals may elect to be interviewed with or without a representative of ████████ Foundation present.

V. REPORTS

The CO of ████████ Foundation shall be responsible for the submission of all reports and notifications to OIG as required by this Agreement.

A. Interim Report

Within one hundred eighty (180) days of the date of execution of this Agreement, ████████ Foundation will provide OIG with an Interim Report demonstrating that ████████ Foundation has complied with all of the Program's requirements contained in Sections III. A, C, D, E, and F of this Agreement. The Interim Report shall also identify the Compliance Officer and the members of the Compliance Committee and identify the steps taken to comply with Section III. B of this Agreement.

B. Annual Reports

████████ Foundation shall make Annual Reports (each one of which is referred to throughout this Agreement as the "Annual Report") to OIG describing the measures ████████ Foundation has taken to implement the Corporate Integrity Program and ensure compliance with the terms of this Agreement. In accordance with the provisions above, the Annual Report shall include the following:

1. In the first Annual Report, copies of the document or documents that comprise ▓▓▓▓▓▓▓ Foundation's Corporate Integrity Program established under section III. of this Agreement as adopted by ▓▓▓▓▓▓▓ Foundation's Board of Directors and implemented by the Corporate Compliance Committee. For subsequent years, ▓▓▓▓▓▓▓ Foundation shall note in the Annual Report any amendments or revisions to the Program documents made during the year covered by the Annual Report.

2. A detailed description of the findings made during the annual audits conducted pursuant to section III. B. of this Agreement relating to the year covered by the Annual Report, a summary of the disclosure or notice documents made by ▓▓▓▓▓▓▓ Foundation pursuant to this section, a description of the corrective actions taken and proof of a refund to the pertinent payor (where applicable).

3. A description of the training programs implemented pursuant to section III. E. of this Agreement and a summary of the activities performed in furtherance of the training programs, including a schedule and topic outline of the training sessions.

4. A summary of communications received from the Confidential Disclosure Program established pursuant to section III. F. and the results of any investigations performed as a result of any disclosures.

5. A summary of the background inquiries conducted pursuant to section III. G. of this Agreement and any personnel actions taken (other than hiring) as a result of these inquiries.

6. A summary of any ongoing investigation or legal proceeding conducted or brought by a governmental entity involving an allegation that ▓▓▓▓▓▓▓ Foundation has committed a crime or has engaged in fraudulent activities. The statement shall include a description of the allegation, the identity of the investigating or prosecuting agency, and the status of such investigation or legal proceeding as required by section III. H. of this Agreement.

7. The names of ▓▓▓▓▓▓▓ Foundation's officers, members of the Board of Directors and Compliance Committee members.

8. A resolution (or its equivalent) from ▇▇▇▇ Foundation's Board of Directors certifying that it has reviewed the Annual Report and agrees with the statements made therein.

Where applicable, the report shall include a statement that no events identified in subparagraphs 1 through 6 of this section occurred. Each Annual Report shall be submitted to OIG one hundred twenty (120) days after the end of the fiscal years ending June 30, 2000, 2001 and 2002. The obligation to submit the last Annual Report will continue despite the other obligations of this Corporate Integrity Agreement having terminated under section I. of this Agreement.

VI. NOTIFICATION AND SUBMISSION OF REPORTS

Unless otherwise stated, subsequent to the execution of this Agreement, all notifications and reports required under the terms of this Agreement shall be submitted, in writing, to the following:

If to OIG:

U.S. Department of Health and Human Services
Office of Counsel to the Inspector General
Civil Recoveries Branch - Compliance Unit
330 Independence Avenue, SW
Cohen Building, Room 5527
Washington, D.C. 20201
Telephone: 202.619.2078
Fax: 202.205.0604

If to ▇▇▇▇ Foundation:

Dr. ▇▇▇▇
Corporate Compliance Officer
▇▇▇▇ Foundation
▇▇▇▇
▇▇▇▇
Telephone: ▇▇▇▇
Fax: ▇▇▇▇
Medicare Provider Number: ▇▇▇▇

-13-

VII. DOCUMENT AND RECORD RETENTION

▓▓▓▓▓▓▓▓ Foundation shall maintain for inspection, documents and records relating to the following: (i) Medicare, Medicaid and other federal health care programs reimbursement; and (ii) its obligations under the terms of this Agreement, for one year longer than the duration of this Agreement, or longer if otherwise required by law, following the execution of this Agreement.

VIII. STIPULATED PENALTIES

▓▓▓▓▓▓▓▓ Foundation's compliance with the terms and conditions of this Agreement shall constitute an element of ▓▓▓▓▓▓▓▓ Foundation's present responsibility with regard to participation in Medicare, Medicaid and other federal health care programs. Pursuant to section XVI. of this Agreement, any and all modifications to this Agreement (including changes to dates on which an obligation is due to be met) shall be requested in writing and agreed to by OIG in writing prior to the date on which the modification is expected to take effect. Absent such written modifications, ▓▓▓▓▓▓▓▓ Foundation agrees to the following stipulated penalties.

A. ▓▓▓▓▓▓▓▓ Foundation shall pay a stipulated penalty of $2,500 for each day it fails to comply with any of the following terms, which stipulated penalty shall begin to accrue one day after the date the obligation becomes due.

   1. The creation of a Corporate Compliance Committee and the appointment of Corporate Compliance Officer within ninety (90) days of the execution of this Agreement.

   2. Submission of the Interim Report within one hundred eighty (180) days of the execution of this Agreement.

   3. Submission of the Annual Report by the due date required in section V. of this Agreement.

   4. Establishment of a confidential disclosure program within ninety (90) days of the execution date of this Agreement.

B. A stipulated penalty of $2,500 for each day ▓▓▓▓▓▓▓▓ Foundation fails to comply by having fully in force during the term of this Agreement any of the following, which stipulated penalty shall begin to accrue on the date of receipt of the OIG's notice of noncompliance or as otherwise indicated in OIG's notice in accordance with section IX. below.

1. Implementation and maintenance of the written Corporate Integrity Policy, as required by section III. D. of this Agreement.

2. Granting access to the information or documentation necessary to exercise OIG's inspection, audit and review rights, as set forth in section IV. of this Agreement.

3. Implementation and maintenance of the information and education program, as required by section III. E. of this Agreement.

4. Notification to OIG of the existence or conclusion of any investigation or legal proceeding, as required by section III. H. of this Agreement.

C. ███████ Foundation shall pay a stipulated penalty of $1,500 for each day it knowingly employs or contracts with or grants staff privileges to an Ineligible Person and that person: (i) has responsibility for, or involvement with, ███████ y Foundation's business operations related to the Federal health care programs or (ii) is in a position for which the person's salary or the items or services rendered, ordered, or prescribed by the person are paid in whole or part, directly or indirectly, by Federal health care programs or otherwise with Federal funds (this Stipulated Penalty shall not be demanded for any time period during which ███████ Foundation can demonstrate that it did not discover the person's exclusion or other ineligibility after making a reasonable inquiry (as described in section III.G) as to the status of the person).

D. A Stipulated Penalty of $500 (which shall begin to accrue ten (10) days after the date that OIG provides written notice by certified mail to ███████ Foundation of the failure to comply) for each day ███████ Foundation fails to comply fully and adequately with any other obligation of this CIA. In its notice to ███████ Foundation, the OIG shall state the specific grounds for its determination that the ███████ Foundation has failed to comply fully and adequately with the CIA obligation(s) at issue.

IX. PAYMENT OF STIPULATED PENALTIES

Upon finding that ███████ Foundation has failed to comply with any of the above-enumerated obligations, OIG shall notify ███████ y Foundation by certified mail of: (i) B███████ Foundation's failure to comply; and (ii) OIG's exercise of its contractual right to demand payment of the stipulated penalties payable under this Agreement (this letter is hereinafter referred to as the "Demand Letter"). The applicable stipulated penalties shall begin to accrue on the date specified in section VIII., which date shall be indicated in the Demand Letter.

Within thirty (30) days of the receipt of the Demand Letter, ▓▓▓ Foundation shall do either of the following: (i) cure the breach to the OIG's satisfaction and pay the applicable stipulated penalties; or (ii) request a hearing before an HHS administrative law judge to dispute the OIG's determination of noncompliance, pursuant to the agreed upon provisions set forth in section XI. of this Agreement. Failure to respond as required above shall constitute a material breach of this Agreement, as set forth in section X. of this Agreement.

Payment of the stipulated penalties shall be made by certified or cashier's check, payable to "Secretary of the Department of Health and Human Services," and submitted to OIG at the address set forth in section VI. of this Agreement.

These provisions for payment of stipulated penalties shall not affect or otherwise set a standard for the OIG's determination that ▓▓▓ Foundation has materially breached this Agreement, which decision shall be made at the OIG's discretion and governed by the provisions in section X. of this Agreement.

If OIG makes a determination to impose stipulated penalties in accordance with this provision, ▓▓▓ Foundation shall have the right to dispute OIG's determination in accordance with the agreed upon provisions set forth in section XI. of this Agreement.

X. REMEDY FOR MATERIAL BREACH OF THIS AGREEMENT

If ▓▓▓ Foundation engages in conduct that OIG determines to be a material breach of this Agreement, OIG may seek an enhanced stipulated penalty of $10,000 per day for each day ▓▓▓ Foundation is determined to be in material breach of this Agreement. Upon making its determination, OIG shall notify ▓▓▓ Foundation of the alleged material breach by certified mail and of its intent to impose this enhanced stipulated penalty as a result thereof (this letter shall be referred to hereinafter as the "Intent to Impose an Enhanced Stipulated Penalty Letter"). ▓▓▓ Foundation shall have thirty-five (35) days from the date of receipt of the letter to proceed as follows:

(1) cure the alleged material breach; or

(2) demonstrate to the OIG's satisfaction that: (a) ▓▓▓ Foundation is in full compliance with this Agreement; or (b) the material breach cannot be cured within the thirty-five (35) day period, but that ▓▓▓ Foundation has begun to take action to cure the material breach, that ▓▓▓ Foundation will pursue such an action with due diligence, and that ▓▓▓ Foundation will give the OIG a timetable for curing the material breach.

If at the conclusion of the thirty-five-day period (or other specific period as subsequently agreed by OIG and ▓▓▓ Foundation), ▓▓▓ Foundation fails to cure the material breach to OIG's satisfaction, subject to the dispute resolution provisions in section XI. of this Agreement, OIG may impose the enhanced stipulated penalty. If OIG elects to impose this enhanced stipulated penalty, OIG shall notify ▓▓▓ Foundation of the imposition of the enhanced penalty in a "Material Breach Letter." The enhanced stipulated penalty shall take effect on the date specified in the Material Breach Letter.

For purposes of this section, a "material breach" is defined as follows: (i) a failure to report a material billing deficiency, take corrective action and pay the appropriate refunds, as provided in section III. B. of this Agreement; (ii) repeated or flagrant violations of the obligations under this Agreement, including, but not limited to, the obligations addressed in section VIII. of this Agreement; or (iii) failure to respond to a Demand Letter in the manner required in section IX of this Agreement.

In connection with the OIG's determination to impose an enhanced stipulated penalty against ▓▓▓ Foundation pursuant to this provision, ▓▓▓ Foundation shall have the right to dispute the OIG's determination in accordance with the agreed upon provisions set forth in section XI. of this Agreement.

XI. DISPUTE RESOLUTION

Upon OIG's delivery to ▓▓▓ Foundation of its Demand Letter or of its Material Breach Letter, and as an agreed upon contractual remedy for the resolution of disputes arising under the obligation of this Agreement, ▓▓▓ Foundation shall be afforded certain review rights comparable to the ones that are provided in 42 U.S.C. § 1320a-7(f) and 42 C.F.R. § 1005 as if they applied to the stipulated penalties or an enhanced stipulated penalty sought pursuant to this Agreement. Specifically, the OIG's determination to demand payment of stipulated penalties or to seek an enhanced stipulated penalty shall be subject to review by an HHS administrative law judge in a manner consistent with the provisions in 42 C.F.R. §§ 1005.2-1005.21. The administrative law judge's decision, in turn, may be appealed to HHS's Departmental Appeals Board ("DAB") in a manner consistent with the provisions in 42 C.F.R. § 1005.21.

Notwithstanding any provision of Title 42 of the United States Code or Chapter 42 of the Code of Federal Regulations, the only issues to be decided in a proceeding for stipulated penalties under this section shall be the following: (i) whether ████ Foundation was in full and timely compliance with the obligations of this Agreement for which OIG demands payment; (ii) whether ████ Foundation failed to cure; and (iii) the period of noncompliance. ████ Foundation shall have the burden of proving that it was in full and timely compliance and the steps taken to effect the cure, if any. The OIG shall have the burden of proving ████ Foundation's failure to cure. For purposes of paying stipulated penalties under this Agreement, and if ████ Foundation chooses to seek review in lieu of curing the breach and paying the stipulated penalties, as set forth above, the administrative law judge's decision shall give rise to ████ Foundation's obligation to pay. Thus, payment will be due immediately after the issuance of the administrative law judge's decision. ████ Foundation's election of its contractual right to appeal to the DAB shall not excuse its obligation to make payment upon the issuance of the administrative law judge's decision.

Notwithstanding any provision of Title 42 of the United States Code or Chapter 42 of the Code of Federal Regulations, the only issues to be decided in a proceeding for an enhanced stipulated penalty based on a material breach of this Agreement shall be the following: (a) whether ████ Foundation was in material breach of one or more of its obligations under this Agreement, (b) whether such material breach was continuing on the date of the Material Breach Letter, and (c) whether the alleged material breach could not be cured within the 35 day period, but that (i) ████ Foundation had begun to take action to cure the material breach, (ii) ████ Foundation is pursuing such action with due diligence, and (iii) ████ Foundation had provided to OIG a reasonable timetable for curing the material breach. For purposes of the enhanced stipulated penalty herein agreed to in the event of material breach of this Agreement, the administrative law judge's decision shall be deemed to make the enhanced stipulated penalty due and owing, if the administrative law judge finds in favor of the OIG. The administrative law judge's decision may be appealed to the DAB in a manner consistent with the provisions in 42 C.F.R. § 1005.21.

All notices required under any of the aforementioned proceedings shall be given to the OIG in accordance with section VI. of this Agreement.

XII. COSTS RELATED TO ADDITIONAL AUDITS

In addition to the obligations assumed by ▓▓▓ Foundation under this Agreement and as described above, if OIG determines that it is necessary to conduct an independent audit or review to determine whether or the extent to which ▓▓▓ Foundation is complying, if at all, with their obligations under this Agreement, ▓▓▓ Foundation agrees to pay for the reasonable costs of any such audit or review by OIG or its duly authorized representative.

XIII. UNALLOWABLE COSTS

It is agreed that all costs (as defined in the Federal Acquisition Regulations ("FAR") 31.205-47) and in Titles XVIII and XIX of the Social Security Act, 42 U.S.C. §§ 1395-1395ddd and 1396-1396v (1997), and the regulations promulgated thereunder) incurred by or on behalf of ▓▓▓ Foundation in connection with (a) the matters covered by this Corporate Integrity Agreement (but not including costs relating to ▓▓▓ Foundation's voluntary Corporate Compliance activities undertaken prior to effective date of this Agreement); (b) the government's audits and investigations of the allegations which are the subject of this Agreement; (c) any of ▓▓▓ Foundation's investigative, defense and collective actions with respect to matters specifically covered by this Agreement, and (d) the negotiation of this Agreement, shall be unallowable costs for government contract accounting purposes and for purposes of seeking reimbursement from either the Medicare, Medicaid or other federal health care programs. ▓▓▓ Foundation shall account separately for these costs for government contract accounting purposes and for purposes of seeking reimbursement from the Medicare and other federal health care programs. Any sums owed by ▓▓▓ Foundation to the United States for payments made to ▓▓▓ Foundation by Medicare and/or Medicaid (federal share) for costs that are unallowable (as defined in this Paragraph) shall be paid by ▓▓▓ Foundation to HHS at HHS' discretion.

XIV. NEW LOCATIONS

In the event that ▓▓▓ Foundation purchases or establishes new business units in which it has a controlling interest after the date of execution of this CIA, ▓▓▓ Foundation shall notify OIG of this fact within thirty (30) days of the date of purchase or establishment. This notification shall include the location of the new operation(s), phone number, fax number, Federal health care program provider number(s) (if any), and the corresponding payor(s) (contractor specific) that has issued each provider number. All employees at such locations shall be subject to the requirements in this CIA that apply to new employees (e.g., completing certifications and undergoing training).

XV. PRIVILEGES AND DISCLOSURES

Nothing in this Agreement shall constitute or be construed as a waiver by ▓▓▓ Foundation of its attorney-client or other applicable privileges. Subject to HHS's Freedom of Information Act ("FOIA") procedures, set forth in 45 C.F.R. Part 5, the OIG shall make a reasonable effort to notify ▓▓▓ Foundation prior to any release by OIG of information submitted by ▓▓▓ Foundation pursuant to its obligations under this Agreement and identified upon submission by ▓▓▓ Foundation as trade secrets, commercial or financial information and privileged or confidential under the FOIA rules. ▓▓▓ Foundation shall refrain from identifying any information as trade secrets, commercial or financial information and privileged or confidential that does not meet the criteria for exemption from disclosure under FOIA.

XVI. EFFECTIVE AND BINDING AGREEMENT

Consistent with the provisions in the settlement agreement pursuant to which this Agreement is entered, and into which this Agreement is incorporated, ▓▓▓ Foundation and the OIG agrees as follows:

1. This Agreement shall be binding on the successors, assigns and transferees of ▓▓▓ Foundation.

2. This Agreement shall become final and binding only upon signing by each respective party hereto.

3. Any modifications to this Agreement shall be made with the prior written consent of the parties to this Agreement.

4. The undersigned signatory for ▓▓▓ Foundation represents and warrants that he is authorized to execute this Agreement. The undersigned OIG signatory represents that he is signing this Agreement in his official capacity and that he is authorized to execute this Agreement.

As Agreed By:

██████████████████████████ **FOUNDATION, INC.**

Date _June 30, 1999_ ██████████████
President

OFFICE OF INSPECTOR GENERAL OF THE DEPARTMENT OF HEALTH AND HUMAN SERVICES

Date _6/9/99_   _____
Lewis Morris, Esquire
Assistant Inspector General
Office of Counsel to the Inspector General
Office of Inspector General
U.S. Department of Health and Human Services